W9-AEI-527

ON THE TRAIL

SILAS CHAMBERLIN

On the Trail
A History of American Hiking

Yale

UNIVERSITY

PRESS

NEW HAVEN AND LONDON

Published with assistance from the foundation established in memory of Philip Hamilton McMillan of the Class of 1894, Yale College.

Yale University Press books may be purchased in quantity for educational, business, or promotional use. For information, please e-mail sales.press@yale.edu (U.S. office) or sales@yaleup.co.uk (U.K. office).

Set in New Aster type by IDS Infotech, Ltd.
Printed in the United States of America.

Library of Congress Control Number: 2016936121
ISBN 978-0-300-21911-1 (hardcover)

A catalogue record for this book is available from the British Library.

This paper meets the requirements of ANSI/NISO Z39.48–1992 (Permanence of Paper).

10 9 8 7 6 5 4 3 2 1

For my parents, Bob and Sue,
my wife, Amanda,
and my daughter, Lily

CONTENTS

PREFACE

In early May 2003, my parents called me at college to report that I had received a strange, handwritten letter in the mail. "The woods are calling. Can you hear?" the letter began. "It's the sound of sweat dripping furiously to the forest floor. It's the sound of muscles begging for relief. It's the sound of satisfied workers, in love with their home." On the back of the letter were black-and-white photos of men in bib overalls wrestling, a man in a skirt and hard hat drunkenly dancing, and several pictures of hikers on the trail, carrying massive backpacks strapped with milk crates, cardboard boxes, Coleman stoves, shovels, rock bars, and pick-mattocks. This was my invitation to join the Adirondack Mountain Club's (ADK) professional trail crew.

Six months earlier, I had visited the club's website and, on a whim, decided to apply for a spot on the trail crew. I convinced my best friend to do the same. Along with fourteen other college-aged men and women, we spent the summer of 2003 in the back-woods of the Adirondacks and Catskills—five days at a time—cutting new trails and maintaining old ones. We learned how to make staircases out of sofa-sized rocks, erect rough-hewn lad-ders from carefully felled trees, and design simple but well-engineered footpaths that appeared to blend into the wilderness setting. We spent our downtime roaming the streets of nearby

Lake Placid or hanging out at the trails cabin, near the ADK's Wilderness Loj at Heart Lake. The bawdy nature of the group is still difficult for me to describe, but a 2006 *Backpacker* article on the trail crew comes close to capturing the atmosphere of a typical trail cabin morning. "I followed [Trails Coordinator] Lampman into the living room, where gangsta rap played at a hard volume," wrote the journalist, Tom Clynes. "In the middle of the floor, a guy with a Mohawk haircut was belly-bucking another guy who had shaved the letters 'TFC' ('Trail Fixing Crew') out of the black mane on his chest. Sprawled on the sagging chairs and beat-up sofa, a dozen more crew members watched the proceedings, hooting and gnawing at eggs grilled in the center of hollowed out bagels."

The crew's tradition—compulsory, I would find—of eating "eggs-in-the-hole" was just one of many forms of culture shock I, a wide-eyed vegan, experienced that summer. Nonetheless, within a few weeks, I was infatuated with the crew's romanticizing of trail work, deep sense of camaraderie, and devotion to the ADK— a club of approximately thirty-five thousand members.

Before my involvement with the crew, I had never given much thought to the idea of a hiking or trail club, although hiking had always been an important pastime for my family and me. Living in rural York County, Pennsylvania, we could simply walk out the back door and into the woods, hiking for miles without a trail, without special equipment, and—perhaps most important—without the company of others. When our backyard was not enough, we camped at nearby Gifford Pinchot State Park, exploring its humble, circuitous trail network. Sometimes we would even make the drive to the nearest section of the Appalachian Trail, at Tumbling Run, and spend an afternoon walking on the famous trail. Even in the presence of other like-minded families sharing the trail or an adjacent campsite, we still considered ourselves to be hiking alone. Indeed, the whole idea of hiking was to get away from other people and workaday cares to immerse ourselves in nature.

My experiences with the Adirondack Mountain Club made me question my previous notions of hiking. I quickly discovered that there were similar clubs throughout New England. The Appalachian Mountain Club had a trail crew in the White Mountains; the Green Mountain Club had a crew for Vermont's Long Trail. There seemed to be clubs like these throughout the country, many of them dating back to the early twentieth century and some even earlier. I learned that in my home state there were groups actively caring for trails, organizing outings, and—of all activities—hiking together. As I learned more, I realized that my experiences with hiking had somehow bypassed any involvement with—or even a basic knowledge of—the rich social life, extensive work, and large membership base of traditional hiking clubs. For me personally, *On the Trail* is an attempt to explain how someone could hike regularly in the late twentieth century and yet be so ignorant of the vibrant culture of organized hiking in the United States. In seeking answers, I found that much of the explanation lies in the fascinating story of the rise and decline of hiking culture in America.

On the Trail is a national history of the American hiking community as it evolved from the pursuit of nineteenth-century urban elites to a mass phenomenon by the 1970s. In contrast to historians' abiding assumption that most environmental institutions flourished during the 1960s and 1970s, I offer a more nuanced account of the disintegration of a remarkably rich culture promoted by organized hiking clubs during the previous one hundred years. Between the end of World War II and the late 1960s, the size of the American hiking community grew exponentially, as tens of millions of people went to the nation's trails for the first time. Yet most of these new hikers eschewed membership in an organized hiking club and instead hiked alone or in small, informal groups. By the 1970s the typical American hiker had evolved from a net producer—of information, maps, well-maintained trails, advocacy, outings, and club culture—to a net consumer—of equipment, national magazines, and federally subsidized trails. As Americans came to see trail access as a basic right—something for which they paid taxes and felt that government should provide—the grassroots, volunteer ethic that had defined the hiking community for more than one hundred years began to lose its hegemony over the hiking community.

On the Trail is written for anyone with an interest in hiking, trails, and how Americans have chosen to engage with nature over time. I endeavor to synthesize the rich but scattered—and, in many cases, privately held—archival collections of the community to trace its evolution from the nineteenth century to the late twentieth century. In the process, I unearth the rich culture of hiking that has always defined and added meaning to the deceivingly simple act of walking in the woods and explain why so many Americans were drawn to this pastime during the last two centuries. Interest in hiking and trails was contingent on many factors, including citizen science and exploration, the development and condition of cities, available modes of transportation, the rise of big business, religion, patriotism, and war. This is not simply a story of a growing interest and concern for nature, wilderness, and the environment but rather a holistic recounting of one of America's most vibrant social communities, how it came to flourish, and why it began to dissolve in the late 1960s.

This is also a cautionary tale of how the success of grassroots movements sometimes paradoxically leads to their demise. The hiking community's successful campaigns to recruit millions of new hikers and to secure federal support for trail development—enshrined in the National Trails System Act of 1968—ultimately undermined the volunteer ethos of the movement and led to the decline in organized hiking. As such, *On the Trail* provides insight about a key question facing the twenty-first-century hiking community: how to recruit and retain a new generation of club members and volunteers, even as club leadership ages and membership rolls shrink.

The origins of U.S. hiking can be found in the culture of nature walking in nineteenth-century American cities. As new modes of transportation freed small groups of wealthy urban residents from lengthy, regular walking, they drew from a body of ideas that celebrated nature—transcendentalism, romanticism, and the pastoral ideal—to re-create pedestrianism as a pleasurable pastime and sport. These ideas would influence walking culture for at least the next century. During this period, rural cemeteries and city parks provided the ideal places to walk because they offered predictable and well-scripted nature experiences near urban residents.

As growing numbers of Americans began to walk for pleasure, they formed groups to promote their goals. The Appalachian Mountain Club was founded in 1876 in Boston, but several smaller clubs had formed during the 1860s that organized and recorded outings, built trails, and provided a model for the larger club's activities. Early hiking clubs could provide opportunities for men to test their mettle against nature and reaffirm fraternal ties established during the Civil War, but most of the clubs were remarkable for their eager acceptance and inclusion of women in regular walks and even the most daunting expeditions. By the early 1890s, the San Francisco–based Sierra Club and Portland-based Mazamas had replicated the northeastern clubs' successes on the West Coast.

These early clubs were led by influential men and women who were adept at using newspapers and their own publications, such as the AMC's journal *Appalachia* and the *Sierra Club Bulletin*, to gain publicity for the clubs' work. As a result, the clubs inspired would-be hikers and club members throughout the country. Hiking clubs and culture proliferated during the first few decades of the twentieth century. In the context of the closing of the frontier, concerns about the future of American masculinity, individual health and virility, and the emerging conservation ethos, hiking clubs provided an especially appealing outlet for the thousands of men and women who founded clubs and provided their organizational impetus. Through newsletters, correspondence, and joint outings, club members developed shared ideas about the benefits of hiking to patriotism, health, and religion. In the process, they invested walking with meaning that elevated what could be seen as an indulgent leisure activity to an irreproachable position even during periods of war and economic instability. By World War II, club-based hiking culture had become a national phenomenon.

Armed with a strong culture and rhetorically rich set of justifications for hiking, club members began to expand their activities beyond organized walks. The most high-profile activity of the hiking community was long-distance trail building. Hiking clubs had always been concerned with building and maintaining trails, but most trails were short and intended to provide access to local natural areas or nearby summits. In the early twentieth century, hikers began to reimagine the trail as offering a longer journey that could take multiple days, weeks, or even months. By the time Benton MacKaye published his proposal for "An Appalachian Trail" in 1921, Vermont's Green Mountain Club had been working on the 273-mile Long Trail for almost a decade. The much longer Appalachian Trail inspired dozens of hiking clubs to reorient their activities toward developing portions of the trail and attracted the attention of the federal government. By the 1930s, western hikers were scouting a Canada-to-Mexico route that would become the Pacific Crest Trail. These long-distance trails overshadowed regional trail projects that occupied the time of many clubs and required them to expand their activities from recreation to landowner outreach, easements and acquisitions, volunteer management, and other requirements of trail development. By the 1960s, most hiking clubs committed at least part of their time to trails, with volunteers regularly participating in work details that kept the nation's trails open and in good shape.

The rapid growth of hiking clubs and construction of trails during the first half of the twentieth century created an apparent boom in the popularity of hiking during the postwar period. The boom, however, had ambiguous ramifications for traditional hiking culture. In the period between World War II and 1968, the hiking community grew in size and complexity. This evolution brought about two ironies that would create tensions among hikers into the twenty-first century. First, beginning in the late 1940s, surplus military equipment, better technology, improved access to nature, and new ideas about wilderness led to rapid growth in the number of Americans hitting the trail—many of whom eschewed club membership in favor of hiking alone or with small, informal groups. Second, many of the new hikers were motivated by the environmental movement to protect and experience natural places but ended up significantly degrading them in the process. Overuse of the nation's trails and other hiking terrain led to a new ethic of hiking and backpacking that ultimately reinforced the autonomy of the individual hiker and ensured federal and state activism in trail development and maintenance, most notably in the form of the National Trails System Act of 1968. By the 1970s, millions of Americans were on the trail, but they were primarily consumers of mass-produced hiking culture rather than active participants in its production.

This transition from production to consumption is the main argument of *On the Trail* and one that has troubling implications for the hiking community. In the years after 1968, many new hikers joined clubs and continued to volunteer time and effort to sustaining the organizations, but many more hikers bypassed membership. By 2005, the Appalachian Mountain Club—the nation's oldest hiking club—had a remarkable 90,000 members. The Mazamas of Portland, Oregon, grew to 3,500 members, while the Seattle-based Mountaineers boasted more than 10,000 active members. Clubs in midsize cities throughout the country often listed between 100 and 400 members. Collectively, an estimated 2 million Americans held membership in a hiking club by the early twenty-first century. In comparison to the 34 million Americans hiking each year, however, club members represented a small portion of the hiking community. Imagine then, the millions of hikers—like myself—who came to take for granted well-maintained trails, carefully plotted maps, favorable public land policy, and other achievements of organized hiking clubs.

Even for those hikers who found their way into clubs, the meaning of club membership changed over time. As the operations of the nation's largest clubs became increasingly professionalized, membership became as much about paying dues to support advocacy or fee-for-service arrangements as it was about regular socialization with fellow hikers. The vast majority of the Sierra Club's 770,000 members, for example, have no expectation of contributing to the day-to-day work of the club. Even smaller, hiking-focused clubs, such as the Appalachian Trail Conservancy, came to think of volunteers as tangential to the day-to-day operational role played by core paid staff. The exception to this trend was at the local level, where membership in small but very active clubs continued to entail weekly hikes, trail work, ice cream socials, Christmas dinners, and square dancing. The volunteer, communal ethos that dominated hiking culture for its first one hundred years may have evolved by the 1970s, but it certainly did not disappear.

The rise of urban bicycle paths, rail trails, and other multiuse trail development—which began in the 1960s but accelerated in the 1990s and the early twenty-first century—also provided new opportunities for volunteer trail organizations to demand significant funding and a voice in regional transportation planning. This led to the investment of tens of millions of dollars for the construction of thousands of miles of new trails. However, as most of the new investment excluded the building of footpaths as a matter of policy, this development had mixed implications for the traditional hiking community.

The decline of the producer hiker and the rise of the consumer hiker could be interpreted as a declensionist narrative, a story about how an ideal golden age of hiking was lost to a less meaningful consumer culture. I hope, however, that most readers will recognize that American hiking culture, although significantly altered, remains vibrant. One need look no further than the communal traditions and volunteer ethos surrounding the Appalachian Trail and similar trails throughout the country to understand that thousands of hikers continue to devote much time, sweat, and love to trails—and to fellow hikers. Twenty-first-century environmental organizations devote great effort to attracting and retaining the next generation of hikers. Some have been incredibly creative in reaching new audiences, especially youth. If we can expose young people to outing organizations early in life, then perhaps they will return to the volunteer clubs that many of their parents left—or never joined—in the 1960s, 1970s, and 1980s.

That approach certainly worked for me. My time on the Adirondack Mountain Club's trail crew exposed me to the power of hiking together, eating together, sweating together, living together.

The trail crew destroyed forever my idealized notion of hiking as an individual escape into nature. And I am glad it did. As the *Backpacker* reporter noted after spending his day with our crew in the Adirondack wilderness, "In their eyes I can see the spark of nature and youth, with its promise of summits within reach, summers without end, and friendships without fail." He understood, as I now do, that on the trail you are never really alone.

ACKNOWLEDGMENTS

The most common question I get about my research is, "Does that mean you get to hike all of the time?" The answer is no. I have a day job for that. Writing the history of hiking includes almost no time on the trail and lots of time sitting behind a computer screen. Fortunately, I have had many colleagues and friends to enliven this experience, provide encouragement, and help make the process fun. Throughout the course of writing *On the Trail,* Steve Cutcliffe has nurtured this project, always sharing my excitement for new discoveries about the characters and clubs that animate this history. I am indebted to Roger Simon and John Pettegrew for providing their perspectives during several stages of my work and to Adam Rome, James Longhurst, Larry Anderson, and Amey Senape, who also read versions of the book and provided excellent feedback. My thoughts on hiking and trails have been reworked for dozens of conference papers at annual meetings of the American Historical Association, American Society for Environmental History, Urban History Association, Society for the History of Technology, Association for Environmental Studies and Sciences, Pennsylvania Historical Association, and many other conferences. I wish to thank those audiences for their feedback. I appreciate the enthusiasm Jean Thomson Black, Samantha Ostrowski, Laura Jones Dooley, and the rest of the team at Yale University Press have shown for *On the Trail* and the improvements they have suggested.

Numerous librarians and individuals throughout the country provided access to public and private archives, recommended sources, scanned photos, or simply provided words of encouragement. I especially wish to recognize Maurice Forrester, longtime newsletter editor for the Keystone Trails Association, and Barb Wiemann of the Allentown Hiking Club. Both have volunteered decades of their lives to ensure that the one-hundred-year legacy of grassroots hiking continues well into the twenty-first century. The guidance and kind words they provided during the first few months of my research have led down a winding path to the publication of this book.

I worked professionally in Pennsylvania's conservation community during most of the time I was writing this book. My colleagues at the Schuylkill River National Heritage Area, the Pennsylvania Department of Conservation and Natural Resources, the Delaware and Lehigh National Heritage Corridor, and dozens of other partner organizations have inspired and informed my work, whether they realized it or not.

Above all, I would like to thank my family for their love, support, and encouragement throughout the process of researching and writing *On the Trail*. My wife, Amanda, and my parents, Bob and Sue, have never questioned why I would spend a decade pursuing a graduate degree, taking jobs building and promoting trails, and writing about walking in the woods. Although hip and knee replacements have made it a struggle for my dad—now in his late sixties—to hike, the memories we made walking out of our backyard and into the woods continue to influence the way I think about the natural world. My sister, Emily, has always been my unofficial editor, and she has read the words of this book many times over.

My daughter, Lily, was born in the midst of this project, and as a result, I wrote many of the following pages in the middle of the night, between putting her to sleep and getting ready for work each morning. Now that she is growing up, we spend at least a few precious hours together every week—on the trail.

The 2003 Adirondack Mountain Club Professional Trail Crew poses for a group photo before spending the week in the woods maintaining and building trails. The author is in the middle row, fifth from left. Courtesy of the Adirondack Mountain Club.

ON THE TRAIL

1 THE ORIGINS OF AMERICAN NATURE WALKING

"SOME of my townsmen, it is true, can remember, and have described to me some walks which they took ten years ago, in which they were so blessed as to lose themselves for half an hour in the woods," noted Henry David Thoreau in his posthumously published 1862 essay "Walking," "but I know very well that they have confined themselves to the highway ever since."[1] In the last years of his life, as Thoreau spent most of his days strolling the Concord, Massachusetts, countryside, he observed the growing detachment of his fellow townspeople from the act of walking. This detachment, he argued, stemmed from the regularization of work hours and practices that kept diligent craftsmen, merchants, and housewives at work most of the day. Rapid changes in forms of transportation were also to blame. From the time of Thoreau's birth in 1817 until his death in 1862, Americans had witnessed a true revolution from horse and foot travel early in the century to halting omnibuses and horse railways in the 1820s and 1830s to the ascent of steam locomotion after the 1840s. With each development in transportation, the need to walk long distances was diminished, and the "art" of walking, as Thoreau called it, was further compromised. Although Thoreau would not live to see the founding of the Appalachian Mountain Club in 1876, that group of thirty-three Boston outdoor enthusiasts and

their vision for New England's landscape represented one antidote to his complaints.

In a fundamental shift of thought and action, leisure walking
evolved from a rare practice of the urban elite in the eighteenth
century to a widespread and multifaceted activity by the late
nineteenth century because it resonated with Americans react-
ing against—and attempting to accommodate—industrialism,
urbanism, and a perceived crisis of masculinity. Their reactions
highlight a central irony of middle-class America. As soon as
people realized some measure of safety and comfort, they spent
considerable time and effort developing new ways to experience
the hardships they had just escaped. For nineteenth-century
Americans, this tension led to a variety of reactions, each of
which added poignancy to the act of walking. Romantic and
transcendental artists and writers, for example, invested walking
with profound meaning and created a new, picturesque aesthetic
that glorified landscapes that were conducive to walking. The
developers of rural cemeteries and urban parks made that
aesthetic tangible and created easily accessible walking opportunities on the periphery of and within cities. Various forms of
pleasure, sport, and explorative walking made contributions to
the emerging culture. Last, and perhaps most important, changes in urban transportation and the spatial layout of cities allowed
an increasing number of residents to avoid walking long distances each day. The transition from walking out of necessity to
walking out of desire constituted one of the primary—but not
sole—origins of American hiking as a leisure activity. Higher
wages, more leisure time, and a growing appreciation for nature
certainly contributed to the increasing number of walkers in the
late nineteenth century, but these factors would not have led to a
walking culture without the liberating force of the omnibus,
horse railway, train, streetcar, and, in the early twentieth century,
automobile, all of which obviated the need to walk and also eventually provided access to walking opportunities on the periphery
of town and in more distant locales. The classes of people most
likely to be freed from walking were also those most likely to join
the nineteenth century's fledging hiking organizations.

As the pace of industrialization accelerated during the nine-teenth century, Americans greeted change with an ambiguous set of ideas about progress, technology, and nature. On one hand, Americans welcomed improvements in their quality of life and took pride in such innovations as mills, canals, steamboats, and trains. On the other hand, they recognized the potential for tech-nology to create larger, dirtier cities inhabited by a class of work-ers with no means of escaping factory life. These dichotomous responses were embedded in the culture of the period and permeated discussions of politics, literature, and society. Nineteenth-century Americans adopted the pastoral ideal, or "middle landscape," as an alternative, more desirable vision.[2]

Nature, which had for most of American history been some-thing to fear and conquer, slowly emerged as an antidote to in-dustrialization. This romantic sensibility included a new set of aesthetic ideals that celebrated nature as beautiful, sublime, and picturesque. The beautiful and the sublime represented the two conflicting emotions Americans experienced when facing the wilderness—ecstasy and fear—while the picturesque often sug-gested the pastoral middle landscape between the two extremes. The picturesque aesthetic promoted the variety and irregularity of nature, as well as man's place in it, and picturesque artists typically included ruins, peasants, or rustic dwellings in their works.

The pursuit of picturesque landscapes required walking. In-deed, walking through a landscape became the primary means of truly understanding its aesthetic qualities. The diaries of Dor-othy Wordsworth, poet William Wordsworth's sister and daily walking partner, reveal the explicit relation between picturesque aesthetics and the act of walking. In her journals of 1800 to 1803, Dorothy records daily walks—often taken both morning and evening—through the pastoral landscape surrounding Grasmere in the Lake District of northwest England. Dorothy described her surroundings as "neither one thing nor the other—neither natural nor wholly cultivated and artificial."[3]

Most of her walks were short and took her no more than one or two miles from home, but Dorothy described a diversity of nature, people, and views close at hand. "We went into the Orchard before dinner," she recorded in the summer of 1802. "We found some torn Bird's nests. The Columbine was growing upon the Rocks, here and there a solitary plant—sheltered and shaded by the tufts and Bowers of trees. It is a graceful slender creature, a female seeking retirement and growing freest and most graceful where it is most alone." Even when Dorothy fell ill, she walked. "I was very unwell," she noted, but "we walked a long time backwards and forwards between John's Grove and the Lane upon the turf." "I was ill in the afternoon, took laudanum," she noted another day, but "we walked in Bainriggs after tea. Saw the juniper—umbrella shaped." Dorothy, William, and fellow poet Samuel Coleridge walked so often—regardless of cold, rain, or heat—that a notation in August 1800 that she "did not walk" is remarkable.[4]

Dorothy Wordsworth and her brother represented one type of walking romantic. In America, Thomas Cole's paintings signaled the emergence of the Hudson River School, which adopted many of the same aesthetics and applied them to the American landscape. Cole's paintings typically merged the wilderness sublime with the picturesque pastoral, as in his famous depiction of an oxbow on the Connecticut River, which transitions from a dark, primitive, and chaotic wilderness to a sunny and well-cultivated middle landscape. Other works, such as *Schroon Lake* (c. 1846), are explicitly picturesque, bringing human habitations into the foreground and pushing the tall but distant mountains of the Adirondacks into the hazy background, which softens their wilderness qualities.[5]

Cole's paintings of northern New York and a flurry of travel guides and accounts made the Adirondacks an appealing destination for artists and other early tourists from the 1840s onward. During the warm seasons, the Keane Valley was crowded with painters who set up their easels in the valley's open farmland or along the shores of the nearby Ausable Lakes. Photos from later in the period show artists, canvases in hand, gathering along the banks of the Ausable River, dressed to both walk and paint. Although the Adirondacks were emerging as a resort destination for wealthy urbanites and tuberculosis patients, accessing the region's most remarkable features, such as Indian Pass, Avalanche Lake, and Mount Marcy, required strenuous hiking. For example, in June 1835, Cole recorded, "I have just returned from an excursion in search of the picturesque towards the headwaters of the Hudson." This journey would have brought Cole up the Opalescent River and toward Feldspar Brook, which penetrates the southern fringe of the High Peaks. In the 1830s, it was a wild place—distant from roads and untouched by extensive logging or other industries—although the proprietors of the McIntyre mine had been seeking iron ore in the area for nearly a decade when Cole visited. The nearby Indian Pass, which even today requires a full day's hike to access, also attracted painters and writers, despite the steep climb. "A more hideous, toilsome breakneck tramp I never took," author Joel Headley related to readers of his popular *The Adirondack; or, Life in the Woods* (1851), but his final evaluation was that the sublime view was worth the trip. The works produced by artists like Cole and authors like Headley popularized the Adirondacks and similar regions and continued the process of investing these landscapes with special meaning that could best be experienced by walking.[6]

In the 1830s and 1840s, transcendentalism emerged as a distinctly American complement to romanticism that celebrated nature experiences as an antidote to a corrupting society, an assertion of self-reliance, and a means of experiencing God. Some transcendentalists, notably Henry David Thoreau, heeded Ralph Waldo Emerson's call to "walk on our own feet" and "work with our own hands" on the margins of society. Thoreau's two years at Walden Pond from 1845 to 1847 are the best-known example, but he also carried the theme throughout his other writings, many of which celebrated walking. "I think that I cannot preserve my health and spirits, unless I spend four hours a day at least—and it is commonly more than that—sauntering through the woods and over the hills and fields, absolutely free from all worldly engagements," Thoreau claimed. He saw walking as an alternative to the "moral insensibility of my neighbors who confine themselves to shops and offices the whole day for weeks and months, ay, and years almost together . . . sitting there now at three o'clock in the afternoon, as if it were three o'clock in the morning."[7]

Despite his criticism of society, Thoreau never sought to leave civilization behind, for Walden Pond even in the 1840s was not a wilderness. Evidence of economy and production surrounded Thoreau, from the ice cutters participating in global commerce outside his door to farmers tending their fields to the nearby train track linking rural Massachusetts's natural resources with increasingly industrial cities. Although Thoreau made "wildness" a central part of his rhetoric—"give me a wildness whose glance no civilization can endure"—when given the opportunity to experience the wildest areas of the Northeast, he recoiled in revulsion and fear. In 1846, Thoreau climbed Maine's Mount Katahdin along a route "scarcely less arduous than Satan's anciently through Chaos." At the summit, he imagined the mountain questioning why a human would attempt such a journey. "Why came you here before your time? This ground is not prepared for you. Is it not enough that I smile in the valleys? I have never made this soil for thy feet, this air for thy breathing, these rocks for thy neighbors. I cannot pit nor fondle thee here, but forever relentlessly drive thee hence to where I *am* kind." Although moved by the adventure, Thoreau returned from the summit believing he might be more comfortable in the pastoral countryside of Concord.[8]

Thoreau is an ambiguous figure in nineteenth-century walking culture. On one hand, he celebrated walking through the same picturesque landscapes promoted by the romantics and other nineteenth-century walking advocates. He also elevated the importance of walking by suggesting it as the primary means of experiencing transcendental thought. On the other hand, Thoreau's writings on walking were not likely to convince others because they set the standard for the experience too high. "We should go forth on the shortest walk, perchance, in the spirit of undying adventure, never to return—prepared to send back our embalmed hearts only as relics to our desolate kingdoms," he suggested. "If you are ready to leave father and mother, and brother and sister, and wife and child and friends, and never see them again—if you have paid your debts, and made your will, and settled all your affairs, and are a free man, then you are ready for a walk." Thoreau was exaggerating the ideal conditions under which to experience a journey free from worldly entanglements, but one must wonder if this rhetoric made walking seem more or less appealing in the minds of his audience.[9]

Encouragements to walk also existed in places other than abstract transcendental thought. Americans' desire for picturesque landscapes took their most tangible form in the rural cemetery movement, which predated large public parks as the nation's first walking grounds. As historian Aaron Sachs notes, Mount Auburn—the nation's first rural cemetery—"had more to do with European landscape traditions than with American wilderness." In 1831, when a group of Boston horticulturalists founded Mount Auburn near Cambridge, Massachusetts, vast territories of the American West remained unexplored and sparsely settled. When placed in its best light by a painter or author, wilderness could have enriching qualities; however, most European Americans, especially those living on the frontiers, continued to view wilderness as something to be feared and conquered. When creating new landscapes in which to bury their dead and experience the rejuvenating qualities of nature, Americans drew from the romantic tradition of the picturesque. The coexistence of gravestones—symbolically resembling the Roman ruins of Europe—and cultivated nature were key picturesque motifs that became tangible in these gardenlike cemeteries. Because the picturesque tradition was closely associated with the thoughtful peripatetic, rural cemeteries fostered America's nascent walking culture of the early and mid-nineteenth century.[10]

Although they appear a remarkable development in landscape architecture today, rural cemeteries resulted from pragmatic concerns about public health and land use. Their proponents believed that moving burial grounds away from churches, where they had traditionally been located, would minimize the health concerns related to the proximity to decaying bodies and provide additional space to avoid the crowding of graves. This idea originated in Europe, where centuries of habitation exacerbated such problems. In 1765, the Parliament of Paris ordered all urban cemeteries closed and authorized the purchase of tracts of land on the outskirts of the city; these were developed into four large municipal cemeteries. The most famous of these cemeteries, Père Lachaise, opened in 1804 to almost complete indifference. The novelty of its setting discouraged all but a small number of burials in its earliest years. However, the cemetery's savvy administrators arranged for a series of transfers of famous remains to the site, including Molière, Jean de La Fontaine, and Abélard and Héloïse, and Parisians scrambled to purchase plots near the famous interments. In 1835, Henry Wadsworth Longfellow described the unconventional qualities of Père Lachaise. "I took a pathway to the left," he recalled, "which conducted me up the hill-side. I soon found myself in the deep shade of heavy foliage, where the branches of the yew and willow mingled, interwoven with the tendrils and blossoms of the honeysuckle." Longfellow remarked on the favorable impression the cemetery made, observing, "The soft melancholy of the scene is rendered still more touching by the warble of birds and the shade of trees, and the grave receives the gentle visit of the sunshine and the shower."[11]

Notwithstanding Longfellow's impressions, Americans hesitated to embrace rural cemeteries until the 1830s, when calls for public health reform, overcrowding of traditional cemeteries, and the rising value of urban land compelled cemetery officials to look beyond city limits. Traditional graveyards located in developed portions of the city caused a number of problems. "Already teaming with dead bodies," wrote one rural cemetery advocate, graveyards exposed those laid to rest "to violations in the opening of streets, and other city improvements . . . not to speak of the incidental and almost necessary exhumation and exposure of the dead, in the daily use of these crowded cemeteries."[12]

Jacob Bigelow, a Harvard University professor of medicine and expert on regional botany, advanced the idea for a rural cemetery near Harvard as early as 1825, but the concept languished for several years, until the Massachusetts Horticultural Society adopted it as an opportunity to establish an experimental arboretum. In 1831, Mount Auburn became America's first large rural cemetery, plotted on 170 acres of former farmland between Cambridge and Watertown, Massachusetts, an area already "noted for its rural beauty, its romantic seclusion and its fine prospect." The cemetery's designers, Henry Alexander Scammell Dearborn and Alexander Wadsworth—Dearborn would go on to design Boston's Forest Hills Cemetery—sought to accommodate both carriage and foot traffic while maintaining the natural topography and ground cover. They eschewed the classical aesthetic of straight roads and grid patterns for winding carriage roads that provided access to the cemetery, while "the more broken and precipitous parts are approached by foot-paths, which are six feet in width." Most of the paths, with names like "Azalea," "Amaranth," and "Lotus," were covered in a smooth, gravel surface and lined with flowers and shrubs. Even as customers developed hundreds of plots, the cemetery managers' efforts "to cultivate trees, shrubs and plants" and prohibit the cutting or destroying of trees ensured that Mount Auburn would continue to look like a park.[13]

Mount Auburn provided a secluded, idyllic resting place for the dead, but the cemetery's proponents also intended the grounds to offer a soothing experience to visitors, who could rest assured that their loved ones were cared for and, perhaps more important, find solace in knowing that they would someday rest in such a setting. An 1839 guide to the cemetery noted this dual purpose. "Here it will be in the power of every one, who may wish it . . . to deposit the mortal remains of his friends; and to provide a place of burial for himself—which while living he may contemplate without dread or disgust . . . surrounded with every thing that can fill the heart with tender and respectful emotions—beneath the shade of a venerable tree, on the slope of the verdant lawn, and within the seclusion of the forest—removed from all the discordant scenes of life."[14]

The distance between Mount Auburn and Boston, roughly six miles, allowed visitors to feel removed from the hustle and bustle of the city but—unlike Père Lachaise—was close enough

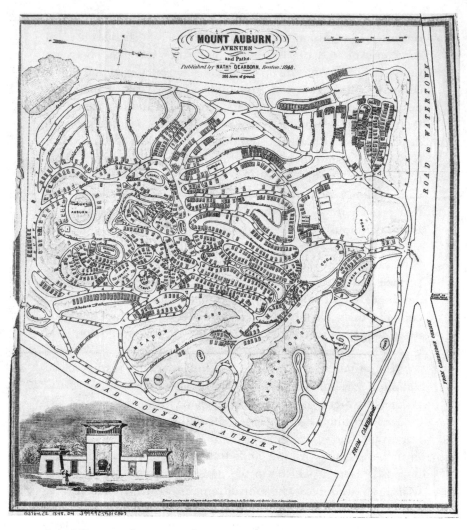

An 1848 map of Mount Auburn Cemetery published by Nathaniel Dearborn shows the circuitous avenues and winding walking paths that made the landscaped grounds an ideal place for Bostonians to stroll. Courtesy of the Norman B. Leventhal Map Center, Boston Public Library.

for them to visit regularly by carriage. The cemetery's promoters hoped that "from its immediate proximity to the Capital of the State, it will attract universal interest, and become a place of healthful, refreshing and agreeable resort, from early spring until the close of autumn." In addition, the cemetery's proximity to Harvard University—less than one and a half miles—made it "the favorite resort of students. There are hundreds now living, who have some of the happiest hours of the happiest periods of their lives, beneath the shade of the trees in this secluded forest."[15]

In the 1830s and 1840s similar rural cemeteries proliferated in cities across the nation. Some were sprawling burial graveyards in large cities, such as Philadelphia's Laurel Hill and Brooklyn's Green-Wood; others, such as Bangor, Maine's Mount Hope and Taunton, Massachusetts's Mount Pleasant, were smaller in scale. In 1839, the editors of the *Knickerbocker* described the view from Green-Wood Cemetery in the same terms that could be used to describe a classic Cole painting: "Views of distant mountains, the melancholy waste of ocean, with bays indenting picturesque shores; of bold headlands, looking down upon noble rivers, and cities sleeping in the sunshine; of rounded eminences and gentle slopes; of calm lakes, reposing in natural basins of surpassing beauty; and of rural villages, gleaming from the landscapes, on every hand." Like Mount Auburn, pedestrians could enter the grounds for free on weekdays to walk the "winding avenues and paths." By 1850, the network of paths was so extensive in this "place of great resort" that a guide to the cemetery recommended that newcomers stick to the main avenue and follow the directional signage. "Unless this caution be observed," the guide warned, "they may find themselves at a loss to discover their way out."[16]

The growing popularity of rural cemeteries as places to walk and recreate disturbed some observers. Andrew Jackson Downing and Frederick Law Olmsted, two of the preeminent landscape architects of their day, supported the establishment of rural cemeteries but decried the sense of pleasure and recreation that permeated these supposedly sacred grounds. "Indeed, the only drawback to these beautiful and highly kept cemeteries," Downing noted in 1848, "is the gala-day air of recreation they present. People seem to go there to enjoy themselves, and not to indulge in any serious recollections or regrets." An article in *Scribner's Monthly* observed "a certain incongruity between a graveyard and a place of recreation," but reasoned that "people were glad to get fresh air, and a sight of grass and trees . . . without considering too deeply whether it might not be better to have it all without the graves and without the funeral processions." However, rural cemeteries offered proof to many observers of Americans' desire for walking opportunities in natural settings, and a growing chorus of voices added the misuse of rural cemeteries to their list of justifications for constructing large public parks in American cities. As historian David Schuyler argues, the popularity of rural cemeteries "marked the confluence of two important ideas: the new attitude toward domesticated nature emerging in landscape painting, literature, and the debate over urban form; and the need for publicly constructed urban parks."[17]

The provision of walking opportunities in landscaped urban settings predated both the rural cemetery movement and the creation of large public parks. One of the most remarkable—and least known—examples was the canal-turned-greenway in Lowell, Massachusetts. Lowell's canal system consisted of several short canals that provided waterpower to the city's famous mills. The Boston Associates—the wealthy group of investors who owned most of Lowell's mills—became concerned about the town's stark appearance. Beginning in the early 1820s, they embarked on tree planting and landscaping projects along their canals and in their factory yards. The first plantings were adjacent to the company's boardinghouses, home to the young women who worked in the mills. Although the land between the street and the canal had been used as an informal promenade for several years, the new landscaping evoked a parklike setting that encouraged more people to use it as a public walk. Textile workers were encouraged to publish their poetry, short stories, and other writing in a monthly periodical called the *Lowell Offering*. An 1841 issue included an article by an admirer of a stand of elms recently planted along the canal. She wrote, "Many pleasant hours have I passed beneath their shade; and often while thus situated, have my thoughts wandered back to my 'far-away home,' and I would almost fancy myself there again, seated beneath some favorite tree on that loved spot." The Boston Associates' landscaping was in line with their overall paternalistic project to create a model community that resisted the negative social tensions of many factory towns. Yet the refinement the company owners tried to project could go only so far. As the Lowell girls, dressed in their best clothing, promenaded along the canals on Sunday afternoons, they commonly passed muddy Irish laborers digging out and repairing the lowered canals—working on the only day of the week when the mills could go without waterpower.[18]

As the Boston Associates manicured new sections of their canals, the greenway became an antidote to the drudgery of the mills, allowing Lowell's workers to walk in a constructed yet green setting. "Thousands swarm forth, who during the week are confined to the mills," wrote John Greenleaf Whittier, the Fireside Poet and outspoken Quaker abolitionist, of a Sunday afternoon along the greenway. "The weekly respite from monotonous in-door toil, afforded by the first day of the week was particularly grateful." When the Northern Canal along the Merrimack River was completed in 1847, city residents could follow the Merrimack, Western, Pawtucket, and Northern Canals in an approximately four-mile circuit of the city that took them through the rural countryside west and north of Lowell. By design, canals are relatively flat, so these four-mile jaunts were hardly strenuous, but they did offer an opportunity to experience walking in a natural setting, especially outside of town.[19]

The experimental greenway had a strong but fleeting influence on local walking culture before mounting demand for urban land allowed railroads and mills to impede on the canalway and disrupt the walk during the 1860s and 1870s. Although Lowell is one of the earliest examples of canal towpaths used as walkways, this became a common use by the late nineteenth and early twentieth centuries. The Lehigh and Delaware Canals in eastern Pennsylvania attracted walkers who picnicked at, sketched, and swam in canals that passed through industrial cities and the pastoral countryside.

Delaware Canal, early twentieth century. Men and women enjoy a
Sunday walk along the towpath of the Delaware Canal in
Uhlerstown, Pennsylvania. In the early twentieth century, the canal
was a popular place to stroll, paddle, and picnic. National Canal
Museum, *Delaware and Lehigh Canals: A Pictorial History of the
Delaware and Lehigh Canals National Heritage Corridor in
Pennsylvania* (Easton, Pa.: Canal History and Technology Press,
2005), 114. Courtesy of the Delaware & Lehigh National Heritage
Corridor and the National Canal Museum.

Unlike the tree-lined and well-manicured power canal at
Lowell, transportation canals, such as the Delaware Canal, were
more utilitarian. The canal companies removed adjacent trees to
prevent tangling with the ropes used to pull barges, and one can
speculate that the passing of thousands of mules meant that
walkers had to keep one eye on the ground before them. The canal waters were notoriously murky with anthracite coal silt, and

one canal historian notes that "swimmers came out of the water speckled with black." Despite these drawbacks, competition from railroads and the impending obsolescence of canals allowed visitors to view them as picturesque rather than industrial. Aqueducts and locks, once essential to the mineral economy of nineteenth-century America, became points of interest for outings. Walks along the canal towpath became a means of temporarily escaping the modernizing nation for a simpler time.[20]

The use of canal corridors as public trails reminds us that many American cities provided informal walking opportunities for their residents that have escaped the historical record, either because they were quickly replaced by new infrastructure or because they were never thought of as "parks" or "trails" in the first place. Lowell's greenways are especially remarkable because they anticipated grander landscaping and park projects, such as Boston's Emerald Necklace of parks, which were still decades in the future. When Frederick Law Olmsted and Calvert Vaux won the opportunity to design New York City's Central Park in 1858, Lowell residents had already been enjoying walks through their city's linear park for more than thirty-five years.

In the mid-nineteenth century, most American cities began to develop large public parks. Public health advocates believed that providing open space would allow cramped urbanites to participate in healthy exercise and, like the residents of Lowell, escape the drudgery of their factory jobs. More important, most nineteenth-century scientists agreed that miasmas—dangerous, foul-smelling gases thought to spread through overcrowding and other social ills—caused recurring epidemics of cholera and other diseases. As Charles Rosenberg recounts, major cholera epidemics plagued New York City in 1832, 1849, and 1866, and each time health officials struggled to find solutions. Parks were thought to act as natural filters to absorb the miasmas and purify the air, even though scientists eventually determined that cholera spread primarily through contact with fecal matter in drinking water, on soiled linens, and in food. During this time, literature advocating the acquisition of land and development of landscaped open space promoted the imagery of parks as "the

2026258 9

lungs of the city." Wealthy residents had the luxury of fleeing the city and epidemics to take up residence in the countryside. Reformers hoped that parks would provide similar relief for city residents left behind. For example, an 1853 *New-York Daily Times* letter to the editor in favor of "a Central Park" warned, "A million people will soon be crowded on this island, and if these Lungs of the City are not furnished, instead of the healthiest, this will become a sickly place. . . . We want a place where all can enjoy the sweet breath of rural life, which this will furnish to tens of thousands by a walk of a few hundred feet."[21]

The letter's recommendation—along with many similar calls—resulted in the purchase of a large tract of Manhattan land and an open design competition, which Frederick Law Olmsted and his colleague Calvert Vaux won in 1858. Although commentators from the landscape design and horticulture community were pleased with the selection of the so-called Greensward Plan for Central Park, many critics questioned the apparent chaos of its naturalistic elements, which closely reflected the picturesque aesthetic and a continuation of the design principles reflected in Mount Auburn and Green-Wood Cemeteries.[22]

Especially in its early years, Central Park encouraged and regulated walking in a number of ways. From the beginning, Olmsted's Greensward Plan sought to accommodate pedestrian traffic as well as horse-drawn vehicles. The network of drives, rides, and walks resembled that found in rural cemeteries, although the need to provide for through-streets and increased traffic required some innovations. Main traverse roads were sunken below grade to render them almost invisible to park users. Where necessary, arched bridges carried vehicles over footpaths, as at Glade Arch, or footpaths over drives, as at Spur Rock Arch. Some of the footpaths resembled trails, such as the narrow passage along the Loch and under the Glen Span in the North Woods ravine. Others were broad and resembled promenades. The experience of walking a footpath would be one of constant discovery, punctuated by open vistas. Olmsted consciously obscured sightlines and followed natural topography to bring variety, surprise, and curiosity to visitors. In the early years, the fresh plantings, turned earth, and graded paths would have intimated the engineers' hands, but soon the carefully planned trails would appear one with nature. Walkers along Olmsted's paths were being trained in what to expect from journeys through natural landscapes.[23]

Like the paintings of the Hudson River School, beneath the naturalistic appearance of Olmsted's picturesque park was a unified theory and order. In Olmsted's opinion, his ability to regulate the use of Central Park would determine the efficacy of the park to enlighten and rejuvenate visitors. Olmsted's fear was that visitors would treat the natural setting as they did woods and other common property on the urban periphery. Rules adopted in 1859 prohibited grazing livestock, swimming, fishing, and any disturbance to shrubbery or plants. He was especially concerned about the maintenance of the park's turf, crafting ordinances that would keep visitors off the lawns and meadows, except in several well-defined areas. These regulations limited the ability of working-class visitors to benefit from the park's amenities, especially since access to some of the common areas was permitted only on Saturdays, when most New York laborers were at work. Olmsted's draconian grass policies provoked harsh criticism. In 1869, a hyperbolic cartoon in *Frank Leslie's Illustrated Newspaper* depicted a corner of Central Park covered in signs listing Olmsted's various prohibitions including several that read "KEEP OFF THE GRASS." In some ways, these prohibitions resembled those imposed at Mount Auburn and Green-Wood, although preserving the sanctity of family plots generated less scorn than preserving Olmsted's manicured lawns. Although Olmsted's class bias certainly influenced his thoughts about social engineering, a more generous interpretation is that he was exercising the same prerogative of any trail builder or landscape architect. By keeping people off the grass and on the paths, the landscape would be revealed to visitors in an orderly manner that maximized the experience and would presumably encourage walking.[24]

The debate over common utilitarian space and manicured open space played out in cities across the country. Late nineteenth-century residents of Worcester, Massachusetts, for example,

THE CENTRAL PARK
A delightful resort for toil-worn NewYorkers

"Keep Off the Grass," 1865. Critics argued that Frederick Law
Olmsted's regulation of Central Park made it unwelcoming for
working-class visitors. "The Central Park," *Frank Leslie's Illustrated
Newspaper,* June 19, 1869, 221. Courtesy of the Library of Congress.

debated how parks should be used and by whom. Working-class
residents desired spaces for active recreation and sports, whereas the city officials charged with designing and managing parks,
along with the city's wealthiest residents, sought to provide themselves and their middle-class allies with well-manicured spaces
modeled on Olmstedian landscape principles. Landscaped parks
were certainly suited for leisure walking and restrained picnicking, but they left little room for sports. Worcester's solution was
to develop scenic parks on its affluent west side and utilitarian
playgrounds on its working-class east side. "The system of 'class

parks,'" notes historian Roy Rosenzweig, "meant both autonomy and inequality for Worcester workers."[25]

The conflict highlighted the varying preferences of different urban groups of the period and suggests why the nation's first walking clubs consisted primarily of middle- and upper-class residents. Given the regulated time of industrial labor, working-class preferences were for near-to-home open space that could be enjoyed for a variety of uses, from baseball games to Fourth of July celebrations. Walking in a natural setting may have been appealing to some of them, but that activity and the landscapes needed for it were not priorities. Of course, there were exceptions. One New England woman remembered waking early for hikes on her days off. "It was our custom to wake one another at four o'clock, and start off on a tramp together over some retired road whose chief charm was its familiarity, returning to a very late breakfast, with draggled gowns and aprons full of dewy roses," she remembered. "No matter if we must get up at five the next morning and go back to our humdrum toil, we should have the roses to take with us for company, and the sweet air of the woodland which lingered about them would scent our thoughts all day, and make us forget the oily smell of the machinery." Despite this woman's enthusiasm, her desire to walk for pleasure was exceptional and did not translate to a significant working-class presence in the nascent walking community.[26]

In addition to these major influences on American walking culture, other types of walking contributed to the emergence of hiking clubs in the late nineteenth century. Rural cemeteries, greenways, and parks provided walking opportunities to urbanites, but most Americans did not live near any amenities devoted specifically to walking or recreation. This did not prevent groups from walking along rural roads, through forests, and to the tops of mountains. Some walkers even identified manmade landscapes in which to walk, as in the case of pedestrianism.

As a formal sport, pedestrianism emerged from British aristocratic practice of placing bets on how far and how long their footmen could walk beside their carriages or around a circular racetrack. A 1663 diarist in London recorded, "The town talk this day is of nothing but the great foot-race run this day on Banstead Downes, between Lee, the Duke of Richmond's footman, and a tyler, a famous runner. And Lee hath beat him; though the King and Duke of York and all men almost did bet three or four to one upon the tyler's head." By 1809, the stakes, audience, and prestige of the pedestrian had grown. In July of that year, Captain Robert Barclay, a wealthy Scot with royal blood, completed his well-choreographed and widely celebrated "thousand miles in 1,000 hours for 1,000 guineas." Barclay, who along with a small team had planned and strategized his approach for more than a year, circled a track for nearly six weeks straight, walking at least one mile every hour. When he completed the feat, he earned, along with side bets, 16,000 guineas, or the equivalent of 320 years of income for the average artisan who composed his audience of thousands. American newspapers picked up the story from London and reported that Barclay finished "with perfect ease and great spirit, amidst an immense concourse of spectators."[27]

By the mid-nineteenth century, reports like these had inspired a small group of celebrity pedestrians in the United States. In the winter of 1861, a professional pedestrian named Edward Payson Weston walked between Boston and Washington, D.C., in eight days. The walk originated in a casual bet with a friend: Weston promised to walk to Abraham Lincoln's inauguration if Lincoln were to be elected. By the time Weston departed the State House in Boston, the journey had attracted crowds, press, and twenty-five thousand dollars in wagers. Throngs of spectators, drummers, and calls for him to speak met Weston at many of the towns along the route. Unfortunately, Weston was also temporarily arrested on several occasions, as his creditors took advantage of his brief visit to their town as an opportunity to demand payment. In the end, Weston made it to Washington in ten days and four hours. Despite missing his goal by two days, a crowd greeted him, and he received celebrity treatment. At the inaugural ball, Weston met Stephen Douglas, who in turn introduced him to Lincoln and the First Lady. "The President offered to pay the pedestrian's fare from Washington to Boston; but Mr. Weston informed him that as he had failed in the first attempt he felt obliged to try it again, and should walk from Washington to Boston." The record is silent on whether he succeeded.[28]

Most pedestrians never met the president or enjoyed the fanfare of Weston's walk, although some received temporary fame. An 1855 article in the *New York Daily Times* described with great enthusiasm the upcoming completion of an attempt by "Curtis" to walk 960 half miles in 960 half hours. "An immense concourse will undoubtedly be in at the death [of the race] and reward the victor, if not with the material wreath which in other ages crowned illustrious athletic effort, at least with the greener and more unfading laurels of public approbation and applause. . . . Nothing will ever surpass it, at least until the age of giants returns to the earth." Unfortunately, we do not know if he was successful. A less hyperbolic and perhaps more representative 1890 article in a Bethlehem, Pennsylvania, newspaper announced that C. Lucas, a local hotel porter who had moved to the South "dead broke," had won a fifty-two-hour walking match. Lucas had a novel approach to the race. "He lounged about the course in a listless sort of way until he heard some one remark that he was tired out. Then with a grin he would start off at a fast run and twice during the evening he turned handsprings just to show his condition." Lucas's prize was seventy-five dollars.[29]

With its emphasis on speed, manmade settings, and cash prizes, pedestrianism bore little resemblance to the rest of nineteenth-century walking culture. Men like Weston and Lucas did not walk as a means of contemplation or to experience picturesque landscapes; they walked to make money. The vast popularity of pedestrianism suggests, however, that Americans of various classes were interested in feats of the feet. Few contemporary accounts suggest why pedestrianism emerged when it did, but it is difficult to ignore the coincidence of industrialization, mechanization, and new forms of transportation—all developments that seemed to dwarf human strength—with pedestrianism's pure tests of endurance and stamina. In that sense, the motivations underlying pedestrianism resemble the desire expressed by public park builders and rural cemetery designers to find counterbalances to the drudgery of factory life and mechanization of society.

As with other forms of leisure walking, the celebration of long-distance or speed walking could occur only within a context of declining required daily walking.[30]

Most pleasure walking occurred as sporadic outings into the countryside rather than well-organized sporting events. On an overcast day in the spring of 1841, for example, a group of about a dozen young men and women piled into a couple of wagons and rode to the foot of central New Hampshire's Moose Mountain for a whortleberry-picking expedition. The climb was steep, but a well-worn path and blazes on trees suggest that the route was popular. "A toilsome way we found it," remembered one of the hikers, "some places being so steep that we were obliged to hold by the twigs, to prevent us from falling." On reaching the berry bushes, the party filled their pails and dippers to the brim, eating as they picked. Someone had packed fresh lemons and sugar to make lemonade with water from a nearby spring, which supplemented the bread and cheese they had packed for lunch. As the hikers moved farther up the mountain, the clouds broke, giving them a view of the countryside below. In terms that could describe a typical Hudson River School painting, the hikers described the picturesque view. "Far as the eye could reach, in a north and north-easterly direction, were to be seen fields of corn and grain, with new-mown grass-land, and potato plants, farmhouses, barns, and orchards—together with a suitable proportion of wood-land, all beautifully interspersed," wrote one of the group. "We could see people at work in their gardens, weeding vegetables, picking cherries, gathering flowers . . . far north might be seen the White Mountains of New Hampshire, whose snow-crowned summits seemed to reach the very skies." After taking in the view, the party descended the mountain on a less grueling trail that led past a grove of sugar maples and across a farm, at which they took tea and made small talk with the old farmer and his wife before returning home.[31]

This was a nineteenth-century walk that bears remarkable resemblance to hikes taken in the twenty-first century—aside, perhaps, from the hospitality of the path's adjacent landowners. There is little doubt that walks such as this were common throughout the century, especially as Americans gained more leisure time. Nineteenth-century hiking was embedded within routines of berry picking, picnicking, traveling, hunting, and even professional tasks, such as surveying.

The reports of Verplanck Colvin, best known as superintendent of the Adirondack Survey, show how a professional surveyor could blend tedious measuring and geological work with a hiker's pleasure and perspective. "The cliff, measured by cord and plummet is here about 126 feet in height. . . . Here you may lunch beside the brook, and gaze out past the Hanging Rock, across the valley," Colvin wrote in an 1869 article for *Harper's New Monthly Magazine*, which he intended as both a report on his survey work in the Helderbergs and encouragement to readers to visit. "From here you see a wide-spread level country, a true basin, bounded by distant mountain chains. . . . You see, nearest, the deep savage valley, with shades predominating, mountain-walled; the checkered fields and woods beyond, in vast perspective; the distant white farm-house and the red barns."[32]

Colvin was among a growing group of Americans who blurred the distinction between science and hiking and began to formalize their interest by founding clubs. The earliest example of this came when John Torrey organized professional and amateur botanists into the Torrey Botanical Club in 1867. Between 1819 and 1858, Torrey published a series of definitive catalogs of New York, Mid-Atlantic, and North American plants that made him a well-known figure in the American scientific community and, in the opinion of Europeans, "the foremost American botanist."[33]

Torrey had led informal outings since the 1840s, but the death of his wife in 1855 and a new position at Columbia University allowed him to devote more time to formalizing the walks. At first, the group consisted of fewer than ten close acquaintances and colleagues who walked to sites in and around New York City, but by 1858 the group was traveling as far as New Jersey's Pine Barrens and Pennsylvania's Poconos. "An attentive study of plants in their native haunts is essential to the advance of the science," Torrey argued, and this required significant time in the

THE CLIFFS.

The Helderberg Escarpment, 1869. Verplanck Colvin's sketch of the Helderberg Escarpment shows a well-dressed couple enjoying the picturesque view. Courtesy of *Harper's Magazine*.

field. In July 1870, one club member twice walked the length of Montauk Point "exploring its Botany very carefully" and reporting to the other members on the abundance of *Oenothera* growing there. Another member based his description of a species of trillium on "observations made in my pretty extensive tramps in the woods of Central and Western New York," during which he "sometimes walked for a whole day." Although club members rarely recorded the specifics of their walks, evidence such as this is embedded in their scientific notes.[34]

In the early years, the small group gravitated to Torrey on a personal level, and his expertise and enthusiasm kept the men coming back to his home and his campus herbarium for sporadic outings and ad hoc meetings. It was not until 1867 that a formal club emerged. "Our beginning was such a gradual accretion that those of us who were among the original members can hardly tell how it came to be called even a 'Club,'" remembered an early leader. By 1870, the group began publishing the *Bulletin of the Torrey Botanical Club*, which further formalized their activities and promoted the club to potential members. The publication also set a precedent of walking organizations publishing their scientific findings and accounts of walks in the form of elaborate journals. The pages of the *Bulletin* consisted primarily of brief reports from members on field observations and experiments conducted in gardens. Most of the content related to New York City and its environs, but the journal also included correspondence and reports related to western exploration and occasional international expeditions undertaken by individual members.[35]

Torrey died in March 1873 at the age of seventy-five, but by then the club had a life of its own that survived the leader's death. Nathaniel Lord Britton and other club members would successfully advocate for the establishment of the New York Botanical Garden in 1891—yet another type of walking landscape. Today, in the twenty-first century, the club is still in existence.[36]

The Torrey Botanical Club was not a hiking organization, and it is difficult to assess members' influence on New York City's walking culture. "Though formally devoted to botanical pursuits," note historians Laura and Guy Waterman, "the club inherited the physically robust interpretation of that science. . . . If not truly a mountain-climbing club, the Torrey Botanical Club has always been a vigorous bunch." Regardless of the club's classification, Torrey and his followers certainly invested walking with yet another meaning—that of scientific exploration. As we will see, managing the delicate balance between science and recreation would become a recurring task within late nineteenth-century hiking organizations.[37]

Although walking had much to do with ideas, aesthetics, and the provision of walking landscapes, one of the most important determinants of one's *desire* to walk was the *need* to walk. Americans who needed to walk everywhere had little incentive to create opportunities for arbitrary strolls, even if there was a set of rich, philosophical ideas available to invest their walking with meaning. In contrast, Americans who were freed—even slightly—from the need to use their feet at all times apparently were eager to adopt gratuitous walking as a pastime. The desire to re-create unnecessary work underlies much of the middle-class leisure experience. As the nineteenth century brought changes to American cities, the number of people who could rely on vehicles—rather than their feet—for transportation substantially increased. This development, perhaps more than the rest, allowed for the emergence of a hiking culture in the late nineteenth century.

Historians refer to most nineteenth-century American cities as "walking cities" for two reasons. First, the cities were geographically small and dense, which allowed residents to walk throughout the city with relative ease. In 1850, for example, Boston proper extended in a two-mile radius from City Hall. The densely developed portion of Philadelphia, at the time of its consolidation with Philadelphia County in 1854, was also roughly two miles in radius from Center Square. The densest portion of New York City extended from the southern tip of Manhattan roughly to Thirtieth Street, a distance of about three miles. Even along congested streets and walking at a leisurely pace, residents could traverse their cities in less than two hours.[38]

Second, the term "walking city" also refers to the need to walk on a daily basis. "Before the invention of the telephone in 1876 and the introduction of street railways in the 1850's," writes urban historian Sam Bass Warner, "face-to-face communications and movement on foot were essential ingredients of city life." Available modes of transportation and the condition of city streets—both closely related—dictated the need to walk. Attempts to pave notoriously muddy and potholed streets began in the 1660s, with the use of, first, cobblestones and then granite blocks, iron, cement, and wood planks. Each paving technique had its flaws, in either the durability of the surface or the cost of the materials. Carriages for personal transportation were rare in American cities, and most cities banned the galloping of horses and forced riders to walk beside their mounts. The emergence of popular horse-drawn public transportation came in the early 1800s, when hacks and cabs—modeled on private carriages— began to offer high-priced passenger service. The idea of the omnibus originated in France in the 1820s, and American operators began similar service in (mostly eastern) American cities. Omnibus use peaked in the 1850s, with 683 buses in New York City in 1854 and 322 buses in Philadelphia in 1858, which daily served as many as 120,000 passengers. In 1834, Charles Dickens, visiting on a lecture tour, described omnibuses as "amusing" but crowded, noisy, and operated by salty, immoral men. "We believe there is no instance on record, of a man's having gone to sleep in one of these vehicles," Dickens observed. The steep fares, bumpy and crowded rides, and slow pace prevented omnibuses from significantly changing the spatial layouts of American cities.[39]

Although improvements continued in the paving of roads throughout the nineteenth century, typically with gravel and cobblestone, most city streets—especially those in the less affluent neighborhoods of the periphery—remained unpaved through the 1890s. All of this is to say that, despite evolutions in paving and transportation, most Americans regularly walked significant distances. However, during the mid-nineteenth century, this began to change for small groups of wealthy people living in major cities. In Boston and its suburbs, such as Cambridge, a hodgepodge network of omnibus routes alleviated or at least supplemented daily walking. During the early 1840s, railroads began to change their policies to attract suburban commuters, prompting more wealthy Boston residents to purchase land and build homes in the suburbs. Historian of suburbanization Henry Binford notes, "By 1860, the number of Boston workers living outside the city rose to more than ten thousand." Indeed, by 1850, 33 percent of Cambridge residents commuted to Boston for work. By 1851, 32 percent of Boston commuters took the train and 30 percent walked. Using omnibuses and trains, some commuters—under the best circumstances—could almost eliminate daily walks. Of course, many suburbanites walked between their home and the train station and between the train station and their place of work. The revolution in travel, however, led to the transition from a walking to a riding city and thus required a reconceptualization of what it meant to walk for necessity and leisure.[40]

Given that the wealthiest Boston residents enjoyed a nascent transportation network that offered alternatives to walking, it should not be surprising that the first permanently organized hiking club emerged from this city. On January 8, 1876, a group of thirty-three men gathered in Room 11 of the Massachusetts Institute of Technology's Rogers Building to start planning the Appalachian Mountain Club (AMC) "for the advancement of the interests of those who visit the mountains of New England and adjacent regions, whether for the purpose of scientific research or summer recreation." This binary mission, expressed in the club's constitution as "scientific and artistic purposes," reflected the nineteenth-century developments that had led to the emergence of a walking culture and prompted the founding of the club. Of the 108 men and women who joined the club in 1876, 45 lived in Boston and 18 lived in Cambridge. The rest of the members were from smaller suburbs of Boston, such as Brookline and Jamaica Plain, and a few other New England cities. The AMC's founding represented both a watershed moment for American hiking and the culmination of nineteenth-century walking culture. Through its regular meetings and publications, the club became a clearinghouse for information about New England's mountains and how to experience them. Never before had a group of people systematically set forth to open access to the mountains by building trails, organizing outings, and sharing research. The founding of the AMC represented the beginning of organized hiking in America.[41]

2 HIKING TOGETHER

O N March 2, 1876, a select group of Boston residents found a simple postcard invitation in their mailboxes. "You are hereby invited to attend a meeting of the Appalachian Mountain Club to be held at the Institute of Technology on Wednesday, March 8th, at 3 1/2 PM," the invitation read. "We wish to bring our objects to the attention of the large class of persons interested in mountain exploration, and shall be indebted to you if you will extend this invitation to such of your friends, both ladies and gentlemen, as you think would be interested in our work." In response, nearly two hundred men and women packed a room at MIT. They looked on as the club's council conducted a short business meeting. The officers discussed filling vacancies and read correspondence, including an invitation from the Reverend John Worcester to use his study at North Conway—a town that served as a gateway to White Mountain trips—as a "summer rendezvous for the club." The club also voted, without fanfare, to admit female members, setting a precedent of relative equity for men and women. After dispatching with logistics, a series of club members addressed the crowd on a number of technical and popular topics, in most cases reading prepared papers. Charles Fay, for example, recounted a twelve-hour hike on the Tripyramids. "A large fraction of the distance could be saved and journey made much less fatiguing if a good path were laid out directly over it," he observed of the existing route. A talk by S. W. Holman on mountain barometers and one by C. H. Hitchcock on the Atlantic system of mountains were more technical but well received by the enthusiastic attendees. Following the paper presentations, the meeting adjourned with the promise of reconvening in April.[1] The large, engaged audience and the expansive agenda would not have suggested to the casual observer that the Appalachian Mountain Club had been founded only several weeks before this meeting. The impetus for the club, however, went back further.

The club and its immediate predecessors, such as the Alpine Club of Williamstown and the White Mountain Club of Portland, initiated organized hiking in the United States. These clubs resonated with potential hikers because, like many other nineteenth-century voluntary associations, they met social and psychological needs that had emerged with urbanism and industrialism. The earliest clubs' activities and organizational structure were a model for hikers who founded San Francisco's Sierra Club in 1892, Portland, Oregon's Mazamas in 1894, and other clubs across the nation in the ensuing years. Despite being separated by thousands of miles, America's first hiking clubs shared many characteristics. Middle- to upper-middle-class city dwellers who were often leaders in business, politics, culture, or education founded the clubs. Membership typically included both men and women, with women often holding important leadership posts. There was usually a twofold mission of scientific exploration and recreation, with members drawn to one or the other but participating in both. Finally, the AMC, Sierra Club, and Mazamas all published fine, detailed journals, which disseminated news of their activities and accomplishments to members, among clubs, and across the nation. In courting members, planning outings, selecting equipment, and documenting their activities, these early clubs invented American hiking and its culture. In the process they transformed nineteenth-century pleasure walking into a popular sport with deep meaning for its participants.[2]

Enthusiasm for founding the Appalachian Mountain Club
came from a small group of men interested in a wilderness area
one hundred miles north of Boston. Edward Charles Pickering,
the AMC's first president, remembered a widespread desire
among the individuals studying the White Mountains during the
mid-nineteenth century for "some means of bringing [their] results to the notice of those most interested." In the early 1870s,
Pickering began climbing with W. G. Nowell, and the two men
began to speculate about a club that would render the mountains more accessible by capitalizing on the increasing popularity of the White Mountains. "I remember in particular the ascent
of one of those many summits said to be unascended and inaccessible, which we have all gone up," Pickering explained to fellow members at the club's annual meeting, "only to find them
frequently visited and presenting no difficulty." He and Nowell
resolved to build trails up those mountains to provide access for
others. However, they felt that they needed a club to recognize
and support the work.[3]

In looking for models, Pickering drew on the expertise of
Samuel Scudder, another influential early member of the AMC,
who had helped to found one of the nation's first hiking clubs,
the Alpine Club of Williamstown, Massachusetts. Scudder had
attended Williams College in the 1850s, studied under Louis Ag-
gasiz at Harvard University's Lawrence Scientific School, and
become one of New England's leading naturalists. "He knew New
England thoroughly," a later biographer tells, "and the rural
beauty of her peaceful valleys, and the majestic boldness of her
mountain peaks were the delight of all his years." In the 1870s,
Scudder was a cofounder of the Appalachian Mountain Club and
one of its most active members, but in 1863, he was a man in his
twenties participating in a fledgling walking club.[4]

In April 1863, Albert Hopkins, a professor at Williams College, founded the Alpine Club "to explore the interesting places
in the vicinity, to become acquainted, to some extent at least,
with the natural history of the localities, and also to improve the
pedestrian powers of the members." On May 2, the club went on
its first outing, "to Birch and Prospect Glens, a six mile tramp

over fields and rough wagon roads." Based in the Berkshires, club members had easy access to a varied landscape. During their hikes, "the whole region was scoured." In 1863, the club made nineteen trips, including several to nearby Mount Greylock and a two-day camping trip to Manchester, Vermont, to climb Mount Equinox. In 1864 and 1865, the club made nearly forty more outings, including camping trips to Pontoosuc Lake, Greylock, and other lakes and mountains in northwestern Massachusetts.[5]

In an article he wrote for *Appalachia* in 1884, Scudder quoted a typical hike description from the club's record book. "The gathering of chestnuts, bright leaves, and berries made the progress up the mountain a slow one, and a slight rain was falling when Laurel Glen was reached," the club's chronicler recorded of a walk near town. "Undeterred by this, however, the Club clambered up the ledge, and, seated on the edge of Pulpit Rock, enjoyed the view of the valley with the shower sweeping over the distant mountains. Just north of this they stood on Solomon's Housetop, and watched the crashing descent of numerous rocks which Professor Hopkins and Mr. Denison, by great exertions, loosed from their resting-places and rolled down the steep."[6]

In 1864, the club made a weekend trip to the Hopper, a deep ravine on the west side of Greylock. It was a favorite destination. "Here we sketched, botanized, penetrated the depths, made various studies in natural history and sociology, and counted as our chief exploit a climb up the steepest face of Greylock." The club members' activities during the trip are evidence of how many aspects of nineteenth-century walking culture merged into a single outing. The club's "chief exploit" was hiking, but the various motives for walking in nature settings—botany, geology, sociology, and recreation—were present.[7]

Outings took up most of the club's energy, and there is no evidence that the club blazed or maintained walking paths. However, in 1865, club members attempted to improve a series of lakes that they had discovered on a hillside near Williamstown. The land around the lakes was marshy, which made it difficult to get to them, and during dry spells, the lakes could almost disappear. "Accordingly the Club dislodged rocks from the mountainside above, and rolled them down to be so placed as to afford a better approach to the shore. . . . At another time our energies were turned in the opposite direction, changing the course of a stream that it might feed the lakes." Efforts to manipulate the landscape would become common among later clubs.[8]

In 1865, the club made what would be its most significant—and last recorded—trip to the White Mountains to climb Mount Washington. Meeting in White River Junction, New Hampshire, they took the train to Littleton, where they hired a team that drove them to Crawford House. From there, the group walked up Mount Willard and arrived at the foot of Mount Madison, via a Pinkham Notch road that was "in a very rough condition." The hikers spent a couple of days enjoying Glen Ellis's Falls, Crystal Cascade, Madison Brook, and Diana's Baths before making their ascent of Mount Washington on Monday. They rode as far as Glen House, walked up the carriage road to the old Tuckerman's Ravine path, dined at Hermit Lake, and summited in late afternoon, "then in the clouds."[9]

By the mid-1860s, Mount Washington was already a tourist destination. In 1819, Ethan Allen Crawford laid out the Crawford Path, by some accounts the oldest hiking trail in the United States. The path served both horses and hikers visiting the summit. In their account of the trip, Alpine Club members referred sarcastically to being "properly introduced to the pleasures of White Mountain travel in those days, by securing a single room for the five ladies and the parlor floor for the three gentlemen." Not all nearby accommodations were as primitive as they claimed. For example, an 1856 visitor to the Profile House in Franconia Notch told New York Times readers, "Its parlors are remarkably tasteful and exceedingly cheerful in their appearance. The drawing room compares favorably, both in dimensions and furniture, with the corresponding apartments of first-class hotels at Saratoga and Lebanon." More affluent visitors to the region typically could afford to sleep in private quarters rather than on parlor floors. Following the White Mountain trip, the official record of the club ends, and historians know little about its fate, only that by 1884 Scudder could write that "the Club is by no means extinct; but it lives rather in the pleasant memories of the past than in the exploits of the present."[10]

The Alpine Club's membership was primarily female. Of the original twelve members, nine were young, unmarried women living in Williamstown. The three male members included Hopkins, another Williams professor, and a reverend. Why was the club led by women? The coincidence of the club's founding with the Civil War may suggest that male residents and Williams undergraduates were preoccupied with other concerns. Between 1863 and 1865—the only years for which there is an official record—women held all the club offices except "chronicler." The chronicler had the important job of creating a narrative of each outing to be read or distributed at the next meeting, and in the Alpine Club, men always held that position. As Scudder explained, "Perhaps this should be expected in a collegiate town where women find no admission to the halls of learning." By the end of the first year, the club had added thirteen hikers, including Scudder, which brought the total to twenty-four members, where it remained. The club's policy of admitting no new members "unless they are possessed of good pedestrian powers, are enthusiastic lovers of Nature, and show a willingness to receive instruction from the members of older standing" apparently meant that no new members would be added at all.[11]

As closely as the Alpine Club of Williamstown resembled future hiking organizations, Pickering never mentioned it as an inspiration for the Appalachian Mountain Club. He did, however, know of another club founded in the early 1870s that had the potential to provide a coordinating influence. A group of engineers, surveyors, and enthusiastic explorers and walkers formalized the White Mountain Club of Portland, Maine, during an 1873 ascent of Mount Carrigain—an isolated and steep peak in the central White Mountains. The men had chosen an adventurous and difficult route, eschewing the range's well-known summits for Carrigain. "It is none of your civilized mountains, the resort of tourists, made easy of ascent by footpaths, carriage ways and railroads, like your tame Mt. Washington," an account of the ascent claimed. "It is a savage peak, rising remote in the wilderness." According to a pamphlet of verse and sketches documenting the outing, the group of six soon-to-be club members rode the train from Portland to the foot of the mountains, where they secured "a sure-eyed guide . . . to track the pathless woods." The route was difficult, and the hikers found themselves struggling over downed trees, tangled in the underbrush, and "tripped up at every step." Despite their slow and strenuous progress, the first night ended on a high note: "How sweet it is in solemn night to lie beneath the sky, and listen to the murmuring brook that drops and gurgles by." Although they had the distant "scars" on Mount Lowell as a landmark, shortly after breaking camp the next morning, the group found themselves lost and heading in the wrong direction. The brooks that should have supplied water were dry, and the climbing became steeper. Handgrips of dusty moss gave way, and some of the men tumbled down the hillside. On locating a small stream, the men drank deeply of its cool water—and of their bottles of brandy—and made camp for the night. The next morning they began the ascent, climbing and scrambling to a false summit, where a thunderstorm forced them back to camp. Soaked thoroughly and reeling from their failed attempt, they decided to go home. Although the final assessment was that the trip was a "disappointment sorest," at some point during the hike, the men resolved to form the White Mountain Club and continue their expeditions throughout the region.[12]

The original group of Carrigain hikers and their associates composed the club's leadership. The backgrounds of the leaders are suggestive of the many nineteenth-century trends that led to the emergence of the White Mountain Club and similar organizations. Engineers, such as George Vose and John F. Anderson, hiked alongside Harrison Bird Brown, a White Mountain landscape artist, and Joseph Thompson, a founding member of the Portland Society of Art. The men were well-educated members of the upper middle class to upper class and held prominent positions in Portland and the region. For example, Edward H. Davies—another early leader—was president of the Portland Gas

Light Company. Many of the men also had served in the Civil War and shared memories of battle and camaraderie.

As a group of relatively wealthy men freed from both combat and daily toil, early hikers sought to reaffirm their masculinity by metaphorically conquering mountains with a martial spirit. Middle- and upper-class American males of the late nineteenth century worried that modern civilization placed undue strain on the nerves. Sitting behind a desk and fretting about business concerns drained men of their competitive strength, they feared. These concerns became more acute as the ordeal of the Civil War—and the personal feats of its heroes—faded into memory. War had provided a means of reaffirming manliness and virility and overcoming the listlessness of modern life. Hiking, with its scaling of mountains, primitive living arrangements, and camaraderie, was one obvious outlet.[13]

Although the White Mountain Club regularly hiked the region surrounding Portland, their major outings avoided well-visited tourist attractions on the resort circuit in favor of isolated and undeveloped mountains, such as Mount Carrigain and the adjacent area known as the Pemigewasset Wilderness. The club also planned many hikes in the Mahoosuc Range, an extension of the White Mountains in western Maine. Modern guides to those mountains credit the club for laying out the original trail system, and some of the placenames still reflect their presence.

Detailed accounts of early hikes are rare, but John Meade Gould—an important member who would draw from his club experiences to publish the popular book *How to Camp Out*—captured one White Mountain Club outing in his diary. The description provides insight into a typical hiking expedition of the 1870s, in this case a return hike to Mount Carrigain planned by a small group of members in 1875. The group departed Portland on a Tuesday afternoon. Gould was a bank teller in downtown Portland, and he remained at the bank until 1:35 pm. He then walked to the Eastern Depot on Commercial Street, where he met Ed and Fred Morse and another club member. The men boarded the Portland and Ogdensberg Railroad bound for Crawford Notch and "played cards about all the way." By 1875, the P and O provided direct access to the White Mountains from Portland. Club members enjoyed some of the special privileges of the line because John F. Anderson, a club founder, was the company's chief engineer. During the club's 1873 and 1875 trips, they could choose between riding in the smoking car, the cab of the engine, or even on the cowcatcher affixed to the front of the engine. From his perilous perch on the catcher, Gould estimated that the train was traveling sixty miles an hour—"the most tremendous speed I ever rode at on the front of an engine." The club took the train to Upper Bartlett, where they spent the night at an inn and secured a guide and a workman.[14]

Although the group thought of their hike as an expedition into wilderness, Gould's notes from the next day reflect the variety of resource extraction and construction then under way throughout the White Mountains. The P and O construction train could take them as far as The Frankenstein, a trestle over one of the Crawford Notch's gorges that Anderson had helped engineer. The hike continued along Sawyer Creek and the granite-hauling roads that paralleled it. As the roads faded, the men followed a blazed path, and "the walking consequently grew harder and the climbing over trees a frequent thing." As the terrain turned more rugged, the men sensed their growing isolation. "The woods were grand," Gould recorded, but "exceedingly wild." He speculated that poor timber and fishing explained the few inroads into the region.[15]

After eight or nine miles of climbing, the men made camp for the evening, instructing their guides to build two shelters with a fire between. Expecting rain, everyone contributed to the effort by gathering brush and spruce bark peeled by the guides, which they used to construct a twelve-foot-by-eight-foot roof. "For sides we had the bank for one and bark for the other and trusted in rubber blankets to cover our feet if it rained." Gould felt comfortable in the shelter, sleeping in a nightshirt and listening to one of the party—a veteran of the Civil War—sing, "We met the Johnny Rebs, and we made the rebels flee, 'til our horses took to water in the Ocmulgee." By the morning, rain and fog had settled in, confining the men to camp. They told stories and talked politics, which led to "the most unmerciful abuse of law, lawyers and courts I had heard for some time." The men spent the next few days near camp, summiting Mount Carrigain for a panoramic view of the mountain range and gorging on the extra food they had brought. On June 11, they descended the same way they came, spent the night at Cobb's house, and then Gould returned home to Portland. Trips like this became an annual tradition for small numbers of White Mountain Club members. They would also provide the model for much larger and regularly scheduled outings of the AMC.[16]

The members of both the Williamstown and Portland clubs were inventing formal hiking with each outing, especially when it came to the equipment. Almost every excursion included a new pack or article of clothing that the men field tested. On their 1877 outing, some of the Portland men used simple packs with two shoulder straps. Gould used a leather haversack—or single-strapped backpack—issued during the Civil War and "wore it as our soldiers did in war times." Two other men brought along a recently concocted "pack-saddle" that "proved to have too limber steel" and "had much trouble from it." Gould notes that poorly designed equipment occasionally caused falls, twisted ankles, and unnecessary fatigue that slowed a hike's progress. Joseph Sanger, one of the men wearing the new pack-saddle, as well as a new pair of shoes, suffered the most. A short distance into their journey, Gould noted, "Sanger's pack now troubled him so that he began to be a burden to the others of us. His new shoes also troubled him." Later in the day, Sanger "kept growing lamer and lamer and his pack-saddle and tin box dangled along every moment threatening to trip him again." At the end of the hike, the poor equipment caused a serious problem. "Sanger's new boots turned over and his sprained ankle gave way every now and then." Most of the men continued without him and sent a horse back to pick him up.[17]

Even when their gear was working well, the men bore heavy loads. In their bag, each man carried his own bread, meat, pickles, rum, clothing, and blankets. Gould carried a blanket, sheet, nightshirt, extra pair of stockings, and rubber tarp. General rations, which were mostly carried by the guide and workman, included coffee, sugar, cooking supplies, two axes, and three canteens.

Gould would eventually compile his knowledge into the guide *How to Camp Out*, published by Scribner, Armstrong, and Company in 1877. Ed Morse, another White Mountain Club member, provided the sketches. The 134-page book included chapters on "getting ready," camping with or without a baggage wagon, clothing, equipment, marching, and hygiene. Unlike most of the nineteenth-century accounts of camping and hiking, such as Adirondack Murray's celebratory *Camp Life in the Adirondacks* (1868), Gould dismissed the idealization of the outdoors and offered blunt advice that would make camping and hiking as comfortable as possible. This played well with an audience of hikers seeking challenging experiences. "This is *very* hard work for a young man to follow daily for any length of time," he wrote of hiking in the backwoods. "Although it may sound romantic, yet let no party of young people think they can find pleasure in it for many days." Gould offered practical advice about cutting down on unnecessary equipment. Although from his diary we know he had interest in trying new gear, he warned against spending money on it. "Every year there is put upon the market some patent knapsack, folding stove, cooking-utensil, or camp trunk and cot combined; and there are always for sale patent knives, forks, and spoons all in one, drinking-cups, folding portfolios, and marvels of tools." He advised, "Let them all alone: carry your pocket-knife, and if you can take more let it be a sheath or butcher knife and a common case-knife." Elsewhere, he suggested the importance of farmers in providing food and places to sleep. "Do not be saucy to the farmers nor treat them as 'country greenhorns.' There is not a class of people in the county of more importance to you in your travels; and you are in honor bound to be respectful to them."[18]

Despite this sound advice, which Gould claimed came from years of observing hiking parties, he ignored what he had almost certainly witnessed when it came to women. Women participated in the leadership of the Alpine Club of Williamstown and the regular outings of the Appalachian Mountain Club, which by the time of the book's publication would have been in existence for at least a year. However, Gould writes, "There are few mountains that it is advisable for ladies to try to climb. Where there is a road, or the way is open and not too steep, they may attempt it; but to climb over loose rocks and through scrub-spruce for miles, is too difficult for them." Perhaps Gould's desire to maintain the highest peaks as a bastion of masculinity led him to disregard women's early climbing accomplishments. His favorite experiences with hiking—as depicted in his diary—were with men, talking bluntly and coarsely of politics and war, and he could not envision a woman taking part in such an experience.[19]

This misrepresentation aside, *How to Camp Out* was a significant contribution to a growing literature of practical advice about hiking and camping. With Gould as author and Morse as illustrator, the book was also a key achievement for the White Mountain Club, even as the group began to slip into obscurity. That a large press was willing to publish the book testifies to the growing market for information about mountain recreation. This was no small feat for Gould and his fellow club members, who after all were literally inventing the methods and culture of hiking with each outing.

Despite the impressive accomplishments of the White Mountain Club and Alpine Club of Williamstown, their small size and relatively limited geographical reach made them imperfect models for larger hiking organizations with more complex missions. As he considered founding the Appalachian Mountain Club, Pickering's final assessment was that "the object of the Portland [White Mountain] Club is . . . amusement rather than scientific study and exploration." He believed that there was a need for a new type of organization and began to move forward with planning a Boston-based club. On New Year's Day, 1876, Pickering sent fifty men an invitation to a meeting at MIT on January 8 for "those interested in mountain exploration." At the first meeting, Pickering laid out his vision for the club, and Charles Fay—a mathematician and linguist at Tufts University who would later found the American Alpine Club in 1902—was elected chair. In the two months between that January meeting and the first public meeting on March 8, a small group of "original members" developed bylaws and a constitution and elected officers. There is no mention of women at those first meetings, and the requirement that inductees secure two member endorsements and a full club vote ensured that early membership was thoroughly controlled.[20]

The first issue of the club's journal, *Appalachia*, described the Appalachian Mountain Club's purpose as "the advancement of the interests of those who visit the mountains of New England and the adjacent regions, whether for the purpose of scientific research or summer recreation." This mission combined two of the major impulses that contributed to the rise of nineteenth-century leisure walking. The club's founders considered including members interested in both art and science as a way of uniting similar pursuits that otherwise would have resulted in the founding of two separate organizations, as the case would be later in the century in Portland, Oregon. "Those familiar with the discussions of the meetings preliminary to the organization of the Club, need not be reminded of the debate which resulted in the wedding of the scientific and aesthetic elements," Councillor of Art Charles Fay explained. "It was felt that the former, like a strong husband, would do the laborious honor-bearing work, and the latter as a graceful enthusiastic consort, would win many friends to the association." In other words, the assumption was that science would earn the club legitimacy, while love of mountain scenery would earn the club members.[21]

This would prove to be a prescient and ultimately successful approach, but the phrasing of Fay's explanation also suggests that men and women interested in scientific pursuits dominated the early years of the club. Elsewhere, Fay explicitly criticized aesthetic hiking, arguing that this motive for entering the mountains led to less astute hikers. "The wish to enjoy the prospect becomes the pretext for repeated halts," he claimed. "The intellect is busy with other materials. The will acts with less vigor." However, this assertion only held for those who, like Fay, believed mountain exploration was an entirely scientific pursuit. In reality, most outings blended aesthetics and science in similar ways to those of Verplanck Colvin and other nineteenth-century surveyors and geologists who mixed their professional, utilitarian outlook on the mountains with a deep appreciation for the landscape. Despite the AMC founders' desire to earn legitimacy for the club through its scientific contributions, the same mixing of motives was certainly true of its members, who often joined for more than one reason.[22]

The Appalachian Mountain Club began publishing *Appalachia* on a shoestring budget in the summer of 1876. The journal quickly became a crucial means of articulating the dual purposes of the club. Throughout the 1870s and 1880s, each issue included several technical articles on surveying calculations and equipment, progress on a pedantic system of mountain nomenclature, discoveries of geological formations and explanations of theory, and detailed lists of flora and fauna with their Latin names. Pages of equations, charts, and lists of surveying stations often accompanied essays. For example, Edward Pickering's seventeen-page article "Heights of the White Mountains" includes seven tables of micrometer-level readings and related data, several taking up multiple pages. The format and tone of Pickering's article suggests that he was writing for an audience already convinced of the topic's importance. His meticulous recounting of each surveying station and calculation indicates that his audience would not have been satisfied with a simple list of mountain heights. Being an AMC member was about joining in the "science" of mountain hiking and sharing in the process of creating scientific knowledge that resulted from club excursions. Indeed, this and other *Appalachia* articles read like a manual for gathering data in the mountains that would allow all members to contribute.[23]

Despite this optimism, one may justifiably wonder how the typical recreational hiker regarded a comment such as Pickering's that the "simplicity of the operation is shown by the formula $A = 0.227\ k\ (r - l + 2 + k) + B$" or the instructions for building plane tables, telemeters, and micrometers. Both appeared in early issues. Many other nineteenth-century walkers were motivated by natural beauty, a deistic spiritualism, and the desire to escape the commotion of towns and cities. Although

AMC Camp Party, 1893. Club members gather at the Perch on
New Hampshire's Mount Adams. From the time of its founding,
the club welcomed both men and women as members. Courtesy of
the Appalachian Mountain Club Library & Archives.

they had a casual interest in geology and botany, most had little
desire to devote their leisure time to scientific work. As the club's
founders anticipated, these members were drawn to the "aesthetic" mandate of the club, which grew in importance throughout the late nineteenth century.[24]

During the first few years of the club's existence, activity focused on the White Mountain regions accessible by rail and near
to lodging, from which small parties launched expeditions into
the backcountry. The time, planning, and cost required for each

outing excluded large numbers of potential members. Beginning in 1879, the itinerary began to reflect a growing interest in more accessible recreational walking, with the club planning several outings relatively near to Boston. "They lack, of course, the grandeur of the mountains, they appeal but slightly, if at all, to the sentiment of the sublime," Fay unenthusiastically wrote to members of Boston's surrounding hills, "but the cultivating influences of the serene and beautiful, the broadening tendency of the extended, the invigorating refreshment of cheerful exercise they can impart." Fay saw local walks as a compromise. The landscape of eastern Massachusetts could not compete with the grandeur of the White Mountains, but perhaps it was good enough to build enthusiasm that would eventually increase membership and lead to more substantial outings to mountain regions. This approach was remarkably successful. An 1879 walk to Mount Wachusett—a short mountain forty miles outside of Boston—brought out 125 participants, while walks around Waltham's Prospect Hill and Milton's Blue Hills attracted dozens of hikers. Fay's enthusiasm grew, and he recommended adding trips for public school students and constructing viewing platforms on nearby hills. "May not this association," he asked, envisioning an expanded mandate for the fledgling club, "be expected to become a centre of influence in the encouragement of a more general and more intimate relationship with nature?"[25]

By the end of the nineteenth century, Fay's initial reservations about promoting Boston's countryside had been swept away by enthusiasm for walks and hikes of all types. In 1897, for example, Houghton Mifflin published *Walks and Rides in the Country round about Boston* on behalf of the club. A local journalist, Edwin M. Bacon, developed the text, which covered thirty-six walks and horse rides within a twelve-mile radius of downtown Boston. Bacon hoped the book would encourage readers "to learn this whole region by heart." Although the club created the book in response to interest in local walking opportunities, Bacon's quasi-apologetic description of Boston's landscape is reminiscent of Fay's words nearly twenty years earlier. "Although much of the natural beauty of the region has been destroyed by

man, and some of the fairest portions are scarred by ugly build-
ings, examples of the most depressing mercantile and domestic
architecture," Bacon wrote, in an apparent attempt to lower ex-
pectations, "it yet remains, if not as Captain John Smith described it before the advent of the European settler, 'the paradise
of all these parts,' the most charming region surrounding any
modern city." Bacon's reluctance to endorse fully Boston's landscape belied a lingering tension within the AMC over its role as a
mountain club and a leading recreational and cultural institution. For his part, Bacon reconciled the various preferences of
club members by advancing a now-familiar aesthetic of walking
to justify the varied landscape surrounding Boston. "Much that
is old is mingled with the new, country roads touch modern thor-
oughfares, and rural by-ways lead from beaten paths directly to
rural parts," he wrote, in language reminiscent of nineteenth-
century landscape painting. "No lovelier or more varied walks
are anywhere to be found," he argued, including, presumably, in
the White Mountains.[26]

Somewhere between the Appalachian Mountain Club's interest in aesthetics and science was the work of making what the
club called "improvements." This meant building shelters, clearing overlooks, erecting signage, and building trails. The AMC
created a department to oversee this work. Regardless of one's
motives for entering the mountains, trails and shelters were essential to a hiker's safe and comfortable experience. "A few only
are fitted by education or natural taste for the scientific investi-
gations that are the most important objects of our society," observed Wilbur B. Parker, councilor of improvements in 1879,
"but all may appreciate at a glance the benefits of better paths to
difficult summits, sheltered camps for passing the night, and
clearings which render accessible new points of view or objects
of special interest." As a result, the councilor of improvements
became an important position within the club hierarchy.[27]

Before 1876, trails were built largely by local residents for
their own use or by proprietors of inns and resorts to entertain
guests. In some cases, this trail building could result in extensive
networks. For example, around 1830, Nathaniel Greeley moved

to New Hampshire's Waterville Valley on the southern side of the White Mountains and began receiving guests suffering from breathing ailments and other tourists. As business picked up, Greeley sought to provide walking and hiking options for his guests. In the 1850s, he began work on a network of hiking and equestrian trails branching out from the valley to surrounding peaks. "Greeley's trail system was ahead of its time," observe Laura and Guy Waterman. "As late as 1875, nowhere else in the mountains of the Northeast was there anything approaching a modern trail system."[28]

The founding of the Appalachian Mountain Club renewed interest in trail building. In its first year, the club ambitiously proposed twenty trails of varying lengths and terrain and identified seven for "speedy construction." The appropriate characteristics of a trail would evolve over time and become contentious at different points in the AMC's—and many clubs'—history. Councillor of Improvements William G. Nowell described the 1876 standards as, "First, that all paths should be made a good width, from six to eight feet; second, that they be cleared of all under-brush and trip-roots; third, that holes in them be filled, so far as practicable." To distinguish official AMC trails from the many old and unmaintained trails crisscrossing the mountains, the councilor approved an official club stamp in the shape of an "A" to be used as blazes along the path. These guidelines were the first attempt to standardize the ancient act of trail building.[29]

Nowell was a good choice for the AMC's first councillor of improvements because he had experience in cutting trails and with contracting with locals for trail construction. In the early 1870s, he worked with another famous trail builder, Charles E. Lowe, to construct a trail from Randolph, New Hampshire— where Lowe lived and Nowell vacationed—southward into the northern Presidential Range. Nowell understood the connection between opening access to the mountains and building a constituency for the club. For example, in 1877, Nowell oversaw the completion of a trail to the summit of Boy Mountain. A group of nonclub volunteers, both male and female, completed the work. The volunteers also cleared more than ten thousand square feet near the summit "in the interest of the topographic and art departments." Nowell reflected on the simple path's importance and his obvious emotional response to the scene. "When the setting sun is flooding the green valley below with misty gold, bathing the shoulders and penetrating the uttermost recesses of the ravines of the Great Range with warm hues of rose and purple, and transmuting the stony gray peaks aloft, into amethyst," he wrote, "those who linger on this little mountain till near the coming of the night shadows, will not fail to perceive why the Club should prize what has been done here in its name during the past season." For Nowell, there was no contradiction between his appreciation for the sun setting over the mountains and his work to improve the summit for taking topographical readings. In the area of "improvements" club members could find both scientific and aesthetic motives.[30]

Nowell and his fellow trail builders, using a combination of volunteer and contracted labor, completed a number of important projects during the first five years of the club's existence. This work was not without inconvenience. Looking back on this prolific period in 1880, Councillor of Improvements A. E. Scott regretted that more work could not be finished:

> We remember . . . with what enthusiasm we looked forward to the November meeting, picturing in our minds a report of twenty smooth paths, eight feet wide, free from trip roots, the trees along their sides spotted with the Club hatchet, and the rocks on the mountain-tops blazing with "A.M.C." And, while we look back with pride on the work that has been accomplished from year to year, our experience forces us to admit, that wielding an axe on a mountain-side, or lugging stones in the ledges with which to build cairns, in midsummer, has a cooling effect on one's ardor in path-building, if not on the temperature of one's body; and that the many so-called improvements must be accomplished slowly, and by hard labor.

As Scott noted in closing, most of that hard labor came from people living near the trails rather than from members themselves. This problem would be addressed in the future, as the club cultivated expertise in construction among its own members as it built more trails across the varied terrain of New England. For now, the club would have to be satisfied with sparking the modern trail-building movement that the rest of the nation would join in the early twentieth century.[31]

By 1898, membership in the Appalachian Mountain Club topped one thousand for the first time. The club's dual mandate of scientific exploration and aesthetic recreational pursuits made it popular with a variety of potential walkers, hikers, and mountaineers. Beginning with its first public meeting, the AMC's progressive stance on permitting female members and allowing women to serve as councilors enabled the organization to court talented new members and encouraged whole families to participate. The club's journal *Appalachia* disseminated the AMC's achievements among members and to other clubs. In short, the AMC had crafted a structure and raison d'être that made it a model for similar organizations across the nation and well positioned for exponential growth in the early twentieth century.

John Muir, the famous advocate for wilderness, was one of the people paying attention. Muir had been a champion of nature walking for many years, though most of his expeditions were solitary. "Since coming to this Pacific land of flowers I have walked with Nature on the sheeted plains, along the broidered foothills of the great Sierra Nevada, and up in the higher piney, balsam-scented forests of the cool mountains," he wrote in December 1868, of his time exploring San Joaquin Valley, the High Sierra, and the Yosemite Valley. The year before, Muir had completed his one-thousand-mile walk from Indiana to Florida. During the walk, Muir usually traveled alone, freeing him to follow his own schedule and routes, which changed on a whim. "My plan," he wrote of his 1867 walk, "was simply to push on in a general southward direction by the wildest, leafiest, and least trodden way I could find." Similarly, during his first summer in the Sierras, Muir eschewed established "trails" for a consciously erratic exploration that he believed mimicked nature. "In these walks there has been no human method—no law—no rule," he recorded in his journal. "A strong butterfly full of sunshine settles not long at any place. It goes by crooked unanticipated paths from flower to flower. Sometimes leaving blossoms of every taste, it alights in the mud of a stream, or glances up into the shadows of high trees, or settles on loose sand or bare rock. Such a life has been mine, every day and night of last summer spent beneath the open sky."[32]

Muir eventually would become a celebrated mountaineer, guide, and promoter of the woods, but his contributions to American hiking are ambiguous. Whereas eastern clubs of the mid- to late twentieth century were shifting toward an emphasis on group hiking, trail development, and improving mountain access, Muir's approach was more nuanced. He hiked most often alone—walking into the backwoods for days, weeks, or entire seasons, returning only when his always meager bread supply had dwindled to starvation level. Although Muir was remarkably comfortable in the mountains, one must wonder how readers and fellow hikers responded to his methods of exploration, such as these directions for accessing a waterfall in "the deepest and most inaccessible" section of Yosemite Gorge: "A view of the lower part may be obtained from a point one hundred and fifty yards farther down the edge on the same side, by holding on to a live-oak branch and leaping out over the rounded brow." Muir's well-known account of slipping behind Yosemite Falls on a narrow ledge and being pelted with water that felt like "a mixture of choking spray and gravel" was similarly daunting.[33] He was inspired to explore in ways that barely resembled nineteenth-century leisure walking or the activities of early eastern hiking clubs. Muir's involvement with the Sierra Club, however, helped channel his enthusiasm for the mountains into writings and activities that would encourage many others to become hikers.[34]

The Sierra Club's origins are remarkably similar to those of the Appalachian Mountain Club. The impetus for the club is typically credited to *Century Magazine* author—and eventual editor—Robert Underwood Johnson. Throughout the late 1880s, Johnson and Muir strategized about how to build a constituency for the designation of Yosemite National Park, then a California state park. Muir had been keeping a journal of his explorations and thoughts, and Johnson encouraged him to turn more of that writing into articles for *Century Magazine*. In November 1889, Johnson wrote to Muir suggesting that he "start an association" that "would have a good influence if you guarded carefully the membership." Muir also received encouragement from a group of University of California professors. William Armes, an English professor at Berkeley, wrote to Muir in the spring of 1891 to suggest founding a club modeled on the AMC and another early club based in Portland, Oregon. "I have corresponded with the officers of the Alpine Club of Portland," Armes wrote, "and they will do all in their power to help us."[35]

The Alpine Club of Portland, sometimes called the Oregon Alpine Club, was a precursor to what would later become the Mazamas. The club started informally in the early 1880s with a group of climbing partners who regularly met at a downtown Portland store to discuss recent climbs and plan future outings. In 1885 and 1887, the men planned trips to "illuminate" or "heliograph" Mount Hood, hoping to light the summit to be seen throughout Oregon and Washington. These expeditions, although limited in success, suggested to many Portland residents the need for an organization to undertake similar mountain activities. The original, small group of climbers decided to host a public meeting in September 1887 to establish a club with membership limited to mountain climbers. However, at the meeting, the public's enthusiasm for a general mountain club—composed of people with various interests, in some cases unrelated to climbing—overwhelmed the wishes of the original climbers. The assembled audience refused to adopt a climbing requirement for membership, and the Portland Alpine Club instead was founded with seventy charter members, open membership, and a broad mandate.[36]

The club defined its object as "the foundation and maintenance of a Public Museum, and advancement and encouragement of Amateur Photography, Alpine and Aquatic exploration, and the protection of our game, fish, birds and animals." The Alpine Club of Portland shared the Appalachian Mountain Club's interest in science and exploration, but their emphasis on protecting game and making the position of "curator-taxidermist" an important club role was unique. The leading men of Portland composed the club's membership. For example, in 1890, the club's president was George B. Markle, a thirty-three-year-old businessman who owned stakes in most of Portland's big businesses, including mining, banks, street railways, railroads, and hotels. Contemporaries attributed Markle's business acumen at least in part to his strong character and healthy body—both presumably honed during club outings in the nearby Olympics. "Mr. Markle is . . . heavy built with a full ruddy face indicative of good health, and a hearty, robust constitution," a contemporary noted. "He is cool and deliberate in manner, and under the most exciting circumstances would not be apt to lose his equilibrium." Preceding Markle as club president was U.S. Senator Henry W. Corbett and Portland mayor and Idaho Territory governor David P. Thompson. Given the club's business-minded leadership, it is not surprising that club activities sometimes blended economics with recreation. An 1890 article in the *Spokane Falls Chronicle* credits the club with organizing a survey and inspection of the Olympic Mountains, with the twofold goal of identifying exceptional scenic features and evaluating the economic uses of the region. The expedition had mixed results. The survey leader described the region as "the Switzerland of America"; he added, however, that it was "of such a uniform sameness that one gets tired of tramping over it."[37]

Muir knew of the earlier club's success. He replied favorably to Armes's proposal, calling himself a "hearty worker" for the cause of establishing the Sierra Club. Muir envisioned the club as a "Defense Association" that would continue the momentum of the Yosemite bill to force preservation throughout the Sierra Nevada. Within the year, the men had recruited twenty-five others who had an interest in Yosemite, the Sierra, or climbing. At the core of this group were lawyer and future progressive Oakland mayor Warren Olney, Hudson River School painter and fellow Scot William Keith, and a number of professors from nearby Stanford and the University of California.[38]

On May 28, 1892, the group gathered at Olney's law office in downtown San Francisco, selecting Muir as president and agreeing to a two-part mission statement that resembled that of the Appalachian Mountain Club and so many clubs to come. The first part of the mission addressed Muir and Johnson's desire for an institution that would apply political pressure for conservation. Thus, the club would "enlist the support and cooperation of the people and the government in preserving the forests and other natural features of the Sierra Nevada Mountains." The second part of the mission reflected the interests of the professors, many of whom were amateur mountaineers, and read: "To explore, enjoy, and render accessible the mountain regions of the Pacific Ocean." At the time, the two missions seemed to be in harmony.[39]

At the Sierra Club's first public meeting in September, 250 people met in the California Academy of Sciences building. The meeting was closely modeled on the Appalachian Mountain Club's format, which by that time had been working well for sixteen years. After Secretary Armes gave an overview of the club and its goals, several papers on natural history and recent outings were presented. Beginning in 1893, the papers would also be reprinted in the *Sierra Club Bulletin*, the club's popular journal, which closely resembled the AMC's *Appalachia*. The second club meeting featured a two-hour talk by John Wesley Powell, chief of the U.S. Geological Survey. Powell's presence at the meeting no doubt attracted potential members and added legitimacy to the new club. At the third meeting, discussion revolved around "the Caminetti bill," which sought to decrease the size of Yosemite National Park. "The Club passed a resolution directing the Board of Directors to prepare a memorial to Congress against it, and to use every effort to defeat it." At the same meeting, a favorable resolution was passed regarding a proposed forestry bill. Although Muir was absent from this and most other early meetings, the club fulfilled the purpose he had envisioned for it—opposing legislation that threatened wilderness and backing conservation efforts.[40]

The Sierra Club was founded during a period of reform in San Francisco, and many Sierra Club members were active in the city's progressive politics. Progressive reform and conservation complemented each other, in that regulating the use of natural resources could lead to more efficient use of public lands. Recreation in those natural areas could lead to healthier, more efficient citizens. During the height of progressive reforms, advocates of open space and recreation constructed urban playgrounds and parks to improve the health and morals of city residents. For middle-class citizens, the same impulse led to the preservation of natural areas farther from the city. In contrast to eastern hikers, who were heavily influenced by the middle landscape ideal, the typical Sierra Club member, observes Michael Cohen, "wanted to retain the wild mountains while he developed his own cities." According to historian Hal Rothman, early Sierra Club members were "aesthetic recreational users of the outdoors who valued the transformation of society in which they engaged but who also felt a personal need for distance from it in their leisure time." This was true even of Muir, who struck a personal balance between time in the mountains and time on his ranch and orchard in Martinez, California. "This seer did not come dressed in sackcloth and ashes; rather, he appeared in a well-tailored suit of broadcloth, signifying a man of worldly accomplishment, a prosperous businessman," Donald Worster has written of Muir. "He lived and entertained in an impressive manor house with flowers and fresh fruit, a bottle of wine and a box of cigars on the dining table. Editors, agriculturalists, businessmen, professors, poets, scientists, and humanists all looked on him as one of them."[41]

In the early years of the club, most hiking and climbing activity took place as individual or small group outings that were reported to other club members at meetings or printed in the *Bulletin*. But in 1901, club secretary William Colby—a twenty-six-year-old lawyer—advocated for annual club trips into the backcountry. The hope was that by experiencing wilderness areas, Colby and other club leaders could inspire the membership to be more politically engaged in their preservation. Unlike the eastern mountain ranges, which were relatively accessible for casual hikers, the Sierra Nevada required planning, pack animals, contracted transportation, and special equipment. The rough terrain limited how many people could experience the

Sierra Club members Helen and Anita Gompertz pause during an
1897 outing to survey the Yosemite Valley. Courtesy of Colby
Library, Sierra Club.

backcountry and thus how many members had personal attach-
ments to these special places that presumably would galvanize
their activism. These High Trips offered less experienced hikers
and climbers their first—and in some cases, only—forays into
the Sierra.

A fictional account of a typical Sierra Club High Trip, written
in 1922, captures the spirit of these outings. "About an equal
number of men and women made up the party. . . . There were
college students who sang well, several natural scientists [who]
. . . would give them a talk now and then on the region they were
passing through, and a representation of professional men and
women, and their families. There was also gray-haired Mr. Nut-
ting who, it was whispered, was a rich man, but who seemed to

enjoy nothing so much as bringing in fire-wood. It was a jolly, hail-fellow-well-met sort of gathering."[42]

The Sierra Club's High Trips would become iconic of the club's emphasis on wilderness recreation and an effective means of cultivating future club leaders. The annual outing would take on added meaning in the early twentieth century, as the Sierra Club became more involved with advocacy. During intense debates that threatened internal division, each High Trip was an opportunity to reconcile differences and reaffirm the club's recreational and aesthetic foundations.

Even in the 1890s, however, some members believed that the Sierra Club was doing too much recreation and not enough advocacy work. The debate over the future of the Yosemite Valley highlights the complexity of Sierra Club politics and philosophy during its formative period. In 1864, Congress granted California the Yosemite Valley to be managed as a state park. The state, having few precedents on which to base its policies, permitted grazing, hogs, and loosely regulated development within park boundaries. To members of the Appalachian Mountain Club, nothing about this arrangement would have been remarkable. The White Mountains and their other hiking grounds were used for lumbering, mining, and farming, and AMC members were accustomed to hiking through working, pastoral landscapes. In contrast, many Sierra Club members desired a clearer demarcation between spaces of work and wilderness and believed that the park should be off-limits to most economic uses. Muir had lived and worked in the valley both as a sawyer and as a guide and was well aware of the problems with state management. Only Johnson's counsel had convinced him to work with the state to address the issues rather than publicly criticize the park and risk being excluded from the process.

Other club leaders were unhappy with this policy and believed it gave tacit consent to the destruction of the valley. They wanted the Sierra Club to make a strong policy statement in favor of federal protection. In October 1892, Charles Robinson, a charter member, wrote to Johnson, complaining that the "Sierra

Club . . . has a mere existence for its own pleasure—that is all. . . . In short the Club, like the state, is nerveless and dead regarding Yosemite." Johnson shared the letter with Olney and Muir. Olney, Johnson, and Muir were, for the time, united in the belief that the Sierra Club's legitimacy required a working relation with the state. If the Sierra Club issued statements in favor of a federal takeover of Yosemite, they risked antagonizing Sacramento politicians. These businessmen and cultural leaders were also in the difficult situation of balancing their desire for a preserved Yosemite with their desire to secure national prestige for California, prestige that would be tarnished if the federal government repossessed the park. By 1895, Muir—having seen the effectiveness of U.S. Army patrols in the valley—began advocating openly for federal management of Yosemite and other western parklands. He also began to shift away from the rhetoric of progressive conservation to emphasize preservation. This placed him at odds with a large bloc of Sierra Club members who eschewed preservation for closely regulated utilitarian use of parks.[43]

This debate would of course continue throughout the twentieth and into the twenty-first century. It is important to note, however, how quickly the Sierra Club found itself embroiled in both external and internal controversy and how this led to a unique trajectory for the club among American hiking organizations. Although the Appalachian Mountain Club and other early hiking clubs would advocate for protection of the mountains and their flora and fauna, no other club would become as politically active as the Sierra Club.

The results for the Sierra Club were mixed. On one hand, its role in the national parks movement and the campaign to protect California's scenic Hetch Hetchy Valley from being dammed with a reservoir would bring the club national attention and make it a leader in the emerging environmental movement. On the other hand, the club's advocacy work distracted members from the hiking and climbing activities that defined most other clubs. Trail building, first ascents, technical climbs, group hikes, and the dissemination of information through the *Bulletin* would certainly continue, and local Sierra Club chapters would expose thousands of Americans to hiking throughout the nation. Hiking and trail development, however, would rarely again supersede environment advocacy as the driving force of the Sierra Club, despite its recreational origins.

In contrast to the Sierra Club, another large western club, the Mazamas, was explicit in its concern for climbing above all else. Enthusiasm for the Portland Alpine Club and its diverse set of outdoor interests waned within a few years of its founding in 1887. With its collapse, the original group of Portland climbers renewed private discussions about forming a true mountaineering club, limited to men and women who had a proven record of ascending mountains. In March 1894, they held a public but informal meeting attended by forty people, at which they decided to hold the first official meeting of the club on the summit of Mount Hood. This location presumably would limit the club's membership to skilled climbers and those willing to learn. Committees formed at once to begin preparations for the climb and outline the formal organization of the club, including a draft constitution. Women held important positions on these committees and would participate in the inaugural climb.

On June 12, 1894, the *Morning Oregonian* published an invitation, entitled "Mazamas" and addressed "To Mountain Climbers and Lovers of Nature," which announced that the Mount Hood meeting and a "typical mountain banquet" would be held on July 19. "The list of charter members will be limited to such as are then there and present," the invitation noted. Making explicit the desire for climbing credentials, the notice read, "No one will be permitted to join thereafter unless he or she has climbed to the summit of a snow-capped mountain acceptable to the club." The unconventional name Mazamas, the invitation noted, was taken from a local Native American name for mountain goat—"the best mountain-climber in the country."[44]

On July 17, nearly three hundred climbers assembled at two base camps on the south and north sides of Mount Hood. The next day, they moved their camps to the timberline and watched the sunset over the Pacific Ocean, some one hundred miles to the west. In the early morning of July 19, parties of climbers began to ascend four different routes toward the summit of Mount Hood. They planned to converge on the summit, share a large but simple banquet, officially announce the club, and light a tar fire to signal to the region the new club's existence. A brief but fierce storm of hail, snow, and strong winds disrupted these plans and forced more than a hundred climbers back down to the tree line. As the storm subsided, small numbers continued to climb, and from eight o'clock in the morning until three o'clock in the afternoon parties of climbers reached the summit. Some chose to stay; others felt uncomfortable on the cramped and windy summit and returned to camp. One of the last parties, a group of forty climbers ascending from the north, reached the summit at three o'clock. There, on a small, sheltered ledge, they organized the club as originally planned, hastily adopting the draft constitution and electing officers. Before descending, the climbers—now officially Mazamas—released three carrier pigeons to carry word back to Portland, and for several hours, smoke signals and mirror flashes from the Willamette Valley and eastern Oregon celebrated the successful ascent. Despite the storm, 155 men and 38 women had successfully and safely reached the 11,225-foot summit of Mount Hood.[45]

The Mazamas were born out of spectacle and hyperbolic enthusiasm. "Never before in the history of the world was a scene like that of July 19 last witnessed on the summit of a mountain so difficult to climb as Hood," the club's president wrote to his members. "With thunder and lightning below us, and the bright sunshine above, we clambered up the mountain and stood on the topmost peak, nearly two hundred strong." The novelty of the outing attracted attention in Portland, where a lengthy *Morning Oregonian* article detailed all aspects of the trip and listed the founding members.[46]

The club's second annual outing was no less ambitious, with the executive committee agreeing "to establish heliographic communication from British Columbia, along the noble peaks of the Cascades and Sierras to Mexico, thus making one of the grandest attempts at the work ever undertaken." Such an event

Founding the Mazamas on Mount Hood, 1894. Climbing prowess was a requirement of membership in the Mazamas. All members had to summit a snow-capped peak before acceptance. Courtesy of the Mazamas Library and Historical Collections, William G. Steel Collection, VM1993.008.002.

required coordination of the various outing clubs across the region, with more than a dozen parties ascending peaks on the given day. Although the Mazamas received the blessing of the U.S. Army Signal Corps and the U.S. Geologic Survey, they admitted that there was no great scientific value to the stunt. However, at least one astute observer realized that "sunbeam signalizing adds an incentive to mountain-climbing, which bids fair to greatly popularize that noble sport throughout the Pacific coast." The significance of the event was not in succeeding—indeed, the club managed to signal from only Mounts Baker, Rainier, Adams, Hood, Jefferson, and Diamond—but in attracting participants in the club's work, elevating mountaineering to an attractive spectacle, and gaining attention in the local and national press. On another occasion, a boastful club historian enthusiastically—if hyperbolically—claimed, "If the United States wants the honor of the discovery of the North Pole, all it has to do is to request our secretary to call a meeting of Mazamas there, guaranteeing all expenses, and the necessary quorum for the transaction of business will be on hand." Apparently, the government did not take them up on the offer, but by all accounts, this early promotional work was successful in promoting the Mazamas both regionally and nationally.[47]

The club's ambitious objectives, as described by E. Fay Fuller, the club's historian, were "to stimulate in people a love of the mountains, and to awaken an interest in the study of them; and yearly to accomplish something which, besides reflecting credit upon the members, should benefit the world." By "benefit the world," Fuller was referring to the widespread belief among the Mazamas that their climbs would contribute substantial scientific knowledge about the relatively unexplored mountain ranges of the West. Beginning in 1896, the club published semiannual issues of *Mazama*—a journal that predictably followed the format of *Appalachia* and the *Sierra Club Bulletin*. In this—and in their rhetoric about natural beauty and opening access to the mountains—the Mazamas echoed both the AMC and the Sierra Club.[48]

But here were also key differences between the Mazamas and the other clubs. The Mazamas, with their emphasis on

technical climbing, excluded significant numbers of potential
hikers from participation, whereas the AMC included walks in a
variety of landscapes—including downtown Boston—and hosted
nonrecreational events, such as art exhibits. Even the Sierra
Club, which included technical climbing in its activities, also
sought—through its High Trips—to accommodate inexperienced
hikers and encourage them to participate in the club. The
Mazamas, at least in the early years, were concerned only with
those who had "borne testimony to their love of nature and their
physical vigor by climbing a snow-draped peak." Although most
Mazama writing suggests that the climbing requirement was intended to ensure an engaged membership, there is some evidence that it also drew from the emerging cultural imperative of
health, purity, and nationalism, which would be most forcefully
articulated in Theodore Roosevelt's "Strenuous Life" ideology
later in the decade. "In the very nature of things our membership
must be limited in number," club president C. H. Sholes wrote in
his annual address for 1896, "some people cannot, and others
will not, climb mountains. And herein lies our greatest strength,
because in either event a sifting process, unprecedented in its
application, tends to guard our society from all elements of
weakness or disaffection." Sholes described a "survival of the fit-
test" for American hikers, in which those who would ascend alpine summits and snow-capped peaks deserved special respect.[49]

In the context of international mountaineering, Sholes's
rhetoric was neither unique nor extreme. In Switzerland, the
birthplace of nineteenth-century mountain climbing, ascents
were closely regulated by a system of tariffs and licensed guides.
At a time when the median household income of an American
was less than five hundred dollars, government fees for a single
ascent of the Matterhorn or Mont Blanc could cost forty dollars
and would be permitted only if one were an experienced climber.
Europeans believed that these barriers deterred inexperienced
climbers, and the required use of at least two guides to a party
ensured that everyone would be outfitted with the proper equipment and expertise. The Mazamas reacted strongly against such
regulations. Sholes, who felt comfortable placing restrictions on

Mazama membership, argued that "the great charm of mountain-climbing in America, and especially in our magnificent ranges on the Pacific Coast, is the fact that the mountains are free to those who seek to derive from them the joy of unaided conquest." With the Mazamas leading the way, American climbers were forging ahead with their own type of comparatively egalitarian hiking independent of the social mores of European climbing culture.[50]

Despite the high-minded talk of climbing restrictions, regulations, and technical expertise, the Mazamas could be remarkably irreverent about the climbing community and made the most comedic use of their name as possible. For example, they marketed the first annual meeting as a "Gathering of the Goats." "The Nannygoat historian and the Billygoat poet will entertain the others with their literary productions, the patriarch Billygoat will cast reflections of Mount Hood and Mount Rainier upon a screen, others will bleat in melodious unison, and all will browse upon the provender provided by the committee." This language masked the important business of the meeting, which included selecting John Muir and Joseph Le Conte for honorary membership. These actions allied the Mazamas with the recently established Sierra Club and with two mountaineering geologists who represented the club's goals. Joint outings of the Sierra Club and Mazamas would be common in the coming years.[51]

As the Mazamas matured, their emphasis on climbing remained, but they compromised on the idea that outings should involve scientific contributions, such as heliographic experiments or field-testing survey equipment. In 1904, the club chose Mount Shasta for their annual outing, and even the outspoken Sholes was satisfied to report that "the only work of a scientific nature (if it could be called such) which the 1904 outing embodied, was an attempt to signal between Mt. Shasta and Mt. Hood." The club's members appeared more concerned with the "science" of technical mountain climbing, which they were either developing as they went or adapting from European alpine clubs and publications. The pages of *Mazama* included sketches of climbing knots and equipment that accompanied narrative accounts of recent outings. One essay described the "complexities of the diamond hitch," a method for tying cargo to pack animals. Pack animals were required for the longer backcountry trips to access the foot of the mountains. This was something the Appalachian Mountain Club had never dealt with, and therefore, the Mazamas—and their counterparts at the Sierra Club—had to borrow methods from professional packers or invent techniques along the way. All of this work contributed to the sense that the Mazamas were leading the way in the American climbing community.[52]

Looking back on the first decade of the Mazamas' existence, Sholes could be optimistic. "Founded upon a rock we have very ancient and high authority to justify our confidence that it will endure," he wrote. "How immensely its field of work has broadened within one short decade! But that it may expand proportionally with this expanding empire between the Rocky Mountains and the Pacific it is necessary to have more members." Sholes failed to acknowledge the connection between his climbing requirement and the need to expand membership. "More members means more workers, more enthusiasm and more funds; more funds in its treasury means increased ability to do the tasks that loom upon our immediate horizon." Sholes could not have known that three years later a large bloc of members would break with the Mazamas to form the Seattle-based Mountaineers. Despite the loss of members, the Mazamas survived the break, and both clubs eventually thrived, adding to the proliferation of successful hiking organizations along the Pacific Coast.[53]

In July 1905, the Sierra Club and Mazamas invited members of the Appalachian Mountain Club to participate in their annual outing—this year a camping trip to Paradise Park on the slope of Mount Rainier, preceded by trips to Mount Hood and up the Columbia River. The AMC members marveled at the view from the summit of Hood but could not help thinking, "with the snow peaks eliminated, the view might have been one in our own White Mountains." A few days later, sixty climbers—fifteen of them women—stood on the summit of Mount Rainier, their numb but smiling faces coated with colorful greasepaint. The

climbers were mutually transformed from their daily appearance. "The man of most ferocious aspect is probably a college
professor, while the piratical appearing athlete with black cheeks
and a bright red forehead may be an erstwhile dignified clergy-
man, lawyer, or physician." These days of hiking and climbing
were followed by evenings of campfires, pageantry, boisterous
laughter, and impromptu speeches.[54]

Beneath the gaiety, the outing had a more substantial meaning to the clubs. By the turn of the century, the nascent American
hiking community was thriving. The Appalachian Mountain
Club would celebrate its thirtieth anniversary in 1906. In the
same year, though San Francisco was reeling from earthquake
and fire, membership in the Sierra Club reached 858 and would
top 1,000 by 1909. The smaller but no less ambitious Mazamas,
with its 200 members, continued to develop the model for a
climbing-oriented club and foster a climbing culture that was
unique from its European precedents. More important than
their individual accomplishments, the clubs had forged a culture
of American hiking, reinforced in presentations, newsletters, accounts of outings, hike schedules, and newspaper stories. Although separated by thousands of miles, the AMC, Sierra Club,
and Mazamas were similarly influenced by the many nineteenth-
century meanings of leisure walking, invested with a new significance in the context of late nineteenth-century progressive
conservation.[55]

Reflecting on the 1905 joint outing to Rainier, an AMC member was optimistic that the excursion "went far to cement a
union that it is hoped will prove in the future to be a powerful
factor in the furtherance of American mountaineering, and a
love of the mountains and the woods by others who may follow."
Indeed, thirty years of organized hiking and club development
had well prepared the American hiking community for the twentieth century—a period when hiking culture would spread across
the nation and result in hundreds of clubs modeled on their
nineteenth-century predecessors.[56]

3 THE RISE OF AMERICAN HIKING CULTURE

O N a rainy, early summer day in 1921, more than a thousand people—some from the surrounding area, others from across the state—ascended Negro Mountain in southwestern Pennsylvania. Earlier in the year, the U.S. Geological Survey had determined the summit's height to be 3,213 feet, making it the highest point in the state. Despite the designation and although the region was known as "the roof garden of Pennsylvania," Negro Mountain was an unimpressive prominence, simply the steepest and tallest point on a thirty-mile ridge that barely rose above the surrounding hills. Regardless, Henry Shoemaker, publisher of the *Altoona Tribune* and founder of the recently organized Pennsylvania Alpine Club, heralded the importance of the event. Accordingly, he contacted the Meyersdale Chamber of Commerce and the local newspaper expressing the Alpine Club's intent to celebrate the designation with a ceremonial hike to the summit and inviting local residents of Elk Lick Township and Somerset County to participate. The response was overwhelming, with two marching bands, Boy Scout and Camp Fire Girl troops, members of the Grand Army of the Republic, and local farmers joining Alpine Club members, dressed in their mountain garb, for the hike. Although vehicles could drive to the top on a dirt road, "The Alpinists do not pick the easy road to the summit, and the rougher the going and the harder the climbing the better it is liked," the club's secretary, J. Herbert Walker, told the *Meyersdale Republican*. "The ascent is made over the rocks and through the brush to test the mettle of the climbers." On reaching the summit, a local dignitary raised the American flag as the bands played patriotic songs and Shoemaker, in the name of the two-thousand-member Pennsylvania Alpine Club, rechristened Negro Mountain as Mount Davis.[1]

Beginning in 1876 and continuing through the turn of the century, members of the Appalachian Mountain Club, Sierra Club, and Mazamas proved that there was widespread interest in organized hiking and that voluntary clubs could catalyze regional conservation initiatives and trail building and generally elevate the simple act of walking to one of national relevance. Despite the impressive work of these clubs, in the early twentieth century organized hiking remained geographically isolated—based primarily in New England, San Francisco, and the Pacific Northwest, where stunning landscapes and strong urban leadership galvanized the founding of clubs. Eventually, however, would-be hikers founded similar clubs along the Appalachian range and throughout the Midwest. The experience of Henry Shoemaker and the Pennsylvania Alpine Club was repeated in dozens of cities and large towns, as community leaders assembled fellow conservationists, bird watchers, geologists, historians, and botanists for organized walks through a variety of landscapes that would eventually attract new hikers of all backgrounds.

As the popularity of hiking spread, club members forged a culture of hiking—shared throughout the nation—that invested the simple act of walking with profound meaning. Far from a frivolous hobby practiced by a small group of elites, club members envisioned hiking as fundamental to American life. One hiker summarized the meaning as, "first, the worship of God, and secondly, a true recreation of our spirits, our courage and our love." As such, hikers advanced an elaborate justification for their activities during the periods of peace, war, and economic instability that characterized the first half of the twentieth century. Central to this justification were the perceived health,

religious, and patriotic implications of hiking, which were repeated in club newsletters, newspapers, magazines, advertising,
and books. These impulses motivated late nineteenth- and early
twentieth-century hikers to commit countless hours to blazing
and maintaining trails, participating in outings, and advocating
for the environment. In the process, the American hiking community forged and spread a distinct culture of hiking that ensured its relevance throughout the twentieth century.[2]

The proliferation of American hiking coincided with a broad
shift in culture that began in the 1890s and continued through
the Great Depression. Americans' ideas about such personal—
and increasingly national—issues as health, masculinity, nature,
and progress took on new meaning. Frederick Jackson Turner's
1893 speech to the American Historical Association on "The Significance of the Frontier in America History" suggested that the
nation was at a turning point. The 1890 census indicated that the
nation had been populated from coast to coast and that westward migration into supposedly unoccupied land, a nearly constant process since the seventeenth century, was no longer possible. For Turner, this development portended a crisis because
the unique American character had been forged by adapting to
primitive, anarchistic conditions on the fringes of civilization.
Those adaptations led to the democratic "traits of the frontier,"
which included "coarseness and strength combined with acute-
ness and inquisitiveness; that practical, inventive turn of mind,
quick to find expedients; that masterful grasp of material things,
lacking in the artistic but powerful to effect great ends; that rest-
less, nervous energy; that dominant individualism, working for
good and for evil, and withal that buoyancy and exuberance
which comes with freedom." With the closing of the frontier, the
implications for the American character were unclear.[3]

One solution to this potential crisis came from an 1899
speech Theodore Roosevelt gave to a Chicago athletic club, in
which he argued that a "strenuous life" was essential to both personal and national health. "A healthy state can exist only when
the men and women who make it up lead clean, vigorous, and
healthy lives," he noted. Through his speeches, published works,

Theodore Roosevelt and John Muir, 1906. Muir served as Roosevelt's guide during his 1906 trip to the Yosemite Valley. Courtesy of the Library of Congress.

and celebrated outdoor and hunting feats, Roosevelt suggested that "frontier" experiences could be created out of wilderness experiences, whether in New York's Adirondacks, California's Sierra, or the wilds of eastern Africa. A man need not live in primitive conditions for years to build character. Instead, he could go on a hunting trip, scale a mountain, or venture into the backwoods to fish, returning quickly to civilization after pushing his body to the limit. This concept provided the foundation of a new culture of masculinity that balanced civilized gentility with regular, but brief, restorative excursions into wilderness. Hiking, backpacking, and camping clearly fit this mold and became popular tenets of the new culture of masculinity.[4]

Roosevelt was not the only figure contributing to the culture shift. The 1890s was a decade of general reorientation within American middle-class culture from the subdued gentility of the previous fifty years to a flourishing of new activities, including outdoor recreation. Football emerged from Yale University in the 1880s, while the Young Men's Christian Association spread the popularity of basketball in the 1890s. The popular ideal of the New Woman encouraged women to participate in sports and be more assertive in demanding leadership roles in organizations, including hiking clubs. Despite its emphasis on breaking with accepted norms, the new culture was not a rejection of modern, mechanized society but rather a means of accommodating and accepting it. Sports, the new culture seemed to argue, provided a temporary release from the rigidity of modern life. This theme would provide a recurring justification for hiking throughout the twentieth century.[5]

Contemporary observers noted the close connection between the competiveness of sports, Roosevelt's rhetoric, and aggressive foreign policy. Imperialism promised to expand the American frontier beyond the nation's borders and offer new opportunities to reinvigorate the nation's strength and pride. The Philippine-American War between 1899 and 1902 provided one surrogate for a domestic frontier that proved deadly for at least thirty-four thousand Filipinos. Pacifist critics, in contrast, argued that martial impulses should be directed at nature and channeled into productive activities. In his 1910 essay "The Moral Equivalent of War," William James described the attraction of battle. "War is the *strong* life," he argued, in terms very similar to those of Roosevelt's strenuous life ideology. "It is life in *extremis.*" In the early twentieth century, however, "reflective criticisms" about the savagery and corruption of war undermined its unquestioned value as a source of American character. James suggested turning "martial virtues" toward American industry through "a conscription of the whole youthful population to form for a certain number of years a part of the army enlisted against *nature.*" Young men would contribute to a variety of industries, from fishing to coal mining to constructing skyscrapers, and, in the process, "preserve in the midst of a pacific civilization the manly virtues which the military party is so afraid of seeing disappear in peace." A similar proposal during the early 1930s would lead to the creation of the Civilian Conservation Corps (CCC).[6]

Others believed the improvement of American communities could absorb the energy of Americans. The progressive movement, which flourished from the 1890s to 1920, was a broad set of ideas about how to reform society—from governments to individuals. Public intellectuals and politicians as dissimilar as Jane Addams, W. E. B. Du Bois, and Theodore Roosevelt turned their energy to such diverse causes as municipal reform, prohibition, regulation of industry, trust busting, food purity and access, family counseling, eugenics, and the modernization of industry. Progressives' interest in efficiency and an equitable distribution of wealth extended to the use of the nation's forests, waterways, and other natural resources and resulted in the conservation movement. Gifford Pinchot, the first chief of the U.S. Forest Service and two-term progressive governor of Pennsylvania, described conservation as making natural resources available for "the greatest good, for the greatest number, for the longest run." The conservation movement elevated the importance of nature, and early twentieth-century Americans began to place an economic value on resources they once took for granted.[7]

In addition to the often technocratic form of utilitarian conservation as advanced by the federal government in its programs and regulations, conservation could also be justified on the grounds of aesthetics and public health. Muir depicted modern society as a world of "over-industry," "luxury," "rust," and "disease" but argued that time spent in nature could help Americans reinvigorate their lives and improve their bodies. "Thousands of tired, nerve-shaken, over-civilized people are beginning to find out that going to the mountains is going home," he wrote in 1901, "that wildness is a necessity; and that mountain parks and reservations are useful not only as fountains of timber and irrigating rivers, but as fountains of life."[8]

Despite their shared belief in the public health and spiritual implications of wilderness, conservationists like Pinchot and Roosevelt would soon find themselves at odds with preservationists like John Muir. Although Muir's influence in the Sierra Club was strong, the club was remarkably divided over natural resource issues, such as an early twentieth-century proposal to create a dam on the Tuolumne River and use the Hetch Hetchy Valley of Yosemite National Park as a reservoir for San Francisco. In general, hiking clubs completely accepted neither the preservationist nor the conservationist belief system, emphasizing the restorative aspects of nature that were relevant to personal health, spiritual renewal, and national strength. Although clubs across the nation could rally against certain projects, such as Hetch Hetchy, a dam proposal near Dinosaur National Monument in the 1950s, and plans to develop New Jersey's Sunfish Pond in the 1960s, preservation had little meaning to clubs founded in states with landscapes altered by lumbering, mining, milldams, and other industrial activities that were hard to ignore. In many cases, especially early in the twentieth century, the leaders of hiking clubs were businessmen who were involved to some degree in extracting value from natural resources. Hikers in landscapes along the East Coast and in the Midwest had meaningful experiences walking through landscapes that preservationists would have considered marginal. Inaccessibly rugged and distant wilderness in the Rockies and the Sierra were worthy of protection, most hikers agreed, but they had little meaning to their daily understanding of the value of nature. As we will see, these values changed over time and by place.[9]

As these various ideological and cultural impulses suggest, modern American culture emerged during the period between 1890 and 1929. American hiking culture was neither the most prominent nor the most influential of these impulses. However, the national culture of hiking that emerged from the dozens of hiking clubs founded in those decades managed to synthesize and simplify complex ideas about modernity, economics, individual and public health, masculinity, character, social reform, self-improvement, national vitality, and the many other diverse ideas of the period to justify and promote a communal action—walking in natural areas.

On a crisp, bright day in the autumn of 1945, George Frank, a member of the Cleveland Hiking Club, spent the morning fixing the old metal roof on the cook shack at Camp Onwego. The camp, situated on a wooded lot with a deep ravine, was located outside the small town of Hinckley, Ohio, some thirty miles south of Cleveland. Since 1933, club members had carpooled to the cabin for overnight and weekend trips full of singing, dancing, pineapple-carrot salad, and even some hiking. A club member later described trips to the camp as "a time to get away from it all—to think and walk and listen to rustling leaves and bird calls and crickets. To sleep like a babe beside a fire that flickers and makes ghostly shadows." On that Sunday, club members were lounging around and doing some light repair work before returning to the city, when Frank collapsed on the ground beside the cook shack. Moments later he was dead of a heart attack. In the camp logbook for the day, a member wrote, "On this date, nearly twelve years to the day, since camp was officially opened by George Frank, he died of a heart attack at 4 o'clock." Following the entry were the names of the twenty-two members present, and then a series of blank pages, after which entries about beef stew dinners and card games resumed. Incidents like this were tragic, but they also suggest the nearly familial ties between the close-knit communities of hikers who laughed, sang, cried, ate, bedded down, and –yes—even died in each other's company. Clubs were both a manifestation of the vibrant culture of hiking and a means of disseminating it to newcomers.[10]

Between 1900 and World War II, dozens of hiking clubs appeared in large cities and smaller communities across the nation. Although the new clubs were concentrated in New England and the Mid-Atlantic, there were also clusters of activity in the Midwest and in the larger cities of the West. The Appalachian Mountain Club continued to absorb most of the hiking energy of New England during this period, but New York City, Philadelphia, Chicago, and smaller cities, such as Washington, D.C., Cleveland, and Allentown, Pennsylvania, began to see the first attempts at organized hiking. These dozens of local clubs resembled their nineteenth-century predecessors in many ways, including the demographic backgrounds of their members and the members' shared emphasis on healthy recreation in fresh air. In some ways mirroring the broader cultural shifts from utilitarian use of the nation's natural resources to preservation for aesthetic reasons, many of the clubs founded after 1900 lacked the Appalachian Mountain Club's and Sierra Club's focus on scientific research, botany, and geology. These topics would be recurring elements of slide shows and lectures at meetings and trailside lessons during hikes, but few of these clubs attempted to justify their activities by tying them back to scientific discovery. Instead, early twentieth-century hikers elaborated on the personal and social benefits of hiking.

Pennsylvania provides an important case study for how these ideas about hiking took form and spread, for between 1900 and World War II the state experienced the most prolific period of hiking club formation anywhere in the nation. The landscape of Pennsylvania hiking was starkly different from that of the northern Appalachians, White Mountains, Sierra Nevada, Olympics, or Cascades. Pennsylvania's highest point, Mount Davis, would have hardly registered as a mountain to hikers accustomed to summits two to three times higher. Furthermore, by the first two decades of the twentieth century, the lumber industry had almost totally consumed Pennsylvania's forests of white pine, hemlock, and hardwoods. Railroad lines penetrated almost every valley of the state, hauling out logs and ore and moving on when those resources were exhausted. Joseph Rothrock and, later, Gifford Pinchot would lead efforts to acquire and reforest these lands, but hikers of the early twentieth century faced a landscape deeply altered by industry. The notion of escaping into an untouched wilderness to test one's strength and bravery bore little relevance to these men and women who walked along country roads and railroad beds and scrambled to the tops of squat prominences. If preservation of hiking grounds motivated members of the Sierra Club, Mazamas, and Appalachian Mountain Club, then socializing with likeminded people while experiencing the culture and history of the landscape motivated Pennsylvania hikers.[11]

In fact, this was the primary motivation for founding the first statewide hiking club. Newspaper publisher Henry Shoemaker had founded the Pennsylvania Alpine Club in 1917 as "a sort of advanced Boy Scouts organization" through which "statesmen, bankers and publishers [could] find surcease of business cares amid the sylvan slopes of the monarchs of our Highlands." More important, these influential men would "strive to protect and preserve [the mountains] for future generations of loyal Pennsylvanians." Shoemaker's concern for Pennsylvania's landscape emerged from a series of trips to the Black Forest, a densely forested area in the north-central part of the state, named for the darkly colored virgin pines that once stood there. From 1898 to 1902, Shoemaker traveled the back roads and trails of the large forest, speaking to lumbermen and, as he referred to them, "mountain people," to collect their stories. Business called him away from the region until 1907, when he returned to continue the work. "But what change those five years had made. Where was the Black Forest?" Shoemaker wondered on his return. "Miles of slashings, fire-swept wastes, emptiness, desolation, ruin met the eye on every side; the lumbermen had done their work." Return trips to what Shoemaker now referred to in quotation marks as the "forest" "only accentuated the sense of sadness for the arboreal paradise that was no more. . . . The hand of man had changed the face of nature from green to brown." In addition to his disgust regarding lumbering, Shoemaker quickly realized that "the ancient legends which were so easy to hear in 1898" were "difficult to obtain in 1910. What were listened to with seeming indifference then, were listened to breathlessly towards the last." The residents of the region who relied on dense forest and clean streams for their livelihoods had been displaced. For Shoemaker, lumbering, mining, and tanneries were to be opposed for their impact on the landscape and for reasons of what would later be termed environmental justice.[12]

Shoemaker and the club's influential members used their newspapers as pulpits for conservation, offering photo opportunities to politicians willing to participate in Alpine Club events and lend support to club causes. Shoemaker also served on the state forest commission, where he edited the Department of Forests and Waters pamphlet *In Penn's Woods*, promoting "the natural wonders and recreational facilities of the state forests of

Pennsylvania." He used the opportunity to spread word about the Alpine Club, including information on how to become a member. Though he was quite critical of the agencies regulating industry in Pennsylvania's forests, Shoemaker recognized ways to work from within the bureaucracy of state government to promote his vision of conservation.[13]

Shoemaker and the Alpine Club enjoyed several early conservation victories. In 1921, the club secured a commitment from the state game commission to end the poisoning of predatory animals in state forests. The club also gathered data "in regard to the pollution of streams of the State by paper mills and tanneries, which pollution killed off millions of food and game fish." Club members provided firsthand accounts of fish kills, and professors from around the state condemned the pollution. Most important, the Alpine Club laid out the Darlington Trail, named in honor of Bishop James Henry Darlington, minister at Saint Stephen's Episcopal Cathedral in Harrisburg and one-time secretary of the club. The trail, probably completed around 1918, followed the ridge of Blue Mountain from the west bank of the Susquehanna River, across from Harrisburg, to Sterrett's Gap, some ten miles to the west. Although this was a relatively short distance, the Darlington Trail was the first modern hiking trail built in Pennsylvania, and it proved that volunteer hiking clubs could effectively establish and maintain trails on a mix of private and public lands. When Shoemaker gave up his position as president in 1930, the club had more than 2,500 members, placing it among the largest outdoor organizations in the nation.[14]

The Pennsylvania Alpine Club spurred the founding of other clubs, primarily concentrated east of the Susquehanna River. The York Hiking Club (YHC), originally called the Back-to-Nature Hiking Club, began scheduling hikes as early as 1922 and organized informally in 1932. In contrast to the Alpine Club's promotional and policy campaigns, the York Hiking Club was most concerned with providing entertainment and exercise to the York community. In fact, some of the passages in their log book mock the serious rhetoric of other clubs. After a 1933 hike, for example, club historian Kenny Young wrote, "There's nothing like a good, honest-to-goodness, upright, God-fearing, one hundred percent American, red-blooded autumn hike." The Blue Mountain Club, founded by Lafayette College chemistry professor Eugene Bingham in 1926, organized hikes on the Kittatinny Ridge north of Easton and became an early source of Appalachian Trail (AT) enthusiasm. Unsurprisingly, several clubs formed in and around Philadelphia, including the Batona—short for "back to nature"—Hiking Club (1928), the Philadelphia Trail Club (1931), and the Horse Shoe Trail Club (1934). The Batona Hiking Club emerged out of a citywide "correct posture campaign" initiated by the *Philadelphia Evening Bulletin,* which included hikes in and around Philadelphia. The Philadelphia Trail Club organized similar hikes but also took on responsibility for maintaining a section of the Appalachian Trail near the Lehigh River. The Horse Shoe Trail Club focused almost solely on building a 140-mile trail for horse riders and hikers between Valley Forge and Manada Gap, near Harrisburg. Finally, in the Wyoming Valley, the Susquehanna Trailers formed in 1932 "to give a greater appreciation of the out of doors, to learn of the beauty spots of the Valley, to keep physically fit by walking regularly and to bring people of the same interest together in a social way."[15]

By 1932, there were nine hiking clubs in Pennsylvania, and they were concentrated in central and eastern Pennsylvania. Even the founding of Allegheny National Forest in 1923 did not lead to an immediate flourishing of hiking activity in northwestern Pennsylvania. The reason for geographic clustering of hiking relates directly to the reasons for the emergence of the original nineteenth-century walking clubs. Hiking clubs formed first in cities, where there were enough people who were relieved of daily walking and physical labor to re-create romanticized versions of those activities as leisure. Much of western Pennsylvania—and entire regions of the nation—lacked such communities and would not see organized hiking until after World War II.

In addition to the role they could play as advocates for tree plantings, regulatory legislation, and trail building, early twentieth-century Pennsylvania hikers developed a remarkably elaborate justification for hiking that elevated the importance of their actions and guarded against the perception that their hiking was a trivial and self-indulgent form of leisure. Pennsylvania hiking clubs, like those of the nineteenth century, faced an especially challenging task: endowing walking with special meaning that the uninitiated could recognize and respect. Hikers achieved this by merging and elaborating on the diverse ideologies that had previously promoted hiking, namely, its positive religious, health, and patriotic effects.

American experiences in nature had been viewed in religious terms since colonial times, slowly gaining a positive, deistic value as industrial society subordinated nature to meet its needs. Americans' struggle to incorporate nature into their moral ideologies had taken many forms. Henry David Thoreau's experiment with transcendental pastoralism may be the best known, but no less a conventional figure than Gifford Pinchot also celebrated the religious value of nature throughout his life. "God's hand is there most wonderfully," Pinchot wrote of his first Grand Canyon experience, "and I thought and sang the doxology." Indeed, the dominant, if paradoxical, trend in American religious thought has been to recognize nature's potential for inspiration and rejuvenation by offering a connection to God while justifying its sometimes destructive use.[16]

Early twentieth-century hikers, like those before them, generally approached the Pennsylvania landscape as Christians, endowed with a traditional sense of the sublime that added meaning to time spent in the woods. The Blue Mountain Eagle Climbing Club, for example, regularly held religious service at Dan's Pulpit, a rock formation on the south side of Blue Mountain, and included hymns and prayer in its annual meetings. Speaking to a local newspaper in 1933, a club member remarked, "Our trips have always embraced . . . first, the worship of God." Somewhat less explicitly, religion motivated hikers across the state. "When you leave a beautiful woodland or descend from a mountain," a Batona Hiking Club publication encouraged members, "stop, turn around, and gaze reverentially awhile. Thank God for the boon our forests are to all mankind." After a Pennsylvania

Alpine Club hike, the club secretary believed that he had achieved "a fuller realization of how great are the works of God." In response to low participation rates, a member of the Susquehanna Trailers warned, "If you don't come on the hikes, you miss . . . enjoying the whole rich cosmos that God intends us to enjoy." In the minds of Pennsylvania hikers, clearly, God condoned hiking.[17]

Whether or not hiking truly constituted a spiritual experience, religious rhetoric dominates the early records of several clubs. The need to hold Sunday hikes offers a partial explanation. At a time when many potential club members worked on Saturdays, Sunday became the only day of the week available for long-distance walks. Combining religious service with a hike was an obvious solution. Another was to emphasize those nineteenth-century associations of nature with God—in turn, elevating simple mountain walks to a spiritual act. This was not a disingenuous strategy. Americans have often used religion—and self-improvement in general—to justify spending time on leisure activities, such as vacations and tourism. Regardless of motivation, the rhetoric of religion allowed Pennsylvania hikers to recreate while minimizing fears of criticism.[18]

Similarly, club members touted hiking's health benefits. According to their purpose statement, the Susquehanna Trailers of Wilkes-Barre formed, in part, "to keep physically fit by walking regularly." Philadelphia's Batona Hiking Club encouraged members to "keep your body and mind in tune by proper exercise and right thinking; commune with nature and you will receive messages of hope, beauty, cheer, and courage that will not let you grow old." An article in the Allentown Hiking Club's newsletter, the *Happy Hiker*, instructed members, "The next time you climb that mountain, and your chest heaves, and you feel like your lungs will explode, remind yourself, IT'S ALL FOR HEALTH'S SAKE." In part, the clubs' references to health drew from the rhetoric of the nineteenth-century back-to-nature and fresh air movements; however, the twentieth-century reformation of these arguments also benefited from a direct relation to patriotism.[19]

Philadelphia hikers on Pulpit Rock, 1940s. A group of Philadelphia
Trail Club members stop for lunch at Berks County, Pennsylvania's
Pulpit Rock near the Appalachian Trail. As the name implies, the
site was regularly used for religious services during hikes. Courtesy
of the Horse Shoe Trail Conservancy.

The leaders of hiking clubs were almost always community
and business leaders who spent significant amounts of time
indoors and, while not expressing explicitly neurasthenic anxieties, certainly longed for temporary escape from what one Pennsylvania hiker described as "the noise and bustle of business
cares." Their longing for "authentic" experience and concern for
well-spent leisure time were elevated during times of war.[20]

Explicit displays of patriotism were common during meetings and apparent in the rhetoric of publications. Despite this
patriotic consistency, war brought out anxieties about the value
of hiking during periods of sacrifice. In 1942, the York Hiking
Club led a series of Hale America hikes intended to "help York
defense workers and all York citizens 'keep fit' for Victory." In the

same year, a Batona hiker exclaimed, "In war as in peace. It's patriotic to keep fit!" In part, these anxieties were generated from the need to use automobiles—and rubber tires and gasoline, both of which were subject to rationing—to access hiking trails. The Blue Mountain Eagle Climbing Club insisted on holding hikes in 1942 and justified the decision in a letter to all members. The letter began "Dear Comrades" and went on to announce that the fall hike would continue as planned. "We hope that our hike, by bringing you health, relaxation, and good fellowship, will strengthen each one of you for your place in our united war efforts. We feel that the genuine love of country that results from hiking in the Great Outdoors nurtures a healthy patriotism." Other clubs decided to avoid driving altogether. "After all," an enthusiastic hiker reminded his fellow members, "hiking is a matter of muscles, not rubber tires and gasoline, and so we need not forego the simplest and yet most glorious of sports." These justifications of hiking were repeated in club newsletters throughout Pennsylvania, forging a cohesive ideology that allowed hiking clubs to flourish in times of peace, war, and economic instability.[21]

The method of founding clubs and justifying hiking in the Midwest was remarkably similar to that of Pennsylvania. The earliest Midwest hiking club, the Prairie Club of Chicago, was an outgrowth of a 1907 meeting of the Playground Association of America, which organized a series of walks in the "Forests, Fields, Hills, and Valleys about the City." Architects Dwight Perkins and Jens Jensen, writer Hamlin Garland, ecologist Henry C. Cowles, and reformer Jane Addams were members of the Playground Association and influential promoters of these walks. At least one member of the Appalachian Mountain Club, Alexander M. Wilson, also led hikes and aided in the transfer of several decades of hiking knowledge to the region. By 1908, the success of the first hikes—some drawing more than one hundred participants—prompted the founding of a separate entity. Known as the Prairie Club, this group intended "to escape the hustle and bustle of Chicago and take hikes through the country." The founders hoped the club would "teach the throngs of the city the

romance of common things. It can make every pool a Walden
Pond. It can lead people away from the glare of artificial lights
and teach them to know and love the constellations, the aurora
and the wonders of dawn and dusk that rarely appear to city
blinded eyes." Despite the emphasis on escaping the city, hike
schedules reveal that most walks actually took place on sparsely
developed land within city limits that was easily accessible by
interurban public transit. The club also purchased cabins at locations both within the city and as far away as Tremont, Illi-
nois.[22]

The Prairie Club, like many of Pennsylvania's clubs, engaged
with local land preservation and conservation issues. Indeed, the
club included some of the region's most prominent conservationists. For example, during the 1890s and 1900s, Jensen was instru-
mental in creating Chicago's Columbus, Humboldt, Garfield, and
Douglas Parks and galvanizing support for the Cook County Forest Preserve and the preservation of the Indiana Dunes. "What
wealth of beauty is revealed in this simple landscape—little understood by man," he wrote of the dunes. Perhaps unsurprisingly,
these later became some of the club's most popular haunts. Another member, Samuel Harper, wrote several books on ecology,
religion, and walking that the club later published. Harper was a
thoughtful critic of the management of the region's nature preserves, questioning if human intervention did more harm than
good. "But if public ownership of the woods will save the trees
and prevent nature from being wholly deforested," he reasoned,
"let us by all means encourage it and then endeavor to unlearn
the ways of man and to learn again the ways of nature so that we
may once more live in harmony with all her living creatures." The
club took this message to the public in a number of ways, including a large display at the Marshall Field's department store in
downtown Chicago. The display included male and female hiking
outfits, club artifacts, maps, and photos of various parks, streams,
and cabins. A poster underneath photos of the Indiana Dunes
read, "Do You Want the Dunes for a Public Park?" and included a
sign-up sheet. As a result of their outreach campaigns, by 1922
the club boasted more than nine hundred members.[23]

Members of the Prairie Club carefully pass through a barbed-wire fence on a 1909 outing. Midwestern hikers were accustomed to passing through urban, suburban, and rural landscapes rather than pristine wilderness. Courtesy of the Prairie Club Archives, Westchester Township History Museum, Chesterton, Indiana.

In contrast to the well-known founders of the Prairie Club, the Cleveland Hiking Club was the brainchild of local journalist Edna K. Wooley and truancy officer Ethel McCarthy. In 1919, McCarthy wrote to Wooley—whom she had never met—to encourage her to write an article in the *Cleveland News* that would promote organized walks around the city. McCarthy had been a member of Washington, D.C.'s Wanderlust Club and lamented the lack of hiking clubs in Cleveland. "There must be many who would walk," she wrote to Wooley, "could they but have company, and if they but knew the interesting points about the city and its environment." Wooley agreed to write an enthusiastic column entitled "D'You Want to Be a Hiker?" in which she told her readers, "We OUGHT to have such a club. . . . Anyone who loves outdoors and is not afraid to wear sensible walking shoes, can belong to it."

She encouraged anyone who was interested to join McCarthy and her for a hike through the Rocky River Reservation, in the western outskirts of Cleveland. The first hike attracted two hundred participants. The outpouring of interest led to the founding of the Cleveland Hiking Club (CHC), the purpose of which, according to its constitution, was "the promotion of outdoor recreation in the form of walks and outings, the encouragement of the love of nature, and the dissemination of knowledge of the attractions of the country adjacent to the city of Cleveland." Like the Prairie Club, most of the club's early hikes took place on the outskirts of Cleveland and in the city's undeveloped river valleys, which in 1919 were only beginning to be acquired as part of Cleveland's famous Emerald Necklace of greenways.[24]

The Milwaukee-based Wisconsin GO Hiking Club also got its start with the work of a journalist—in this case, J. Craft McCracken of the *Milwaukee Journal.* Beginning in 1921, McCracken used his column to organize frequent hikes, of which the *Journal* published notice and served as the unofficial sponsor. In 1923, McCracken moved to another paper, and the *Journal* stopped printing notices. Not willing to see organized hiking end in Milwaukee, a group of McCracken's regulars held an organizational meeting and, in 1924, officially founded the Wisconsin GO Hiking Club—the GO standing for "Genuine Oldtimers," although it would quickly take on the meaning of the imperative verb "go." "In those early years business meetings were very informal, usually being held on regular hikes, along a country road," remembered one early member. "Once I recall the President and Secretary were perched in an old wagon and the rest of us were down below on the ground in some field." Outings were a mix of half- and full-day hikes, "with, of course, parties on any and all occasions." One member even suggested altogether throwing out business meetings, wondering "what all this ado about revising, rescinding, and undoing has to do with hiking?" The levity of the group is clear in a hike announcement from the 1920s promising that participants would "Drink from the Fountain of Youth, see the African Jungles of Chardon and the Valley of Death. All for $1.25!"[25]

This approach apparently served the GO Club well. In 1935, the club's president, Carl Hub, could report, "Even in these 'depression' years this club has functioned with scarcely any loss of membership." A tally of the preceding year's hikes shows that Hub was not exaggerating. The schedule included thirty-nine hikes of varying types and distances that attracted 689 people, each walking, on average, more than ten miles. In general, the Great Depression had few effects on hiking clubs, whether in the Midwest or in eastern cities. Hiking was an inexpensive pastime, and those Americans hit hardest by the economic downturn were those already less likely to be active hiking club members.[26]

The GO Club, like most hiking clubs of the period, kept a close eye on what other clubs were doing throughout the country. The *GO Club News* had a regular column called "The Snoopers," which excerpted material from clubs across the country. A 1935 edition of "The Snoopers" included a reprinted article from a Connecticut club that reported, "Some practical idealists who went walking in Germany and discovered the far flung network of hotels for young people are trying to establish a similar chain in this country." Soon after, the *GO Club News* included a detailed write-up of a hostelry presentation held in Milwaukee and suggested that the club should become more engaged with what they now called "a national movement." During the 1920s and 1930s, it was not uncommon for GO Club officers to read from letters, newsletters, and hike schedules of the nearby Prairie Club and other outing organizations during official meetings. The *GO Club News* covered national hiking topics as diverse as progress on the Appalachian Trail, federal investment in trails and bicycle paths, bridle paths and accommodations in the Northeast, the Prairie Club's recent railroad excursion to Ontario, and other selections copied out of *Nature Magazine*. The newsletter contained information from clubs not only in the Midwest but also as far away as Portland, Oregon.[27]

Midwestern hiking clubs' interest in the activities of hikers throughout the country extended to the ways in which they spoke and wrote about hiking. Their justifications for hiking closely resembled those of their Pennsylvania counterparts.

Language that evoked the spiritual, health, and patriotic benefits of hiking appeared throughout their speeches, newsletters, scrapbooks, and other club material. Many hikers, for example, described hiking as a form of worship because it allowed for immersion in God's creation. Although the Prairie Club's Jensen was a landscape architect engaged in reshaping the natural world, he described hiking as a means of experiencing the "work of the Great Master." Club members also never tired of quoting Scripture, although they sometimes used it to playfully chastise speedy walkers, as was the case with the Cleveland Hiking Club's use of Luke 13:30 on some of its publications: "And, behold, there are last which shall be first, and there are first which shall be last." Overall, midwesterners used less religious language than Pennsylvanians, but they clearly associated hiking with spirituality.[28]

Midwestern hikers faced the same problem as Pennsylvania hikers when the United States entered World War II in 1941. At first, hikers were concerned that their recreational pursuits would appear inappropriate at a time when fellow citizens were serving abroad. In the spring and summer of 1942, however, the problem became more acute. Hiking clubs had to justify the use of rationed materials, such as rubber tires and gasoline, to access traditional hiking locations. In some cases, the rationing made little impact. For example, during wartime, members of the CHC visited Camp Onwego at least twenty-five times, although a notation in the cabin logbook observed that there was always a "flag waving bravely" outside. Club events regularly featured lectures on the Civilian Defense Fund and appeals for donations, and the club's newsletter highlighted accommodations made for wartime rationing, such as moving the annual banquet to a downtown location next to a transit line and requiring meat ration vouchers and sugar donations at club dinners. GO Club members appeared to be similarly unimpeded by wartime restrictions. "Every driver will of course be mindful of the use of their car," the club's newsletter noted in 1942, but "as long as there is some rubber left and we can buy gas, we're going out for some fun!" This rhetoric was the same as that used during the

Great Depression, when a club member, trying to convince others or perhaps himself, wrote, "Isn't it something to know . . . that no matter how depressing the material things of life may be, we can still go out under the skies, along the roads, over the hills, to hike and play and laugh with . . . our good pals. Nothing can take that from us, as long as we have our health and happy spirits."[29]

Despite the apparent enthusiasm, GO Club membership took a hit from the war, as nearly a third of the club either enlisted or left Milwaukee for work in defense plants. A 1943 newspaper article noted that once-popular hikes were attracting meager groups of as few as ten members. To maintain morale, the club organized correspondence with members—seventeen male and one female—serving in the military "to show that at heart they are still in our midst." They also made small keepsake booklets that contained thirty pages of CHC photos with humorous captions. The last page featured a group photo of the club and was captioned, "Wish You Were Here."[30]

For their part during World War II, Prairie Club members turned rationing into an opportunity to expand their "Get to Know Your Chicago" walk series, during which the group visited different Chicago neighborhoods and interesting sites near the city. Their urban walks adopted the spirit of the nineteenth-century flâneur in that they explored not just scenic stretches of the lakefront or river valleys but also numerous industrial plants, Hull House, the YMCA, hospitals, colleges, prisons, police stations, the city's new sewage disposal plant, the airport, churches, and the mayor's office, always reporting back on their experiences. "The club being cosmopolitan, a number of visits were made to the so-called foreign colonies located in various parts of Chicago," a member wrote of the hikes. "Our party was always entertained, by pre-arrangement, with songs, dances, and hospitality of the Japanese, Chinese, Russian, Mexican, and German colonies." Midwestern hikers faced serious obstacles during World War II, but the need to invest hiking with meaning to justify leisure during a period of sacrifice led to an articulation of hiking's benefits that resulted in a stronger culture of hiking.[31]

Although religion and patriotism motivated hiking club members at different times, the primary rhetorical justification for midwestern hiking was its health benefits. The fact that influential, nationally recognized leaders of the Playground Association of America founded the Prairie Club meant that they recognized the potential for hiking to reform the health and morals of participants. Although getting urban residents to walk in natural areas was a much simpler task than reforming public education, providing fresh and pure foods, or retooling urban sewer and waterworks, the leaders of the Prairie Club—and hiking organizations throughout the nation—saw hiking as part of the progressive campaign to improve public health and make city life more livable. Early members described themselves as "a band of nature lovers who have never surrendered to the thralldom of the city" and as a result find "health and enjoyment beyond price." The Cleveland Hiking Club stressed that members could enjoy rigorous exercise made more palatable through stimulating experiences in the company of others. "Hiking is a tonic because it brings the hikers to fresh air. . . . The weariness that comes after the strenuous walk is highly enjoyable. So, too, is the soreness of muscles that may be the next day's testimonial that legs have been doing unaccustomed work," wrote CHC member Carl T. Robertson. "The real joy of hiking is that it is highly healthful and at the same time interesting." This emphasis on health was echoed throughout CHC publications and even within the club's official song, the lyrics of which read in part, "Fellowship and faithful service we will pledge anew. Hike for health and recreation to our creed be true. Field and wood, the open spaces always call to me. Though the trail be steep and stony, hike with CHC."[32]

This emphasis on health was shared—song and verse—by the GO Club. The club's slogan in the early years—first listed in its articles of incorporation and repeated on its letterhead and throughout publications—was "Health and Good Fellowship through Hiking." The basis for the GO Club's claims was their belief that time spent in the outdoors offered a release from the concerns of the modern world and that freeing the mind ultimately benefited the whole body. According to a club member in the 1930s, hiking offered "release from cares, fears, doubts, and obligations. Release from regrets over the business contract you failed to land last week, and worry over the one you hope to snare next week. Best and most important of all, there's release from YOURSELF. Who," the club member asked, "can continue to think of problems while in his nostrils is the smell of good clean loam—with perhaps a distant whiff of equally good barn-yard aroma!"[33]

The club member envisioned leaving "city-born" worries behind and engaging one's mind and body with the sights and sounds of a healthier landscape. Hikers need not seek out reserves of pristine nature, for the salubrious landscape described in this passage is one of old farm houses, orchards, country roads, stone walls, and even dusty barnyards—a rustic built environment. This preference for nearby pastoral landscapes closely resembled that of hikers in the East who regularly walked through altered lands, but it also clashed with an arcadian vision of pristine nature promoted by western hiking clubs, such as the Sierra Club, during the same period.

In addition to the mental benefits of hiking, the GO Club promoted the physical transformation that hiking provided. "The American foot is determined to be glorified," claimed one enthusiastic member. "All we need are a few more trails . . . and the color of young Americans will soon turn from putty to bronze." A few lines from a 1934 poem entitled "Our Club" promised that hiking would yield "two rosy cheeks, a coat of tan, a sunny, happy smile; Just lots and lots of energy, and tons of pep a mile."[34]

The three midwestern clubs' focus on religion, patriotism, and health provided a body of ideas resembling that of Pennsylvania hikers during the same period. This loose ideology of hiking justified the hobby to outsiders and coalesced as a national hiking culture in the 1920s. There are several reasons why the ideological underpinning of midwestern and Pennsylvania hiking culture reflect each other so closely. First, both drew from the various impulses already at work in American cities in the late nineteenth and early twentieth centuries, such as the health, back-to-nature, arts and craft, and—most important—progressive reform movements, many of which celebrated recreation in natural settings and an escape from the city. Another reason is that there was a limited but influential exchange of ideas between eastern clubs and midwestern cities. Club newsletters often reprinted summaries of hikes, lectures, and other events throughout the region and the nation, spreading the cluster of ideas and activities that constituted American hiking culture.

In some cases, the proliferation of hiking clubs also resulted from the movements of people. On a local level, hiking clubs often hosted joint outings or took longer trips to visit a friendly club's cabin, during which hikers undoubtedly shared their ideas about walking and its meaning. Sometimes this happened on a national level. The Cleveland Hiking Club originated out of Ethel McCarthy's desire to replicate Washington, D.C.'s Wanderlust Club, with whose members she had previously walked. More than one founding member of the Prairie Club was also a member of the Appalachian Mountain Club, which by the 1920s was the most successful hiking club in the nation. As hiking club members moved throughout the country, they transferred their version of hiking culture—where, how, and why to hike—with them. They also brought with them an institutional knowledge of how small, volunteer hiking clubs functioned, how to develop membership lists, what to charge for membership, how often to hold social events, what content newsletters should contain, and the many other administrative functions that almost all hiking clubs shared during this period.

By the 1920s, there was also a literature of hiking available to anyone interested in finding it. The Appalachian Mountain Club's journal *Appalachia* had been in publication since 1876 and the *Sierra Club Bulletin* since 1893. Both publications spread ideas about hiking and trails across the country, including to readers who were more concerned with the scientific articles than the recreational accounts. Articles on hiking and the outdoor life also regularly appeared in national magazines. Typical volumes of *Outing Magazine, Boys' Life, Nature,* and *Outdoor Life* depicted hiking and nature walking as two of a variety of outdoor activities in which Americans participated.[35] The general public also learned more about hiking during this period. Most hiking club officers were influential in their communities and had few problems convincing local newspapers to announce hikes or reprint accounts of outings. Anyone living in an area with a hiking club would have gained some knowledge of it by reading the local paper. Even if they never actually hiked, increasing numbers of Americans recognized the sport's growing popularity. However, the most effective means of transferring hiking culture was through the small, homemade newsletters published by most hiking clubs. The quality of the newsletters varied widely based on the capacity and resources of each club, but even simple, mimeographed newsletters required a significant investment of time and money. Some clubs treated each issue as a work of art. Every issue of the *GO Club News*, for example, had a different cover, typically featuring a drawing depicting club members on the trail. The Cleveland Hiking Club had a simpler newsletter, but its annual banquet invitations, which often included brief club histories, song lyrics, and other information, were handmade, elaborate crafts that would have taken hours to assemble. The time and care club members invested suggests that they understood that their mailings played an important role in spreading news about their club and ideas about hiking. They assumed that others would read and then share the information the newsletters contained. These vibrant channels of communication allowed members of hiking clubs— and Americans in general—to follow developments regionally and in other parts of the country. This was the most crucial mechanism for spreading American hiking culture.

By the onset of World War II, there were plenty of new developments to watch throughout the country. Not only did the Appalachian Mountain Club, Sierra Club, and Mazamas grow in size and expand their hiking and trail-building activities, but new hiking clubs proliferated near large cities and in some smaller communities previously without walking organizations. Beyond the hotbeds of hiking activity in Pennsylvania and the Midwest, clubs formed throughout the country, especially in New York, where the New York–New Jersey Trail Conference and the Adirondack Mountain Club were both founded during a series of meetings in the replica log cabin atop the Abercrombie and Fitch store.

Dozens of other clubs were founded during this period, many with the shared goal of developing and maintaining the Appalachian Trail. For example, in 1924, the Smoky Mountain Club—a club notable in retrospect for limiting its membership to "whites" until 1946—began advocating for the trail to receive national park status, clearing portions of the trail, and planning, first, monthly and, then, bimonthly hikes in the mountains near Gatlinburg, Tennessee. In 1927, Washington, D.C., area hikers, many of whom had previously been members of the Wildflower Preservation Society, formed the Potomac Appalachian Trail Club (PATC). The club and its dedicated leadership would spearhead the early development of the Appalachian Trail. In 1934, a group of Maryland-based PATC members decided to break away and form the Maryland Mountain Club so that they could hike and maintain the section of trail nearest to home. In 1923, a large contingent of the Appalachian Mountain Club's Southern Chapter splintered off to form the Carolina Mountain Club, which in turn enveloped the Carolina Appalachian Trail Club in 1930. The club promoted its hikes, lectures, and social events in the *Asheville Citizen Times* and grew steadily in membership and capacity. In the period just after World War II, the club maintained more than ninety miles of the Appalachian Trail. The Georgia Appalachian Trail Club (1930), Natural Bridge Appalachian Trail Club (1930), Roanoke Appalachian Trail Club (1932), and Maine Appalachian Trail Club (1935) all formed to develop and maintain sections of the Appalachian Trail. As early as 1925, the Appalachian Trail Conference (ATC) attempted to bring these various "maintaining clubs" together to coordinate their work and hone their collective voice in advocating for the trail. Although the Appalachian Trail was important to these clubs, they also organized hikes and other outings throughout their respective regions that resembled the midwestern and Pennsylvania clubs described above. In this way, American hiking culture spread throughout the Appalachians.[36]

A member of the Potomac Appalachian Trail Club surveys a section of the trail in the late 1930s. Courtesy of the Appalachian Trail Conservancy.

By World War II, then, the East Coast and Midwest shared a thriving hiking culture, but there were also attempts to establish clubs in other parts of the nation. The most successful were those more closely devoted to technical climbing and mountaineering, including Seattle's Mountaineers and Denver's Colorado Mountain Club (CMC). The Mountaineers were formed in 1906 by a small group of Seattle-based Mazamas who envisioned "a small club of perhaps twenty folks" who would spend their time exploring the nearby mountains. This simple vision quickly evolved into plans for a citywide club, as 192 members stepped forward during the first year. Within a short time, the Mountaineers rivaled the Mazamas for the position of top climbing club in

the Pacific Northwest. The Colorado Mountain Club was founded in the Denver area in 1912 and by 1918 had 437 members, 270
of whom had reached at least one 14,000-foot summit to become
"qualified" members. Outing accounts from the CMC's journal,
Trail and Timberline, show that many early climbs were to nearby, relatively short peaks, and although the club would promote
mountaineering throughout Colorado and the region, it also
continued to hold accessible hikes of moderate length that attracted large parties.[37] On a national level, in 1902, the American
Alpine Club (AAC) emerged as the leading force for mountaineering. John Muir served as the club's second president, and
members of the Appalachian Mountain Club and other climbing
organizations filled key posts. The AAC would become America's
international face of mountaineering, but the club also held
climbs and hikes throughout the United States.

   This small but active group of climbing clubs was influential
in creating a national culture of mountaineering that disseminated information about climbing through club events, published journals, and newspaper coverage, eventually sending
American climbers throughout the world to claim first ascents of
peaks. Despite their success, climbing clubs both implicitly and
consciously limited membership to those who had the money to
invest in equipment, guides, and transportation, as well as the
disposable leisure time to spend countless hours training and
more than a week approaching and scaling the nation's highest
and least accessible mountains. As a result, hiking clubs and
their members always outnumbered the climbing clubs.[38]

   While adults focused their energy on expanding hiking and
climbing culture to cities and towns throughout the country, students at some of America's leading colleges organized outing
clubs with financial resources and ambitious schedules that
rivaled those of even the largest private clubs. Many of these
college clubs took on regional leadership roles building and
maintaining trail networks and cabins, organizing events, and
publishing accounts of their exploits. They also played an important role in institutionalizing hiking as an upper-middle-class
activity. The Dartmouth Outing Club, one of the nation's first, led

this movement in the early twentieth century, but the concept quickly spread to private and public colleges across the nation.

"What is there to do at Dartmouth in the winter?" undergraduate Fred Harris asked in a 1909 letter published in the student newspaper the *Dartmouth*. Hanover, New Hampshire, nestled along the placid Connecticut River—a stone's throw from Vermont—seems isolated in the twenty-first century and must have seemed even more remote in the early twentieth. The town's location amid steep and rolling hills situated within Lake Ontario's snowbelt assured that Dartmouth winters were typically spent indoors, gathered around fireplaces. Harris sought to change that. Citing successful winter carnivals in Montreal and ski jumping events in the West, he suggested "that a ski and snowshoe club be formed," with the primary purpose being "to stimulate interest in out of door winter sports." Although Norwegian immigrants had brought skiing to the Midwest in the mid-nineteenth century and formed clubs to promote the sport within their ethnic communities, skiing clubs were relatively scarce in 1909, especially in New England. Carl Tellefesen, a Norwegian working to promote skiing and standardize ski jumping competitions, had formed the National Ski Association as recently as 1905. Harris, therefore, was covering fresh ground by founding an East Coast ski club that was not dominated by European skiers. Moreover, he planned to do so with undergraduates. "By taking the initiative in this matter," Harris noted in the conclusion to his letter, "Dartmouth might well become the originator of a branch of college organized sport hitherto undeveloped by American colleges."[39]

Harris's letter struck a chord. Several days later, sixty men came to the organizational meeting of what they would call the Dartmouth Outing Club (DOC). The new membership, which included several faculty members, immediately elected Harris the club's president. A discussion ensued of what activities the club would pursue. Although Harris had only mentioned winter sports in his letter, the newly formed club now expanded its interests to include camping, hiking, and canoeing. One especially enthusiastic member even suggested the club "build a log cabin or camp in the college grant, which could serve as a terminus for tramps."[40]

In the first year of its existence, the DOC enjoyed popularity among undergraduates and faculty who already had an interest in spending time outdoors, during both periods of snow and more temperate weather. Their most popular event was a February gathering that came to be known as Winter Carnival. The 1910 carnival featured a hockey game, performances by Dartmouth's thespian group, a ball, a number of races on skis and snowshoes, and—the most popular attraction—a ski jump competition. Fifty special guests, including members of the press, were invited to watch Dartmouth's most daring men soar through the air for distances of up to forty-five feet. "Each man had five jumps," wrote Harris in a summary of the event, and points were "awarded for style and distance." The event was exciting enough to draw Dartmouth's entire student body out into the snow and endear them to the fledgling club.[41]

In the following years, the popularity of Winter Carnival grew to epic proportions. "The hills in all directions are dotted with flying toboggans, the roads with jingling sleighs," a 1914 description of the event recorded. "From the Vale comes the clear call of a bugle announcing the downward swoop of the ski-jump, while the staccato crack of the starter's pistols speeds the panting racers on their snowy course on snowshoe or ski. Everywhere gay mackinaws, toques and ribbons liven the snow-banked hills." The carnival took on national prominence in 1920, when Harris managed to get an article about the club published in *National Geographic*. Although the piece dutifully described the variety of club activities, it was the description of the carnival as the Mardi Gras of the North that caught the attention of some two million readers. "Thousands of spectators can be accommodated on the slopes surrounding Dartmouth's great ski-jumping event," Harris wrote in the article of the growing stature of the carnival. "McGill College, of Montreal, Canada frequently sends a team of jumpers to the carnival, when the struggle for supremacy assumes an intercollegiate and an international flavor." Beginning in 1915, other regional colleges had been invited to

Colden Camp, 1935. Members of the Dartmouth Outing Club join
the Intercollegiate Outing Club Association for a trip to the
Adirondacks. Courtesy of Dartmouth College Library.

participate in the carnival, and by 1936, German, Swiss, and
Chilean ski teams were making their way to Hanover to compete
against DOC skiers. In 1922, the DOC began to charge a small fee
for attendance, and the number of paid admissions through the
1920s averaged more than two thousand. Success came with a
high price tag—in 1930, the winter carnival cost the DOC
$5,266.46 of a $11,624.03 total club budget—but the event's role
in getting Dartmouth undergraduates to join the club and promoting the DOC to the region and nation was clear.[42]

In the meantime, the DOC was also attracting attention for
its nonwinter activities. In its first year, the club followed through
on its idea of maintaining a cabin for hiking members' use in an
old lumber shanty near Moose Mountain, northeast of Hanover.
The shanty was accessible by a ten-mile trail out from Hanover,
which would eventually become the route of the Appalachian
Trail. Within the year, the club had raised enough funds to build

a new, full-size cabin nearby the original site. This development eventually caught the attention of the *Boston Herald*, which in April 1913 ran an article entitled, "Dartmouth Men Plan Line of Camps in White Mountains"—written, not surprisingly, by Harris. The article announced the upcoming dedication of the new Moose Cabin and depicted it as the first of a long chain of cabins that would reach more than one hundred miles northeast toward the Dartmouth Grant.[43]

The appearance of this article turned out to be one of the most fortuitous developments in the history of the club, for it enticed a minister and businessman named John E. Johnson to make the trip to Hanover for the cabin's dedication. Johnson began attending Dartmouth in 1862, but service in the Civil War—in which he served as a U.S. Army captain—temporarily drew him away from academic life. A bout with a severe fever caused him to be honorably discharged in September 1865, and he finally graduated with the class of 1866. Johnson then attended Cambridge Divinity School and became an Episcopal minister in churches in New Jersey and southeastern Pennsylvania. He earned a reputation as an unconventional and sometimes vulgar preacher, and he soon left a traditional church setting for Theater Services of Philadelphia, a theater ministry that attempted to bring religion to the secular masses by offering discounted theater tickets for audience members who also attended service. The public liked Johnson for his humor and realistic approach to preaching, and he continued with Theater Services for more than twenty years.[44]

Johnson summered at a one-hundred-acre home in Littleton, New Hampshire—in north central New Hampshire—known as Sky Line Farm, and this shaped many of his ideas about the importance of wilderness and his future relationship with the DOC. Sky Line Farm was located in the heart of the White Mountains, and Johnson enjoyed views of the Franconia and Presidential ranges to the south and east. By the late nineteenth century, however, intensive logging had decimated large swathes of the White Mountains. In 1867, New Hampshire governor Walter Harriman sold 172,000 acres of forest to private companies, opening the region to resource extraction at a time when the American Industrial Revolution was demanding increasing amounts of raw materials.[45]

Johnson was attentive to the toll logging took on the region, and he became one of several outraged voices calling for regulation. In 1900, he published a short pamphlet entitled "The Boa Constrictor of the White Mountains," which targeted the actions of the New Hampshire Land Company. Johnson described the company's strategy of buying up large swathes of forest at low prices and then refusing to sell to the locals, thus interrupting the traditional balance of subsistence agriculture and selective lumbering that the locals had developed. When the land company had acquired a large enough tract of land, the company "cuts everything, rolls it down the mountain, crushing the saplings, and not content with that, often burns the refuse for charcoal." Complaints such as Johnson's led to passage of the Weeks Act in 1911, which allowed the federal government to purchase private land to create national forests that would protect important headwaters and watersheds from overlogging and fire. In 1918, Congress created the White Mountain National Forest from precisely those lands in New Hampshire and Maine that Johnson sought to protect.[46]

By 1913, therefore, Johnson was already familiar with the need to protect and enjoy the natural places of New England. The Dartmouth Outing Club's proposal to build a chain of cabins reaching deep within the White Mountains most likely seemed like a good opportunity to promote both interests. When Johnson arrived at the dedication of the Moose Mountain Cabin, he was unknown to anyone, but he approached Carl Shumway and Ernest Nichols, two DOC leaders, and asked if he could have an opportunity to speak because he had something he wanted to give to the club. Shumway and Nichols obliged, although they had no idea what gift the stranger had in mind. "When I called upon Mr. Johnson to speak he gave a very long talk which mainly emphasized that if he was to go through college again he would spend less time in classes and studies and much more time in the out-of-doors in the line of endeavors promoted by the Outing Club," Shumway later recalled, noting that Nichols, a

Dartmouth professor, was a little startled by the content of the speech. The bewilderment—and excitement—grew as Johnson announced that he was giving Sky Line Farm to the club and handed the deed to the DOC president, suggesting that the cabin chain extend eighty miles north to reach it.[47]

From that point on, Johnson was the DOC's greatest benefactor, ultimately giving over $69,000 to the club in the form of land, cabins, life insurance, endowments, and cash. In 1913 and 1914, Johnson constructed two cabins on another tract of land purchased mostly with his funds. In 1915, Johnson attended the winter carnival and was so moved that, writing on letterhead from the Hanover Inn—next to Dartmouth's campus—he sent a check to the DOC "to be applied towards forwarding the interests of the club in Hanover and the line of its cabins." The same year he built one club cabin for the cost of materials and at his own cost constructed a cabin in the Agassiz Basin and a four-room chalet at Sky Line Farm. In addition, he provided five cords of split and stacked firewood as a gift. In 1916, he turned over $25,000 worth of Tacoma, Washington, property to the DOC as a gift. In 1918, he purchased a tract called Happy Hill and designed and built a cabin there. By 1921, Johnson had established the Harrison Memorial Fund—an endowment of more than $55,000—and published an open letter to the Dartmouth community to raise that figure to $100,000. "I think I began to see what looks wonderfully like the bottom of my barrel," he wrote, giving an honest assessment of his quickly dwindling personal wealth, "but I will try to 'cough up' five one thousand dollar bonds for a starter." In his impassioned appeal, the rhetorical flourishes of a seasoned minister are apparent. "We may not always be able to define 'The Dartmouth Spirit' but we know what The Spirit of The Dartmouth Outing Club is. It is the spirit of The Outdoor God! . . . Now are we going to 'lie down' on this proposition? If so then blaze a trail over into the old cemetery at Hanover and drag the Club over there and leave it there!" Dartmouth undergraduates and alumni were apparently prepared to meet the challenge. By 1930, the endowment stood at $100,000, with over 60 percent coming from Johnson.[48]

All of this generosity allowed Johnson to influence club policy. His influence extended from the minutiae of the types of medals members received and the price of food at the club's kiosk to determinative decisions about the incorporation of the club and the content of its constitution and bylaws. In 1915, for example, Johnson sought legal advice about incorporation of the club and strategized about whether the club should reside under the alumni-operated Athletic Council or the non-Athletic Council, which was under the control of Dartmouth faculty. "I believe that the club will attain a more healthy and vigorous growth under its own officers, backed by Alumni who have the scent of wood smoke in their lungs, than it ever would as an accessory to the Drama and Jews Harp clubs," wrote one of Johnson's confidants. Not surprisingly, the club was soon after incorporated and placed under the control of the Athletic Council.[49]

At times, DOC officers gingerly worked to satisfy their benefactor's wishes while operating the club as they thought best. Johnson was a prolific letter writer, typically addressing the DOC's current officers as "Mr. President" or "Mr. Secretary" at the beginning of each letter. The undergraduate officers often found themselves writing to justify certain expenditures or defending their decisions. For example, a 1920 letter enclosed with a copy of the club's recently drafted bylaws timidly warned Johnson, "Possibly you will disapprove of some of it, but I know it to be the fact that everyone concerned had the improvement of the club at heart."[50]

When Johnson died in 1934, it was a severe loss for the club; however, Johnson had placed the club on a fiscal footing enjoyed by almost no other hiking club in the country. The DOC had eighteen cabins, ninety-five miles of trails, and physical assets worth over $200,000, whereas many hiking club composed of middle-class adults struggled to purchase a single cabin or organize the maintenance of more than a few miles of trail on an annual budget of several hundred dollars. Wealth was one reason for the club's success. Johnson was not alone in his generosity, and the club enjoyed large donations of both land and cash from a number of alumni. In addition, most Dartmouth undergraduates had personal wealth. In 1928, for example, a young man named

Nelson Rockefeller, whose father was worth an estimated $995 million, was unanimously inducted into the Cabin and Trail Committee of the DOC.[51]

Another reason for the health of the club was that it inculcated Dartmouth undergraduates with a culture of outdoor sport that they found fulfilling and exciting. DOC participation could become the defining college experience for students. Over the year, an inexperienced hiker could become an expert prepared to welcome and train newcomers the following autumn. The DOC attracted undergraduates who may have known little about hiking, trails, or the White Mountains and exposed them to a variety of experiences—some recreational, some laborious, but all social—that resulted not only in skilled hikers and skiers but also in deeply committed club members. On graduation, these men spread their hiking and administrative skills throughout the country, providing regional hiking clubs with devoted members and leaders.

Thanks to the success of this indoctrination process, membership grew rapidly during the first two decades of the Dartmouth Outing Club's existence, both in numbers of members and in percentage of the student body. When Fred Harris founded the club in early 1911, there were 79 members, which represented only 6 percent of students. By 1930, the club had 1,568 members representing 62 percent of the student body. Unlike the hiking clubs that preceded it, the DOC did not develop a strong, rhetorical justification of hiking based on religion, patriotism, and health, although the young men surely believed that outdoor sport contributed to all three. The primary goal of the club was to foster a sense of community through democratic access to the club activities and an emphasis on the shared character of manliness. As Harris explained, "Unlike football, baseball, hockey, and basket-ball teams, each of which in its ultimate development enlists the active efforts at play of a limited number of athletes," the DOC was open "to all who love the wide spaces, all who delight in the stillness of the winter woods, all who feel the lure of the frozen trail."[52]

Dartmouth's yearbook, *The Aegis*, also linked the democratic spirit of the club to its outings. "The democracy of the trail has

served to eliminate all distinction; the intimate contact of the
drifted hills and woodlands has broken down even the barriers
between student and instructor, and has resulted in a newer
comradeship, a deeper sympathy and understanding worth
much to those who would foster the true spirit of Dartmouth,"
the yearbook's editors wrote. "The whole idea of the club has
been to keep its membership democratic, to keep its financial
obligations low that no man need be excluded from its whole-
some activity on the score of expense." This concern for expense
extended to all facets of the club. For example, Johnson once
wrote to the club's president asking him to replace the "Delmo-
nico prices" at the DOC food stand in order to "preserve the democratic character of the club in small matters as well as great."
On a more important issue, club dues, Johnson also suggested
that a fee of one dollar was a fair price that would not prevent
participation. "We want to keep this Club as near the ground as
possible," he wrote in a piece that appeared in several campus
publications.[53]

The growth of the club between 1910 and 1931 suggests that
the Dartmouth Outing Club truly was democratic in its membership. Membership was composed almost solely of Dartmouth
undergraduates and faculty, an already self-selecting group of
relatively affluent men, so there was no obvious need to prevent
unwanted members. There is no indication of why, even in the
club's most popular year, 26 percent of the student body declined
to join. In addition to personal preferences about how best to
spend leisure time, unspoken social or financial barriers to
membership may have limited participation. Within the club's
structure, the Cabin and Trail council members were those who
actually controlled the club, so induction into the council served
as a means of selecting men of a certain physical and social stature. All of this is to say that the rhetoric of democracy, for all its
nobleness, veiled the obvious fact that the DOC was an elite
organization composed solely of well-to-do men.

What concerned the DOC more than democracy was a sense
of community and tight-knit bonds of masculinity born of time
spent on the trail, eating a large "feed" together, and sleeping

next to one another in cabin bunks. The DOC was similar to most hiking clubs of the period in that ultimately the club was about socializing with friends. The time spent together was invaluable. "To travel out to Moose [cabin] and eat an unusual dinner in the novel informality of the cabin, and around the fire have a bit of speaking and more of straight out talk, is worth a dozen lifeless dinners at the Newton Inn," wrote a Cabin and Trail officer. This network of friends eating and playing together became a surrogate family for undergraduates far from home, especially those unable to travel during the holidays. Income from a special pot of money, known as the Rum and Molasses Fund, purchased Thanksgiving meals for the group of men remaining in Hanover, which they often ate at one of the DOC's cabins.[54]

Dartmouth undergraduates in their late teens and early twenties grew up during a period when America was redefining cultures of masculinity. Virility became an increasingly important marker of manliness, as men sought to prove that the modern world had not sapped their strength. Time spent scaling mountains, laboring on trails, and sleeping on hard cots complemented time spent in classrooms preparing for the business world or academia. Harris, as founder of the club and its most influential alumnus, regularly articulated the relationship between the DOC and manliness. He once described the ideal club president as "a man who loves the woods, woodcraft, campcraft, and outdoor life." He noted, "The man who spends hours and days working on the trails might not have his work so well recognized as the ski jumper but he is working for the best interests of the club just the same." On another occasion, Harris wrote to complain that the DOC was growing "soft" because the Cabin and Trail group had purchased firewood and had it delivered to the cabins instead of cutting it and hauling it themselves. He contrasted this weakness with the recent efforts of a small group "to open a trail in wilder country and build shelter camps on it." The DOC men working on the trail and shelters had "hair on their chests," he noted, and "will never ask anybody to cut or buy wood for them." As a result, "I'll bet they will know more about real woodcraft and camping than the fellows who follow the easier trails."[55]

Despite the focus on manliness, the DOC rarely emphasized competition—outside of its skiing events—or used martial rhetoric to describe its outings. As one club leader explained, "Competition is not desirable on the trips owing to the danger entailed in high mountain work, and the lack of pleasure in racing by good views, in getting over fatigued, etc." In addition to the safety issue, open competition would have undermined the club officers' attempts to achieve democracy and community within the DOC.[56]

By 1931, the Dartmouth Outing Club's 1,700 members owned eighteen cabins and maintained ninety-five miles of skiing and hiking trails. Sky Line Cabin, on the farthest end of the chain, was more than eighty-four miles from Hanover. Most of the club's activities consisted of hiking or skiing along the chain and performing maintenance on the cabins, but there were also large outings to some wilder and less explored areas, such as the Adirondacks, Pemigewasset Wilderness, and Mount Katahdin, as well as recently added cabins on the periphery of the usual hiking territory. *Dartmouth Out-o'-Doors*, the club's official journal, resembled issues of *Appalachia* from the same period, with most of the essays written by individual members to recount recent group outings and personal trips well beyond Hanover.[57]

By World War II, the Dartmouth Outing Club had become one of the Northeast's premier hiking organizations, on par with private groups several decades older. As historians Laura and Guy Waterman have noted, "Dartmouth can be taken as the starting point of the college outing club movement in more than just chronological terms." The club's founding and prolific activity between 1910 and World War II provided a model to students at colleges across the country. During this period, students and faculty at more than two dozen colleges came together to form outing clubs modeled on the DOC. For example, in 1923, when students at the University of Maine began plans for their club, the goal was to create "a real organization similar to the well-known Dartmouth Outing Club." Like the DOC, these clubs organized trips to nearby mountains for hiking and climbing, but they also planned other outdoor activities, including skiing and climbing, and constructed cabins and trails for club use. In 1932, members of the DOC spearheaded the founding of the Intercollegiate Outing Club Association (IOCA), an organization intended "to keep the different outing clubs in touch with each other." With fourteen charter member schools, IOCA was one of the largest outing organizations in the world at the time.[58]

One major difference between the DOC and the clubs that followed was that most allowed men and women to participate, and equality of the sexes was an important aspect of the clubs. The DOC was reserved solely for men. This was in part because Dartmouth was an all-male school until 1972, but it does not explain why the DOC could not open its membership to women living in Hanover, as the Alpine Club of Williamstown had done as early as 1863. While other clubs prided themselves on equity, the DOC maintained its emphasis on a culture of manliness. Progressive private hiking clubs across the country were already encouraging women to participate by the early twentieth century, and many women held influential leadership roles in the Appalachian Mountain Club, Sierra Club, and other clubs. Coed college outing clubs facilitated this process by introducing young women to hiking early and giving them the woodcraft skills that they may not have received in childhood. The result was a new generation of educated young women with interest and experiences in hiking that made them more likely to join and lead clubs on graduation.

College outing clubs were most active in the Northeast, but students formed similar clubs at schools across the nation. In 1919, a group of Norwegian American students at the University of Wisconsin erected a wooden scaffold for a ski jump and landing slide at Muir Knoll, a knob on the shore of Lake Mendota. By 1930, the jump had deteriorated to the point that it was condemned, prohibiting ski jumping. As a result, Harold Bradley, chairman of the Physiological Chemistry Department and a leader of the Union Council, assisted a small group of students seeking a club that would be able to support maintenance of the jumps.[59]

For several years, Bradley had been informally planning winter excursions, canoe trips, and other outings for small groups of students and council officers, such as Director Porter Butts. On the trips, the men asked themselves, "If this is as fun and rewarding as it was . . . why not make it possible for students generally?" In 1931, the group posted a signup sheet on the Union bulletin board that read, "Please sign here if you're interested in participating in an outing club with skiing, camping, and canoeing as a prospect." The sheet gathered a number of names, and out of this list the Wisconsin Hoofers was founded. "Hoofers" was chosen as a play on the DOC's use of "heel" to describe their new recruits. In the early years, the club focused on skiing. At the time, skiing was not a popular sport in Wisconsin, except among small numbers of Norwegian and Finnish Americans, and it was difficult to find skiing equipment in the state. The Hoofers contacted the DOC and arranged to receive hickory skis with leather bindings, poles, and boots from their Swiss outfitter. They rented the equipment at the Union to any student interested in skiing or learning how to ski. They also hosted large events at the renovated steel jumps in the 1930s that attracted as many as four thousand spectators to cheer on the region's best skiers.[60]

Although much of the Hoofers' energy went toward skiing activities, hiking grew in importance as the club matured. In the early years, the club held a biannual hike around Lake Mendota and awarded prizes to the people completing the twenty-two-mile circuit in the fastest time. In the 1930s, hiking events had become so common that members could claim, "There isn't a crow's nest we haven't explored, nor a ravine that has been left untrod by Hoofer feet, not even a cornfield stands to wave that has not been traversed by some Hoofer group at one time or another." Scrapbooks from the period show a balance between skiing and hiking, canoeing, climbing, and other nonwinter sports.[61]

Like the DOC, the Hoofers envisioned their club as a democratic institution "that would cut across the different strata that are bound to appear at any university." The members prided themselves on their diverse backgrounds. "Heinz and his '57' hasn't anything on us Hoofers," one member bragged. A club

Members of the Hoofers' leadership convene in their Memorial
Union office during the early 1950s. Lessons learned from leading
college outing clubs empowered young men and women to found
or expand community hiking organizations on graduation.
Courtesy of University of Wisconsin–Madison Archives, #06021410.

member, looking back on the period between 1937 and 1942, believed, "The Hoofers provided students with a unique experience
of comradeship." Within the club, members made the distinction
between "heels" and "Hoofers of the first degree," who had attended more than three meetings, participated in more than one
activity, and paid the one-dollar initiation fee. In the mid-1950s,
the club would also add a requirement that incoming Hoofers
earn a certain number of points by attending events and meetings and undergo a thirty- to fifty-minute interview, during which
the heel answered questions about the club's constitution, history, and day-to-day operations.[62]

Despite this structure, like many hiking clubs, the Hoofers
could also be irreverent about their sport. A typical event

announcement from 1939 read, "Nobody likes to climb rocks and stuff to get poor views of the surrounding country especially on these awful fall days. For those that do, we'll climb the Wisconsin Rockies." The announcement also included a bleak advertisement for an outing to Pewits Nest. "An uninteresting region in the glaciated Baraboo section drags out another bunch of lazy folk who are foolish enough to enjoy hiking. Stan Sprecher leads."[63]

In other parts of the country, college outing clubs played important local roles in fostering outdoor recreation but rarely became regional leaders. In contrast, the Hoofers became one of the premier groups in Midwest outdoor culture by the end of the 1930s, in part because few other clubs—college or private—were organizing hikers in the region. The Wisconsin GO Hiking Club had formed in 1924 but was based in Milwaukee, and the next nearest club was the Chicago-based Prairie Club. The Hoofers and the GO Hiking Club did not have significant interaction before World War II, aside from monitoring each other's activities, but their proximity helped to make the Midwest a hub of hiking culture.

College outing clubs were crucial to building and spreading a national culture of hiking during the interwar period. Outing clubs exposed men and women to hiking, camping, and trail-building experiences and taught hiking and woodcraft skills that were quickly fading from America's collective memory, as the frontier closed and the modern nation industrialized, mechanized, and urbanized. Along with the Boy Scouts and Girl Scouts, founded in 1910 and 1912, respectively, college outing clubs created a process of hiking and camping training that could take an individual from youth to adulthood, with the outcome being someone experienced and skilled in the outdoors who would be very likely to join a hiking organization. Perhaps more important, managing outing clubs prepared young men and women for the task of institution building, promoting membership, planning outings and events, leveraging typically limited resources, and the other day-to-day work of running a hiking club. On graduation, members of the Dartmouth Outing Club's Cabin and Trail or a Wisconsin Hoofer would be prepared to help lead any hiking club in the nation or return to their hometown and found a new club. Although the influence of most college outing clubs would wane following World War II, they played a crucial role during the formative period of American hiking culture.

By the end of World War II, the American hiking culture that developed out of small, nineteenth-century gatherings of mountain walkers, such as the Appalachian Mountain Club and Sierra Club, had taken root and spread throughout the country. Dozens of clubs organized middle- and upper-class hikers in cities and large towns along the East Coast and in the Midwest and Pacific Northwest. At the nation's leading colleges, young men—and some women—built trails, visited cabins, and hiked to the summits of mountains. Despite the growing popularity of hiking, however, large portions of the country showed little interest. Before World War II, few hiking clubs formed in the Plains states, the Southwest, or the Deep South, and many small towns and cities throughout the nation failed to organize clubs. Of course, Americans who did not form clubs had no reason to record their reasons, so we are left to guess why hiking did not catch on in places like Texas or Florida or Kansas in those years. One possible explanation is that hiking, though it took place in rural areas, was ultimately an urban form of recreation. Typical hikers lived in towns or cities, which meant that they were likely to be employed in a job that did not require manual labor. They were likely to have disposable income to spend on hiking clothing and trips to the mountains. They were likely to have been influenced by writing, art, and speeches that romanticized time spent in nature as an antidote to crowded, dirty, ungodly, effeminizing cities. In contrast to the places where such hikers lived, large regions of the country—not to mention the majority of the population—were rural through 1920. In the country's interior, there were few large cities, with only Saint Louis, Kansas City, and New Orleans among the twenty largest American cities between 1900 and 1940. These cities did not have formal hiking clubs, or if they did, they were so short-lived that they left little evidence of their existence. Outside of cities, Americans who made their living in traditional industries, such as farming and mills, remained subject to the whims of nature and worked with their bodies in ways that many of their urban counterparts no longer did. The proposition that someone waking before dawn to tend animals and fields or standing behind a loom six days a week would carve out half a day for the unnecessary labor of walking was unlikely. Despite the rich justifications hikers developed for their sport, walking for leisure just did not make sense to most early twentieth-century Americans.

Where hiking did emerge, it was an important cultural act with a sophisticated set of rationales that included health, religion, and patriotism. Most important, however, hiking was about socializing with others. Hiking generally was a group activity. For members of hiking clubs, meetings, dances, meals, and simple companionship were almost as important as the act of walking itself. Take, for example, the wedding of two Prairie Club members. "The top of a dune on which Arthur had camped many a time during his bachelor days, was the chosen spot and a group of beautiful pine trees formed the altar," the official club history notes. "The wedding breakfast was served on top of this dune; the wedding garments were hiking clothes, khaki and flannel which Ruth had made herself. . . . Could there be anything more romantic?"[64]

Thousands of American hikers—like Arthur, Ruth, and their wedding party of fellow club members— ate, slept, and experienced life's important milestones together, in the process forging a cohesive community that transcended weekly outings and the logistics of club administration. "You see," one hiker of the early 1940s noted, "there is no better way to get to know a person than on a hike or outing. Their true nature is soon revealed." But despite the power of hiking to bring people together, the communal aspects of hiking would begin to change in the postwar period, as new technologies, evolving ideas about nature, and other developments would help Americans reenvision hiking as an individual, therapeutic pursuit not directly connected to groups of any type. As a result, many of the clubs founded in the first half of the twentieth century would struggle to recruit and maintain members by the late twentieth century. In the period between 1900 and World War II, members of newly formed and extremely active hiking clubs across the nation would have found that fate hard to imagine.[65]

As hiking culture spread across the nation and hikers founded clubs in dozens of cities, some began to turn their attention from simply organizing outings to protecting and expanding hiking opportunities in the form of trails. Trail building became an integral and highly visible aspect of American hiking culture. Volunteers from hiking clubs, at times in partnership with federal and state agencies, constructed several long-distance trails, including the Long, Appalachian, and Pacific Crest Trails, during this period. The blazing, maintenance, and protection of these trails would become the defining goals of many clubs and a rallying point that helped the American hiking community coalesce around shared principles. At the same time, however, the new trails provided an opportunity for a few hardy souls to prove they could "thru-hike" the trails on solo expeditions of many months. Although a community of hikers constructed the trails, individual hikers would make them iconic.

4 BUILDING TRAILS

IN the autumn of 1921, a small group of volunteers from the Palisades Interstate Park Conference assembled at dawn for a day of work in Harriman State Park, thirty miles north of New York City. It was a Sunday, a day of rest for most people, but these hikers would spend most of the day bent over with picks, shovels, and bow saws or reaching high with loppers to clear a narrow path through the forest. The hikers were responding to changes in the Mid-Atlantic landscapes through which they had once hiked. "Ever increasing automobile traffic on highways and even on secondary roads which were once delightful paths for the pedestrian, has spoiled many fine country walks," a popular guidebook of the period observed. This was especially true on Sundays and holidays, "when most trampers find their only opportunities to enjoy such recreation." The changing nature of roads coincided with "the remarkable growth of interest in walking as a means of recreation." By the early 1920s, there were at least sixty hiking or walking clubs in or near the city, highlighting the need for new places to hike.[1]

On this particular Sunday, the Palisades crew was building a brand-new trail just to the west of Bear Mountain. Their first step was "laying a string along the top of the cliffs on the western side of the ridge" that would indicate the approximate route of the trail. After the leaders had approved the route—based on a balance between maximum scenic quality and ease of travel—the rest of the crew would begin to clear the path. However, before the volunteers could chop the first root or saw the first limb, a group of Sunday hikers came upon them, having followed the string along the ridge. Smiling and excited to be charting a new course, the group of hikers called out to the volunteers. "You are public benefactors," they said breathlessly and continued to follow the string out of sight. As stunned journalist and trail advocate Raymond Torrey would write in his next *New York Evening Post* column, "Demand for trails by hikers is just barely ahead of the supply." In this case, it was ahead by only a matter of hours.[2]

Building trails had been an important job for nineteenth-century hiking clubs, but, as the popularity of hiking increased during the first half of the twentieth century, the construction and maintenance of hiking trails became a crucial and very visible task for the American hiking community. Hikers created short, regional paths, such as the one the Palisades crew built, as well as entire networks of trails that spread out from hubs in state and national parks and major city park systems. The most high-profile projects were long-distance trails that spanned hundreds or thousands of miles and sometimes multiple states. In the 1910s and 1920s, the Green Mountain Club's Long Trail, which ran the length of Vermont, became the nation's first long-distance trail. By the time the club finished the Long Trail, however, the much longer Appalachian Trail had also come into being. By the late 1930s, the Pacific Crest Trail (PCT), which linked Canada to Mexico, became the West's first long-distance trail.[3]

If concepts of religion, health, patriotism, and community motivated hikers and helped them forge a culture of hiking, then trails served as the tangible rallying point for that culture. Trails were something physical over which hikers could take ownership—either literally or in spirit. They were a manifestation of the various impulses that had guided the hiking community since its earliest days, including the pastoral ideal of wedding human artifice with wild nature. Despite their importance, however, trails led the hiking community toward a less tenable culture that celebrated solo "through" hikers and, in the postwar period, provided access to thousands of new recreationists who bypassed club membership and took the creation of trails for granted.

As early as 1910, James P. Taylor envisioned a trail that would follow the ridge line of the Green Mountains between the Vermont-Massachusetts border and the Canadian border—a distance of roughly 270 miles. Taylor was the associate principal at the Vermont Academy in Saxtons River. The academy, which advertised itself as giving "special attention to life in the open," was founded in 1876 as a college preparatory school with close ties to Dartmouth. After sketching out a route for the path, Taylor approached the Appalachian Mountain Club to see if he could interest the club in the trail project. The disinterested group of mountain climbers turned him down, reportedly saying, "The Green Mountain state was as flat as a pancake." Undeterred, Taylor focused on generating enthusiasm among influential Vermonters, including the governor and the state forester, whom he visited map in hand. After securing a reasonable amount of support, Taylor convened an organizational meeting for a club that would not only fulfill his vision for a long trail but also promote the exploration of Vermont's mountains and forests. In his invitation to potential members, he envisioned that "the work of the Club would be to awaken an interest in the mountains of Vermont, to encourage mountain climbing, to make trails, build shelters, and aid in the preparation of maps and guidebooks." On March 11, an audience composed of twenty-three lawyers, journalists, clergymen, businessmen, judges, a fish and game commissioner, a future governor, and—not surprisingly, given Taylor's background—a number of educators assembled for the meeting. They discussed Taylor's plans, developed a constitution, and founded the Green Mountain Club (GMC).[4]

By 1910, trail building was already well under way in Vermont. Like the Prairie Club and others, the Green Mountain Club traced the history of early hiking paths back to Native American trails. "There are paths in use today in southwestern Vermont," a publication from the 1920s noted, "that must have been trod by the feet of redskins untold years ago." By 1847, there were rough trails to the summits of Mount Mansfield, Mount Ascutney, and a few other peaks, which were typically built by locals and only periodically maintained. In the 1850s and 1860s, trail-building activity temporarily flourished, as the proprietors of local inns and lodges cut bridle paths from their establishments to the nearest outlooks. For example, the owner of the Equinox House in Manchester cleared a bridle path between Beartown Notch and a spur of Mount Equinox. Equestrians could also follow trails up Mount Mansfield and Camel's Hump, and several paths were later finished—at least partially— as permanent carriage roads. After this flurry of activity, bridle path construction slowed, and most of the trails became overgrown.[5]

Beginning in the 1870s, walking for pleasure became more popular, and inns and early resorts once again responded, but this time by constructing hiking trails. By 1910, when Taylor hosted the first meeting of the Green Mountain Club, there were paths to the summits of Mansfield, Camel's Hump, Lincoln, Killington, Haystack, Jay Peak, Equinox, and Ascutney. Guests at the Pavilion Hotel in Montpelier often visited the summit of Mount Hunger, riding a carriage road "to a point half a mile below the top and from there a path ascended the mountain, surmounting the ledges by means of stairs." Another lodge near Warren constructed a buckboard road up Mount Abraham and a trail along the skyline of Lincoln Mountain to service visitors.[6]

Vermont trail building was not entirely commercial. For example, in 1906, a small group of people near Windsor founded the Ascutney Mountain Association after they purchased the mountain summit and surrounding land. The association maintained a stone hut and trail to the ridge, with the overall goal to "preserve the natural beauty of the [sides and] summit of Ascutney . . . to improve and keep in good repair the trails leading to its summit and in general encourage the making of the summit [of the] mountain a resort for recreation and pleasure." Camel's Hump had a wood-framed hotel at its summit from 1859 to 1875, when it burned down. In 1908, the Camel's Hump Club reopened the old path to the summit and erected canvas tents that could sleep more than fifty hikers. Soon thereafter, the club added three simple, galvanized metal cabins and stationed a caretaker at the summit to service guests. According to an account from 1915, the club also continued to improve the path to the summit using a unique technique. "Two men in a buggy carrying 10 pounds of dynamite reached the top intact and not prematurely. It was not done on a bet, the dynamite being used to blast out boulders on the way." The club's work led to a rapid increase in visitation, with seven hundred hikers reaching the summit that year and most spending the night.[7]

The Green Mountain Club was not the first trail-building organization in Vermont, but it would become the first to institutionalize trail building and coordinate these numerous short, local paths under Taylor's unified vision for the Long Trail. The idea of a long-distance trail across Vermont proved to be a relatively easy pitch. Less than a year after its founding, the GMC's Burlington Chapter, for example, had ninety-five members. The process of actually constructing the trail took more effort. "No trail construction was carried out in 1910," a 1926 club history reports, "but logging roads were explored and possible routes were tried out for new trails." Taylor also began approaching private landowners to secure their permission for the trail. Two years later, roughly twenty miles of the trail were in place, linking Sterling Pond (northeast of Mount Mansfield) with Camel's Hump by following old logging roads and short sections of new trail. This was admittedly slow progress. In response, the club entered into an innovative relationship—a "public-private partnership" in twenty-first-century parlance—with the state's Forestry Department. If the club could raise the funds for trail construction, the Forestry Department agreed to build portions of the trail. Rising to the challenge, in 1912, the club raised the considerable sum of $1,065 from several sources, including $100 from the Appalachian Mountain Club, $25 from the Woodstock Inn, and the remainder from the GMC treasury and wealthy members. Using the funds to pay for staff time and equipment, in 1913, the Forestry Department opened more than fifty miles of trail south of Camel's Hump to Killington Peak. With the additional mileage, the club began to construct log lean-tos that would provide temporary shelters for hikers. The first were built at Birch Glen, at Broad Loaf Glen, and south of Mount Horrid with the private funds of Emily Dutton Proctor, the philanthropist daughter of Redfield Proctor, founder of the Vermont Marble Company and U.S. senator from Vermont. Already ambitiously planning for the day when hikers would walk the entire trail, the club spaced the shelters five to eight miles apart, which was the estimated distance a hiker could cover each day.[8]

In order to supplement the state's work, the GMC formed new chapters throughout the state, including one in Bennington that, in 1914, began exploring miles of abandoned highways and old logging roads to identify a route to the Massachusetts border in southern Vermont. In the meantime, other chapters helped to extend the trail further north, from Sterling Pond to Johnson, along the Lamoille River, using their knowledge of local conditions to connect the general route outlined on Taylor's map. In 1915, the club published its first guidebook to the trail. The simple, fifteen-page pamphlet was based on an article published in the *Burlington Free Press* entitled "Along the Skyline over the Long Trail." The article, written by club member Louis Parker, matter-of-factly described his hike on the completed trail between Sterling Mountain and Camel's Hump. The guide is remarkable for its general descriptions, and although Parker references his pedometer for the total miles walked each day, he does not give precise distances between key landmarks or points on the trail. The pamphlet includes dozens of suggested one-day trips from Burlington and other locations, and Parker suggests, "By combining, reversing and rearranging trips an endless number of excursions can be made into the mountains." Partnering once again with the state's publicity department, along with the region's railroads and hotels, the club printed and distributed sixty thousand copies of the guide, vastly expanding awareness of the trail.[9]

Despite this apparently productive relationship, Green Mountain Club members realized that conflicting visions about how the trail was to be used could adversely affect its design and construction. "The purpose to be served by a trail useful to the Forestry Department was not always the same as that of a path desirable for pleasure tramping," the club noted. "In the former case the need was for access to the forested foothills of the mountains, while in the latter the desire naturally led to a skyline path along summits, preferably to places where there was an outlook because there was no timber." The Forestry Department was willing to construct the Long Trail because it hoped to use the path to access its holdings and patrol for fires. As a result, the foresters sought a route no steeper than a 15 percent grade to facilitate towing their firefighting equipment into the backcountry. Critics claimed that the smooth grades, which required valley and mountainside routes—often through previously logged areas—undermined the original vision of providing access to the mountaintops. "The necessities of the forest patrol did not harmonize with the ideals of the tramper," observed Appalachian Mountain Club president Allen Chamberlain in 1919. "A route across the ridges was too meandering and laborious to meet the foresters' needs, and the trail that they ran on easy grades along the slopes was far too tame and unspectacular for those whose quest was scenery." Other critics suspected the graded paths would allow the foresters to take pack animals on the trail, as was the custom in the West. Due to these divergent preferences, portions of the state's route south of Camel's Hump were eventually abandoned, but others—especially near Killington—were "well adapted to both purposes and have remained in use."[10]

As the experience of later trail organizations will show, the Green Mountain Club's questioning of the trail's route was not unique. The design, layout, and construction of trails revealed deeply held ideas about the purpose of trails, their use, and the role of man-made features in the wilderness. These questions, tied as they were to personal values, had the potential to cause internal divisions and intense debate within clubs. Controversy over the government-built section of the Long Trail pitted GMC leaders against one another. The club's corresponding secretary, Roderic Olzendam, and the Proctor family, the GMC's wealthiest patrons, supported the Forestry Department's work. Furthermore, the Forestry Department's commissioner, Austin Hawes, was also GMC's chairman of trails and shelters. Olzendam considered the issue to be one of access, which he expressed in gendered terms. "A small number of enthusiastic men laid out the first trail," he wrote of the sections along the ridgeline and over rough terrain, "but the Long Trail is to be for women too." During a 1919 Long Trail hike, Allen Chamberlain made a similar comment about female hikers. "It was pathetic to note the track of a woman's foot in a muddy bit of trail, the pointed toe, the narrow shank, and peg heel, all spelling plainly the fatigue and general discomfort that must have been the wearer's lot for days after that experience." Both comments ignored more than fifty years of hiking history, during which women had joined men on the nation's toughest trails.[11]

A newcomer to the club in the 1910s, Will Monroe, was perhaps the most vehement critic of the state's trail. Monroe lived in New Jersey, where he had experience with volunteer trail building. He was also a seasoned climber and was comfortable working in the backwoods. Beginning in 1914, Monroe taught at the University of Vermont's summer school, which meant that he was nearby the Green Mountains for several months each year. After experiencing several sections of the trail and deeming it unfit for safe travel, Monroe complained directly to the club's officers about the state's work. Chamberlain agreed that the trail was rough in some locations, but he disagreed with Monroe about the safety issue. "There are stretches, in fact, that are rough enough to please the fancy of the toughest woodsman," he noted, "and yet the way is sufficiently clear for any one familiar with mountain trails to follow safely." Regardless, Monroe's persistent criticism brought the question of trail design to the fore.[12]

In the summer of 1916, he volunteered to lead the Green Mountain Club's efforts to continue the trail south of Camel's Hump. Monroe recruited several helpers, who joined him in pulling an "oxcart with a single pair of enormous wheels" into a mountain camp near Camel's Hump, which they used as a base for their trail-building activities. Throughout the summer, they scouted logging roads and cleared new paths roughly thirteen miles south to Glen Ellen. The next summer and fall, Monroe and his team extended the trail farther south—first to Lincoln Mountain and then to Middleburg Gap. This thirty-five-mile section was later christened the Monroe Skyline. Monroe used the trail as a model for well-engineered ridgeline paths in contrast to those cleared by the state, yet even sections built by his crew could be very rough, narrow footpaths that required squeezing through boulders and blow-down and scaling rock ledges by means of rustic ladders.[13]

The Skyline Trail quickly earned a reputation throughout New England for being well constructed and thoughtfully routed. In 1919, the Appalachian Mountain Club's Chamberlain noted, "In its construction . . . the trail is as near perfection as a mountain tramper has any right to expect. Not that it is a graded path, that horror of the pedestrian," he added quickly. Rather than building up the tread of the trail, Monroe and his crew painstakingly removed roots and small stones that could trip up hikers. In the canopy above, they cut back encroaching limbs and brush, leaving a six-foot corridor for easy passage. Chamberlain also observed that Monroe blazed the trail at short, regular intervals and included wayfinding at intersections and access points. Indeed, the signage was so excessive that Chamberlain presumed an experienced hiker would consider it "an affront to his woodcraft." However, he argued, "This trail was designed to open that mountain picture-gallery to every one, old and young, and especially to the tenderfoot, to conduct him through its mazes with certainty and safety."[14]

Chamberlain also noted that the Skyline Trail followed a circuitous route dictated by scenery rather than expediency. "Not only does it find every high spot where broad views abound," he reported, "but it hunts out every intervening charming dell and glade and ravine, every picturesque cliff, every refreshing spring, that could possibly be brought within the line of march without undue departure from the course." This was ideal for people seeking natural wonders, as Monroe intended, but impractical for foresters, firefighters, and other travelers seeking a direct route through the mountains.[15]

Long Trail sign, 1924. In the 1920s, Vermont's Long Trail became the nation's first long-distance trail. Courtesy of University of Vermont Special Collections Library.

The debate over trail design came to a head in January 1917. As Monroe constructed the trail, he recruited a number of like-minded volunteers from the New York and New Jersey area to help. Having given generously of their time, money, and labor, these volunteers reasonably desired to join the Green Mountain Club by forming a New York area chapter. In 1916, Monroe formally requested permission to do so. Club officers who had grown increasingly frustrated with Monroe opposed the chapter, first, because Monroe's contingent threatened their control over trail policy and, second, because they believed that the club was intended primarily for Vermont residents. Monroe, now angry that the club accepted the volunteers' free labor but denied them membership, asked whether the club's constitution prohibited forming out-of-state chapters. Sensing a crisis that might split the club, President Proctor organized a meeting between the two groups. Monroe's backers stated their case for skyline trails and chapter status, while traditionalists spoke of 15 percent grades and a club for Vermonters. The heated discussion threatened to derail the meeting, until the seasoned Taylor rose and stated definitively that he envisioned the Long Trail as "a high, scenic mountain pathway." This statement, from the man who founded the club, implicitly endorsed Monroe's approach and effectively undermined the opposition. Within a year, the New York chapter had more than 150 members, and the club shifted from graded mountainside paths to ridgeline trails.[16]

By 1920, the club had resolved its vision and, thanks in large part to Monroe's volunteer trail building, the Long Trail extended 209 miles, from the Massachusetts border to Johnson. As the Long Trail became a reality, the Green Mountain Club grew in membership and capacity. The club continued building shelters along the trail and added several elaborate, multi-room lodges. For example, the Proctor family once again stepped forward to fund Long Trail Lodge at Shelburne Pass, which provided an unheard-of level of luxury in the backwoods. "This artistic structure fits into its wild, natural setting without a jarring note," one hiker recalled. "One finds a family atmosphere with all of the conveniences of a hotel, and the club's hospitality remains one of the delightful episodes of the trip." Meanwhile, Robert Hulburd, an attorney and former lieutenant governor of Vermont, funded an extension of the trail fifteen miles northward from Johnson to Belvidere Mountain.[17]

At the Green Mountain Club's organizational meeting in 1910, members said that their goal was "to make Vermont's mountains play a larger part in the life of the people." By 1926, they could look back on more than fifteen years of progress toward fulfilling that vision. "Where eight or ten summits were provided with paths twenty years ago, fifty or more are now within reach," the club's chronicler wrote. "Where the trails available then were sometimes vaguely marked or poorly planned, the paths to-day are designed not only to help the tramper safely to the top, but to afford outlooks and near-by pleasure while on the way. Where the paths then existing were isolated one from another, there is now a great system of trails with a central path extending from the Massachusetts line almost through to Canada. Along the route there are thirty-one shelters for the overnight use of trampers." Four years later, the club cleared the final few miles to the Canadian border, erecting a stone monument at the northern terminus. Although the Appalachian Trail would shortly exceed the Long Trail in fame and length, the GMC's 1,500 members and 270 miles demonstrated the plausibility of long-distance trail building at a time when lengthy sections of the Appalachian Trail remained unimproved.[18]

But the Green Mountain Club's importance transcended the physical trail, for although they spent these years scouting, blazing, and constructing paths, they also developed a culture of trail building that would influence other clubs. At the root of this culture was the idea that cutting trail was reserved for only the heartiest hikers who were willing to live under primitive conditions and commit to "tremendous" labor. "The site has to be chosen with care," wrote a trail builder in the 1920s, "regardless of how inaccessible this may be, the axes and saws, hammers and spikes, chains and shovels, and other tools all have to be lugged up on the backs of the men. A bushel of potatoes, canned goods, beef and bacon and pork, fruit and milk and coffee, cocoa and

tea, cereals, and a large outfit of cooking utensils and inciden-
tals, all have to go up in the packs too. . . . This may not sound
like work. But carry fifty to sixty pounds on your back up four
miles of steep, rough trail and you will agree that it feels like
something."[19]

Trail builders could use this "work" to differentiate themselves from others, even other club members who had never
spent time in the backcountry constructing trails. "Only those
who have helped cut trail and to build shelters can know what
this means, both in the labor involved and in the pleasure resulting," the trail builder claimed. In theory, this pleasure came from
"the satisfaction of building that which those who follow, the
friends whom you do not know and never will meet, will enjoy."
Chamberlain noted that "the actual work of construction through
weather foul and fair, and often under the torment of ravenous
swarms of flies, calls for a degree of courage and persistency of
an uncommon sort."[20]

Although the Green Mountain Club was the leading force in
Vermont trail building, it was by no means the only organization
concerned with providing paths to access the Green Mountains.
For example, faculty from Norwich University opened trails on
Bald, Scragg, and Paine Mountains, while the Stratton Mountain
Club developed a trail from West Wardsboro and placed an observation tower on the summit. One of the better-known projects
of the day was the Brattleboro Outing Club's forty-mile Winged
Ski Trail between Brattleboro and Stratton Mountain, where
it connected with the Long Trail. "The trail runs through a ski
runner's paradise," Fred Harris, also an active member of the
Brattleboro Outing Club, observed. "In laying it out, the needs of
ski-runners have always been kept in mind." Conditions on the
trail were reported in the *Brooklyn Eagle* and other news outlets,
suggesting that skiers would travel long distances to reach it. In
1923, the Brattleboro Outing Club hosted the Amateur National
Ski Championships, which daily brought as many as six hundred
skiers and spectators to the trail and the nearby ski jumps. Of
course, during warmer months, the path also met the needs of
hikers quite well. The Dartmouth Outing Club was also active in

clearing trails—for both hiking and skiing—in western New Hampshire and Vermont. As Allen Chamberlain observed, "The trails are stretching out north and south along the main ranges year by year." In the process, the Long Trail became the "spine" of a regional network of interconnected paths.[21]

Trail-building activity was so advanced in the region that as early as 1919, Allen Chamberlain, who would later become president of the Appalachian Mountain Club, wrote a book-length guide about the "tramper's paradise." In *Vacation Tramps in New England Highlands*, Chamberlain—using the now-familiar rhetoric of health, religion, and patriotism—espoused the benefits of hiking, made recommendations for the ideal "hiker's kit," and described the emerging trail network. "Everywhere throughout New England mountain hamlets are found local clubs devoted to the development of their surrounding heights as trampers' havens," he wrote. "In recent years the mountaineering clubs have opened mile after mile of trail, even to the remotest ravines and summits, and latterly the hotels . . . have built pretty paths for ramblers and good trails for the walkers who may chance to be guests beneath their roofs." Chamberlain partially credited the automobile for this flourishing of activity. "The advent of the automobile drove the bicycle off the roads, but to the gentle art of tramping it is destined to be a stimulation." He went on, in terms that would appear naive in the coming decades, to note, "No car can ever encroach upon the mountain trails, which will always remain sacred to the hiker, while out on the open road, the auto is his friend, helping him cover monotonous stretches of hot highway."[22]

Vacation Tramps included chapters on the Long Trail's Skyline section, winter hiking in the White Mountains, and outings on a number of other trails. Chamberlain gave the impression that New England, even in the early twentieth century, had enough trail and hiking opportunities to exhaust even the heartiest walker. But he also recognized that, for all the trails in place, the region was on the cusp of a new hiking boom as a truly regional network of trails emerged. He envisioned "a more complete opening-up of the scenery, particularly of the hill and mountain country, through the development of a system of trunk trails, to be built and maintained as a coordinated enterprise, and linking up the great National Forest in the White Mountains, the State wild parks, State Forests, and certain quasi-public forests and reservations maintained by educational and other institutions." The firm establishment of the Long Trail, soon to be followed by the Appalachian Trail, made this system a reality by the 1930s.[23]

As the Green Mountain Club neared completion of the Long Trail, the better-known Appalachian Trail—envisioned as a continuous footpath between Maine and Georgia—already began to overshadow the club's accomplishment. Visionary trail advocates had discussed a trail along the Appalachian range since the late nineteenth century, but Benton MacKaye—a regional planner and forester by training—was the first to flesh out the plans in writing. MacKaye had pitched his ideas to prominent members of the planning community for several years and received encouragement from Lewis Mumford, Clarence Stein, and others. In July 1921, MacKaye, Stein, and the American Institute of Architects' journal editor, Charles Whitaker, met at Hudson Guild Farm in New Jersey. Whitaker agreed to publish an article if MacKaye could translate his many ideas into a concise piece. His article, "An Appalachian Trail: A Project in Regional Planning," appeared in the October 1921 issue of the *Journal of the American Institute of Architects.* In the article, MacKaye called out the successes of the Appalachian Mountain Club and Green Mountain Club and the opportunity to expand those projects. "What the Green Mountains are to Vermont the Appalachians are to the eastern United States. What is suggested, therefore is a 'long' trail over the full length of the Appalachian skyline, from the highest peak in the north to the highest peak in the south— from Mt. Washington to Mt. Mitchell." The trail, he hoped, would provide a productive outlet for urban Americans' expanding leisure time and serve as an antidote to "the problems of life" in modern society. MacKaye did not have to wait long for others to take up the idea of an Appalachian trail.[24]

The greatest enthusiasm for MacKaye's project came from a group of trail builders based in New York and New Jersey, many of whom would become leaders in the national trail movement. In the 1890s, a quarry operation began dynamiting the Palisades—a series of cliffs along the Hudson River north of Manhattan—to produce paving stones. In response, a coalition of civic and outdoor groups led by the New Jersey Federation of Women's Clubs began an advocacy campaign that, by 1900, resulted in the creation of Palisades Interstate Park. In 1912, "Major" William Welch, an engineer with international railroad and park design experience, became manager of the park. Welch had the difficult task of building interest and providing access for the park, which was composed of fire-scarred second- and third-growth forests on difficult terrain. Welch recognized that there was already significant trail-building expertise among New England's hiking community, and he reached out to members of the Green Mountain Club and Appalachian Mountain Club for assistance. He also fortuitously joined forces with Raymond Torrey, the author of a weekly column in the *New York Evening Post* that served as the clearinghouse for New York City's hiking community. Through his contacts in the hiking clubs and Torrey's column, Welch spread the idea for a trail network within his park and a major, twenty-mile through trail that would transcend park boundaries. This growing enthusiasm resulted in an October 19, 1920, meeting in the log cabin atop Manhattan's Abercrombie and Fitch store. The group of trail and hiking leaders agreed to found the Palisades Interstate Park Trail Conference, with the goals of promoting "a deeper interest in the use of the Palisades Interstate Park for recreational purposes," "the development of trails and shelter systems," and trail development in "regions contiguous thereto, with power to invite other groups to join."[25]

By the following spring, the conference had already built the Tuxedo-Jones Point Trail (also known as the Ramapo-Dunderberg Trail), a twenty-four-mile path that allowed New York City residents to make an overnight trip with convenient rail access on both ends. The trail-building process was typical of its time. Welch first mapped out the basic route of the trail. Will Monroe led the volunteers, bringing to the task his experience building the Green Mountain Club's Skyline Trail. "The working parties were divided according to experience and ability, into scouting, clearing, and marking squads," Torrey wrote in his column. "The scouts were those who knew how to lay out a trail to include the highest scenic qualities: directness of route, supplies of water . . . and occasional ledges and cliff climbs to make the routes interesting. They went out ahead of the rest and made temporary small blazes on rock cairns. When everyone had agreed to the best route, it was primarily marked with a line of cotton string looped over the bushes and trees." The next group, known as the "elephant squad," followed the line and cleared the brush with hatchets and pruning shears. Finally, the marking crews blazed trees, built cairns, and nailed metal trail markers to the trees. Torrey described the routing of the trail around swamps and other hazards as "an interesting game." With the trail completed, the conference expanded its vision to include connecting its trails with the Delaware Water Gap to the south and the Long Trail to the north.[26]

MacKaye's *Journal* article appeared in print when the Palisades Interstate Park Trail Conference was considering a trail that would have spanned several states. MacKaye's proposal gave their work a national relevance, and they responded with enthusiasm. On April 25, 1922, the leading members of the New York hiking community, including the Palisades group and its constituent members, again met at Abercrombie and Fitch's log cabin. After a discussion of the Appalachian Trail proposal, the group voted to dissolve the Palisades Park Trails Conference and form the New York–New Jersey Trail Conference. This new, expanded group would focus on building the Appalachian Trail between Kent, Connecticut, and the Delaware Water Gap at New Jersey's border with Pennsylvania. By October 1923, the conference, supported by Adirondack Mountain Club volunteers, blazed and cleared the first sixteen-mile section of the Appalachian Trail, which began at the Hudson River, climbed to the summit of Bear Mountain, and ran westward to the Ramapo River. This short section was a powerful sign that the Appalachian Trail could become a reality.[27]

Like the New York–New Jersey Trail Conference, hiking organizations along the East Coast responded to MacKaye's vision for the Appalachian Trail during the 1920s and 1930s. In places along the Appalachians where well-established trail clubs existed, the AT could be built very quickly. For example, a handful of Pennsylvania hiking clubs built the state's 230 miles of trail by 1931. Beginning in the late 1920s, members of Easton's Blue Mountain Club, guided by Lafayette College chemistry professor Eugene Bingham, constructed 35 miles of trail along the Kittatinny Ridge between the Delaware and Lehigh Rivers. Between 1930 and 1931, several clubs from Maryland and Virginia worked with Pennsylvania state forest staff to establish the AT on existing trails and wood roads between the Maryland border and the Susquehanna River. Last, in 1931, the Blue Mountain Eagle Climbing Club of Reading completed the herculean task of routing the 102-mile section between the Lehigh and Susquehanna Rivers, in part by paying men who were out of work because of the Depression.

In regions where hiking had been localized or informal, the Appalachian Trail proposal served as a catalyst for the formation of formal hiking organizations. The most important example came in 1927, when Washington, D.C., area hikers, many of whom had previously been members of the Wildflower Preservation Society, formed the Potomac Appalachian Trail Club. This club enthusiastically assumed responsibility for the trail in southern Pennsylvania, Maryland, and Virginia. By their own account, however, members had little experience with trail building and did not realize how difficult their work would be. J. F. Schairer, the club's supervisor of trails, wrote of an early work trip to the section near Harpers Ferry, West Virginia, "We had to learn from sad experience how canteens are needed in the Blue Ridge, and we didn't have the kind of tools used today, clippers, and weeders. We learned our trail technique the hard way. We used, that day, mainly Boy Scout axes. We were all dying of thirst after getting to the top. It took us all day to get from south of Chimney Rock to a point about a half mile beyond. Our axes got so dull we couldn't cut with them. We just had to saw off the twigs." The club learned quickly from this negative experience and adapted its approach, yet building the trail remained a

Myron Avery, right, discusses an Appalachian Trail sign with a fellow Potomac Appalachian Trail Club member. In the 1920s and 1930s, a number of regional clubs stepped forward to build or maintain sections of the trail. Courtesy of the Appalachian Trail Conservancy.

struggle. "After the first trip, we got to using pruning shears. Each fellow had to buy his tool. The club hadn't any money to buy tools. . . . Anyways, we kept pushing the Trail, and we had to pick old wood roads and faint mountain paths. We couldn't pick the perfect route then because it was too tough."[28]

Early club records repeatedly stress the difficulty of accessing their isolated trail sections. The club organized car pools, rented buses and trucks, and hosted regular work weekends to get their members on the trail. Coming as they did from Washington and its suburbs, PATC members were also shocked by the Appalachian culture they encountered, which sometimes seemed otherworldly. In most cases, club members won over locals by offering to help at harvest time or by providing homesteading families with extra income in the form of rental fees for camping space. However, reports of trail workers stumbling upon illegal moonshine stills, encountering shotgun-toting drifters, and out-running intentionally set forest fires were common enough to make the work of clearing and maintaining the Appalachian Trail seem like a great adventure.[29]

Dozens of hiking organizations, including the Potomac Appalachian Trail Club and clubs in New York, New Jersey, and Pennsylvania, contributed countless hours to clearing, marking, and maintaining the Appalachian Trail. As early as 1925, the Appalachian Trail Conference coordinated their work, with the Palisades' Welch serving as president. During the 1930s and 1940s, annual ATC meetings became an opportunity to share best practices, network with other members, and set policies on signage, construction standards, and other issues that would maintain consistency along the 2,200-mile trail. When members of a Civilian Conservation Corps crew finished a short section in the Maine wilderness in August 1937, the trail was officially complete.[30]

Although the completion of the trail was an impressive feat, Appalachian Trail advocates knew that the next step would be providing for its permanent protection from encroachments and closings due to private land. For this work, the Appalachian Trail Conference would need to partner closely with the federal government. In 1938, the ATC signed the Appalachian Trailway Agreement with the National Park Service and the National Forest Service, which protected a one-mile corridor on either side of the trail on federal land. This was a watershed moment for hiking trail development in the United States and would serve as a precedent for even more ambitious legislation in the late 1960s. PATC president Myron Avery saw the agreement as "the beginning of a second era . . . a distinct epoch in Appalachian Trail history," during which the ATC would focus less on constructing the physical trail and more on stewardship of the surrounding corridor.[31]

As observers to the rapid development of eastern trails, hikers in the West sought to create a long-distance trail of their own. Through more than twenty years of work by the Sierra Club,

Mazamas, and others, several trails already traversed major western wilderness areas. For example, Washington's Cascade Crest Trail linked the Columbia River to the Canadian border. Constructed between 1909 and 1920, Oregon's Skyline Trail led from Mount Hood to Crater Lake. In California, the 181-mile Tahoe-Yosemite Trail linked Lake Tahoe to the Tuolumne Meadows. The grandest trail project of the period was the roughly 228-mile John Muir Trail, which connected Yosemite with Kings Canyon. Joseph Le Conte and a party scouted the route in twenty-eight days during 1908. In 1914, the Sierra Club entered into a partnership with the California state government and the U.S. Forest Service to fund construction of a portion of the scouted route. The state committed its engineer to plot the trail's route and ultimately paid more than fifty thousand dollars to construct the trail. Meanwhile, the Forest Service supervised construction. Although the partners had completed a majority of the trail by 1929, when the Depression ended California's financial support, it was not until 1938 that the Forest Service and the National Park Service partnered to complete two especially difficult passes.[32]

Throughout this lengthy construction process, the trail grew in fame. For example, adventure novelist Allen Chaffee celebrated the John Muir Trail in his 1922 work *Unexplored!* The engaging but corny tale features an old professor, a young U.S. Geological Survey man, and three boys in their late teens who go on a pack-burro trip along the trail that leads them through an unlikely series of adventures, including fighting wildfires, riding in airplanes, participating in a rodeo, and prospecting for gold. As a Sierra Club supporter, Chaffee knew the trail conditions well. Instead of promising readers a completed and predictable trail, as eastern trail builders often boasted, his novel emphasized the unknown journey that awaited packers or hikers on the John Muir Trail. "Why should they choose a route that was all cut and dried for them, as it were—where each day they would know when they started out just about where night would find them and what they would meet with on the way?" Chaffee's narrator asked. "Who wanted their views labeled anyway?"[33]

Despite these long-distance trails through magnificent landscapes, the West lacked a single trail that could connect the various projects as the Appalachian Trail had done for the East. During the 1930s, Clinton C. Clarke, a successful oilman and leader in the Boy Scout movement, promoted the idea of a border-to-border trail that would traverse the West's most scenic and rugged terrain, making use of the four major existing trails. Unlike MacKaye, who envisioned a symbiotic relation between the urban areas of the eastern seaboard and the AT, Clarke believed that the Pacific Crest Trail should provide access only to those Americans hearty enough to appreciate and endure true wilderness. "The Pacific Crest Trailway is not a recreational project for the casual camper or hiker," he wrote. "It is a serious educational program for building sturdy bodies, sound minds, and active, patriotic citizenship." In the first guide to the trail, Clarke implored, "Care should be taken that the TRAIL never be made popular for the average tourist type of recreation seeker, but that it be kept intact for the true wilderness lover and nature worshipper."[34]

In 1932, Clarke founded the Pacific Crest Trail System Conference—later to become the Pacific Crest Trail Association—as an organ for trail advocacy. The conference was modeled on the Appalachian Trail Conference and included representatives of the Sierra Club, Mazamas, Mountaineers, YMCA, and Boy Scouts, along with influential individuals. Clarke and the Conference members immediately established a working relationship with the National Park Service and National Forest Service. Between the two federal agencies, the federal government owned the land for all but 160 miles of the trail's 2,156-mile route. By the early 1940s, the agencies, with significant support from nearby Civilian Conservation Corps camps, had established a functional route between Canada and Mexico.[35]

Construction of the Pacific Crest Trail required a reorientation within the federal agencies. When Clarke initially approached the Forest Service about the trail during the early 1930s, the regional foresters balked at the construction and maintenance of such a long trail, let alone the adjacent corridor.

Since its creation, trails in the national forests served primarily pragmatic purposes, as the Green Mountain Club had found in Vermont. For example, the Forest Service's 1907 "use book," *The Use of the National Forests*, mentions trails only in the context of communication and fire control, listing them along with roads, bridges, and telephone lines. However, the Emergency Conservation Work Act of 1933, which created the CCC, provided the agency with an abundance of labor and the ability to work on trails that served primarily recreational purposes, including construction of PCT sections. Clarke had misgivings about the CCC's heavy-handed methods in constructing roads deep into the wilderness and creating trails that were obviously graded, but like many trail builders before and after, he had little choice but to accept the assistance and guide the work as best a civilian participant could. "Appreciation is due to the officials of the United States Forestry Service and the National Park Service," Clarke wrote in 1935, "for their enthusiastic cooperation and assistance in making this Trail possible." He singled out for praise "the hardy mountaineers—the Forest Rangers—who have done the actual work of locating, building and mapping the Trail."

Clarke's ties to the YMCA and Boy Scouts proved determinative in scouting the route of the Pacific Crest Trail and promoting the project to the general public. Between 1935 and 1937, Scout and YMCA crews traveled northward from the Mexico border along the entire length of trail in a series of relays. The crews carried fifty-five-pound packs and letters bound for Canada. Clarke believed the rigors of the trail would "develop a sounder physique, offer cross-country exploration that creates self-reliance and leadership; the romance and adventure of pioneering."[36]

Clarke hoped the expeditions would serve his purposes as well. During their excursions, the young men logged the condition of the trail, explored the surroundings, and evaluated alternative routes. Log books from their journey indicate how tenuous the route really was. "Again map incorrect," a 1938 log book noted: "Map said trail up creek but after one-hour search with no success we decided to try and break trail. We spent three

YMCA Relay Team, 1937. On their second day on the trail, Pacific
Crest Trail Relay Team 31 crosses a meadow near Mowich Lake in
central Oregon. Gordon Petrie leads the way, followed by Norman
Rupp, Bud Moran, and Lloyd Craft. The relay teams had the dual
purpose of scouting the route and proving that it could be hiked.
Courtesy of Barney Scout Mann.

grueling hours of fighting brush up the mountain only to be
turned back by sheer rock walls and an 80-foot waterfall. Finally
decided to fight our way back to White River which we reached
at 7 pm very tired and discouraged. By mutual agreement the
first thing we did was to pray—first we were thankful for a safe
return to our starting point—then we asked for guidance in the
3 days ahead."[37] Despite the blunt language, the relay teams' can-
did reports helped Clarke, the trails conference, and the government agencies keep tabs on the vast wilderness trail, while press
coverage of the relays in the *New York Times* and local papers
conveyed to the public that the PCT was truly a complete—if
primitive—trail.

During the first half of the twentieth century, the Long, Appalachian, and Pacific Crest Trails inspired hikers throughout the country. The common goal of completing a trail could unite hiking clubs from multiple states and regions, often with assistance from federal and state agencies. Long days of shared labor were required in scouting, clearing, building, and maintaining the trails, and a shared philosophy of trail construction ensured at least a minimal level of uniformity. The result was a close-knit community of men and women with a shared culture of hiking and trail building.

But even as long-distance trails brought the hiking community together, they also resulted in a new type of hiker who foreshadowed the dissolution of that community. The idea of through-hiking a long-distance trail—walking from end to end in a continuous journey—had its roots in the nineteenth-century pedestrianism movement, which emphasized endurance and speed in walking very long distances. But the idea of doing this on a wilderness path really began on the Long Trail in the 1920s. In 1926, with 278 miles of the trail in place, a milk salesman and member of the GMC and AMC named Irving Appleby claimed to have walked the entire trail in twelve days and five hours. The news was not unwelcome. Green Mountain Club founder James P. Taylor thought that the feat was a "good chance to get something for the Associated Press" and envisioned an ongoing competition "where hiker after hiker tries to better the record already made." The following year, Appleby completed a second hike, this time claiming to have broken his old record thanks to "his knowledge of the trail gained by last year's hike and also due to better equipment and more complete arrangements." This time the club's leadership balked, asking for substantiation of the claims. A perturbed Appleby repeated the hike, this time with a cameraman. Again the GMC refused to accept the record. Meanwhile, Appleby made the Boston papers, and his fame grew with the public as "store windows exhibited his trail clothes, sweat-stained shirt, battered pack and the worn boots."[38]

In 1927, a group of three women—two teachers and a college student—walked the Long Trail in twenty-seven days.

Known as the Three Musketeers, the women received a warm reception and validation from the Green Mountain Club. Appleby complained that the club accepted their achievement with no substantiation by a photographer or detailed itinerary. The controversy continued as other hikers claimed faster records and demanded recognition. "End-to-end" hiking had quickly turned from a potential boon to the trail to a divisive spectacle. In April 1928, the GMC passed a resolution saying that speed records undermined the intention of the trail, and—although the club would eventually begin issuing certificates for end-to-end hikes— it would no longer recognize other hiking feats.[39]

The New York–New Jersey Trail Conference also had to deal with speedy hikers. In May 1921, three hikers crossed the twenty-four-mile Ramapo-Dunderberg Trail in less than nine hours. Then, a member of the Fresh Air Club completed the trail in five and a half hours. "They run up the hills and stagger down. Their motto is 'hurry, hurry, hurry!'" conference member Dick Barton complained. "[There's] no chance for relaxation, no chance for long and inspiring views from the hilltops."[40]

Many hikers agreed with Barton. Through-hiking seemed to threaten the philosophical underpinnings of their sport. Americans viewed hiking as an opportunity to escape regimentation, slow down, enjoy the scenery, restore energy, test one's will, and even worship God. Traditionally, a journey along the trail was seen as an end in itself, without a need to complete the entire trail or earn recognition. In the case of through-hiking, there appeared to be other goals: speed, accomplishment, and fame. More troubling, club culture held that hiking was something done in the company of others, and the opportunity for socialization often trumped other motives for walking and climbing. Through-hikers typically walked alone or in small groups, circumventing the well-established clubs that had built the trails and organized outings. Their expeditions proved that it was possible to hike without a camp cook, heavy equipment, experienced guides, or other benefits of club outings. Traditionalists, such as those in the GMC leadership, recognized the threat and harshly criticized this new form of hiking. However, this criticism often

unfairly simplified the complex reasons people chose to complete through-hikes.

The motives behind the nation's most famous through-hike,
Earl Shaffer's 1947 traverse of the Appalachian Trail, were quite
modest. At the age of five, Shaffer and his family moved to the
small rural community of Shiloh, just outside of York, Pennsylvania. Now increasingly subdivided and built on, in 1923, Shiloh
was a rural landscape of farms, scattered forests, and the winding watersheds of the Codorus and Conewago Creeks. Shaffer
and his best friend, Walter Winemiller, made regular Sunday
jaunts through the countryside, sometimes hunting, trapping,
and fishing their way for miles. "We often walked as much as
twelve or fifteen miles on these afternoon hikes, poking into
every woodland or meadow," Shaffer later recalled. "We knew
almost every woodchuck hole, squirrel tree, or similar attraction
for miles around."[41]

Nonetheless, Shaffer was not a natural-born outdoorsman.
The first "mountain" he scaled was Roundtop, a pleasant but di-
minutive hill near Gifford Pinchot State Park in south central
Pennsylvania. "We climbed the steep and rocky western side,"
Shaffer remembered, "and Dan [his oldest brother] almost had
to drag me the last few hundred feet." Even after gaining more
experience in nature, Shaffer continued to consider himself a
novice relative to Winemiller, who "was the more natural woodsman. He seemed to know by instinct many things his partner
had to learn." In 1937, Shaffer and his brother Evan walked from
Caledonia State Park to Dillsburg, but—aside from that thirty-
mile trek—it seems that the soon-to-be long-distance hiker remained close to home.[42]

By the time Earl and Dan Shaffer and Walter Winemiller
were taking their regular walks, the nearby York Hiking Club
had been offering organized hikes for more than a decade. There
is no evidence, however, that either man participated in the club's
organized hikes during the 1930s. One of the city's most prominent families provided the organizational impetus for the York
club, and judging by the rate of automobile ownership and commitment of leisure time, many of the members were also social

elites. As the son of a welder, Shaffer, who had lost his mother in his mid-teens, was of a different socioeconomic class than the YHC's leadership. These were also Depression years, and Shaffer struggled to find steady employment, laboring on local farms and working as a carpenter when he could. Shaffer's and Winemiller's fishing and hunting probably supplemented meager family incomes, and in the 1930s, York County still provided opportunities to trap for the fur trade. It is also possible that Shaffer simply preferred the freedom of walking alone or with Winemiller and had little need for the regimentation of a club.[43]

As happy as Shaffer and Winemiller were hiking in their backyards, they often dreamed of more exotic locales. "Sometimes we would meet along the creek of a late evening and build a little fire, then sit by it and talk of woodcraft and outdoor travel. Alaska, Canada, South America, and other places were in our dreams and we said that someday we would see them all," Shaffer wrote, adding, "We never did mention the South sea islands, where we were destined to go." Both men would serve in World War II, and the experience would change the trajectory of Shaffer's life.[44]

Shaffer enlisted in the army in 1941 and, following the Japanese attack on Pearl Harbor, headed to the South Pacific, where he served in the Signal Corps. As a forward-area radar technician, Shaffer set up radar stations and built airstrips, under difficult and dangerous conditions. He left the service in 1945. Winemiller joined the marines and also ended up in the South Pacific. The pair had kept up a correspondence throughout the war, sharing mixed emotions of combat and plans for after the war. In the days preceding the assault on Iwo Jima, Winemiller wrote one of his customary letters to Shaffer and concluded with the foreboding comment, "If I'm still afloat after the noise, I'll tell you more." On February 15, 1945, Winemiller was one of 6,822 marines to die in the invasion.[45]

Returning home to York, Shaffer struggled to find employment, supplementing carpentry work with antique dealing and restoration. Worse, he suffered from depression and felt unable to restore meaning to his life in the wake of his friend's death and his own traumatic war experiences. The loss of his childhood friend and hiking partner had a profound impact on Shaffer. An entry from his diary at that time reads, "Miss your voice, the touch of your hand. My buddy, my buddy. Your buddy misses you." Then, in 1947, Shaffer read a short article about the Appalachian Trail and the fact that no one had walked it in a continuous journey. He resolved to become the first and, in the process, to "walk the army out of my system, both mentally and physically."[46]

MacKaye and other Appalachian Trail Conference leaders had never intended hikers to travel the entire trail. Contemporary articles in the *Appalachian Trailway News* questioned whether a through-hike was even possible, and discouraging proclamations from the Conference suggested, "Such expeditions are somewhat in the nature of stunts." In light of these misgivings, Shaffer was the ideal person to make the first trip. His modesty made him an appealing figure, while his naive confidence allowed the grueling trip to seem like a pleasant outing or, as he would call it, a "Long Cruise." On April 4, 1948, Shaffer began his journey alone and without fanfare. That June, the Appalachian Trail Conference was meeting in Fontana Village, North Carolina, when a letter arrived from Shaffer notifying them of his journey and saying he was already passing through eastern New York. On August 5, he was standing on top of Mount Katahdin. "The Long Cruise was finished," he wrote in the classic *Walking with Spring.* "Already it seemed like a vivid dream, through sunshine, shadow, and rain. Already I knew that many times I would want to be back again— on the cloud-high hills where the whole world lies below and far away."[47]

As news of Shaffer's journey spread, articles appeared in dozens of newspapers from the towns through which he passed. Unconvinced of his feat, long-time ATC secretary Jean Stephenson took the first opportunity to grill Shaffer. "The discussion was long," Shaffer remembered, "a charming but thorough cross examination." When Shaffer produced his day-by-day diary of the trip and the hundreds of color slides taken with his Retina camera, however, the conference had no choice but to endorse Shaffer as the first AT through-hiker.[48]

The effect was immediate. Maintenance of the Appalachian Trail had languished during World War II because of rationing of rubber tires and gasoline, but Shaffer's walk resulted in prominent articles in popular publications extolling the value of the trail. A lengthy article in the August 1949 *National Geographic* described the trail as "one of the seven wonders of the outdoorsman's world" and documented its different regions with dozens of photographs—many in color—depicting hikers scaling rocky cliffs, overlooking uninterrupted forests, and taking in the history and culture of the trail's many towns. The public relations boon resulted in a renewed interest in the trail that would continue to grow throughout the postwar period. Of course, other hikers also hoped to travel the entire trail. Following Shaffer's lead, in 1951, Georgia Tech student Gene Espy repeated the south-to-north through-hike following his graduation. The same year, Chester Dziengielewski and Martin Papendick completed the first north-to-south hike. In 1952, Papendick would become the first person to hike between British Columbia and Mexico along the general route of the PCT, but the first official through-hike is credited to Eric Ryback, an eighteen-year-old college student who completed the hike in 1970.[49]

Through-hiking, whether on the Long, Appalachian, or Pacific Crest Trails, remained uncommon before and immediately after World War II. In the postwar period, however, the idea of hiking alone for long distances and without assistance from fellow hikers would become an increasingly important part of American hiking culture. By the backpacking boom of the 1960s and 1970s, the model of the lone hiker would compete directly with organized hiking and threaten to undermine the dominance of the country's strongest and most active hiking clubs.

The prominence of the Long, Appalachian, and Pacific Crest Trails inspired but also obscured the many shorter, regional trails being developed throughout the country during the first half of the twentieth century, many of which never received the recognition or government assistance that the long-distance trails enjoyed. A typical example comes from southeastern Pennsylvania, where a group of volunteers formed the Horse Shoe

Earl Shaffer on the summit of Mount Katahdin, 1948. Shaffer became the first person to walk the trail in one continuous trip, sparking renewed interest in the trail in the post–World War II period. Earl Shaffer Collection, Archives Center, National Museum of American History, Smithsonian Institution.

Trail Club (HSTC) and constructed the 116-mile Horse Shoe
Trail at roughly the same time that other nearby clubs were fin-
ishing the Appalachian Trail.[50]

The Horse Shoe Trail Club, founded in Philadelphia in the
1930s, was unusual among Pennsylvania hiking clubs because
its members focused almost solely on trail maintenance and protection rather than social outings and pleasure walking. Henry
Woolman, a University of Pennsylvania graduate, provided the
visionary and organizational impetus for the club and its trail. In
the autumn of 1926, Woolman and soon-to-be HSTC secretary
W. Nelson West traveled to Gatlinburg, Tennessee, for two weeks
of horseback riding through the Smoky Mountains. "In the
smoky atmosphere of a clear October morning," remembered
Woolman some years later, "I spied a tiny [AT] marker on a large
balsam tree. . . . It made a lasting impression on me." He returned to Tennessee three times in the next four years to work on
"opening the foot trail to horseback travel."[51]

Woolman carried those experiences with him on his rides
through the maze of old logging and mining roads that covered
the low hills of southeastern Pennsylvania and stumbled on inspiration. "I rode farther afield and found other ridges with old woods
roads," Woolman wrote, "and gradually the idea germinated in my
mind that here at home we could have a little Smoky Mountain
Trail and although the depths of the valleys were in hundreds of
feet instead of thousands, the colors of the sunrises and sunsets
were just as gorgeous." So Woolman set about the task of recreating the Appalachian Trail on the outskirts of Philadelphia.[52]

In March 1934, a handful of hiking and equestrian clubs, as
well as representatives from the Pennsylvania Forestry and Parks
Associations, gathered at Penn's University Club "to discuss the
possibilities of opening a hiking trail and bridle path connecting
Fairmount Park with the Appalachian Trail on the Blue
Mountains near Harrisburg." In part, the group felt they were
responding to changes in how Philadelphians spent their increasing leisure time and recognized "the growing desire to pass
those hours in the open air amid natural surroundings." Like
many trail projects of the time, Woolman and those assembled

catered to horseback riders as well as hikers. Horse Shoe, the suggested name for the club, reflected hope for a harmonious coexistence between those who traveled on shoes and those who rode on horses.[53]

At the close of the first organizational meeting, the participants appointed Woolman as chairman, who in turn quickly recruited others to join in the surveying work he had already started on his horseback rides. Crews, under the direction of the chairman, spent the spring and summer of 1934 temporarily marking the entire trail. Woolman obtained topographical maps for the region and sketched out a "tentative route" in red pencil. "Then I took my automobile," wrote Woolman, describing his early solo efforts, "and skirted the route checking where old trails left the highway, then circling around to the next valley to see where they came out." Like many other trail builders, Woolman used existing paths wherever possible. According to a 1938 guide produced by the Federal Writers' Project, portions of the trail followed "old logging roads, charcoal roads, cowpaths, and paths used by Indians and early settlers." Woolman also made extensive use of an unnamed path that once linked the numerous forges, furnaces, and mines of Robert Coleman's Cornwall Iron Furnace. When surveys had determined the general path, crews, partially composed of National Youth Administration workers, went to work clearing and marking the trail, borrowing methods of directional and side trail marking from the Appalachian Trail system. Originally, the path was marked with horseshoes, but the trail workers were forced to implement a system of dots after "it was reported that the men from a broken-down truck were pitching quoits with yellow horseshoes." By December, a large and diverse coalition of outdoor groups had contributed time to the project, and the final section of trail at Manada Gap, Dauphin County, was complete.[54]

A testament to the enthusiasm of Woolman and his volunteers, the majority of trail work was accomplished before the club was formalized. Not until July 1935 did a small group of leaders convene at Woolman's Cressbrook Farm in Valley Forge to found the Horse Shoe Trail Club. According to the articles of incorporation, the club was formed "to open, develop,

extend and maintain trails for horseback riders, hikers, mountain climbers and nature students in the wooded and mountain
regions accessible from Philadelphia and Harrisburg." Almost a
year later, the club held its first general meeting and reported
a membership of 115. In addition to that number, members of
the Batona Club, the Nature Ramblers, and the Philadelphia
Trail Club maintained sections of the Horse Shoe Trail,
establishing the trail and the club in the Philadelphia hiking
community and giving others a vested interest in the continuation of both.[55]

But no amount of enthusiasm or volunteerism could protect
the HSTC from the whims of landowners over whose land the
trail passed. Unlike his counterparts at the Green Mountain
Club, Appalachian Trail Conference, New York–New Jersey Trail
Conference, and other larger trail organizations, Woolman did
not enjoy influence with the federal or state legislature or its
various agencies that might be able to put money toward protection of the Horse Shoe Trail. What is more significant, very little
of the trail crossed over public lands, so its protection required
acceptance of an agenda of substantive and costly acquisition
efforts that—incidentally—would infringe on the private property rights of landowners along the 116 miles of trail. Although
Woolman was able to report in 1937 that "everyone along the
line has been most helpful, and we are always welcomed as we
ride by," permission to cross private property was typically secured through verbal agreement, subject to change at any time,
especially when property changed hands. At a 1936 meeting, the
club extended honorary membership to all landowners over
whose land the trail crossed, but even property owners well-
disposed toward the trail could be deterred by fears of misuse,
vandalism, or lawsuits. Members could chuckle over rumors that
"a certain number of well-known persons had fallen off their
horses recently," but landowners justly feared trail users sustaining injuries while crossing their land. Furthermore, although
suburbanization would only begin in earnest after World War II,
subdivisions in land were already occurring, complicating the
work of securing permission and making it difficult to cultivate

the high-quality face-to-face relationships necessary to maintain public trails on private lands.[56]

In addition to fickle landowners, developments on the Appalachian Trail forced Woolman to recognize the need for strong government protection. Since 1931, portions of the trail in Virginia- -originally constructed by the Potomac Appalachian Trail Conference from 1927 to 1931—had been displaced by construction of the Skyline Drive and Blue Ridge Parkway in Shenandoah National Park. The road building and subsequent trail relocation were intended to provide emergency relief employment for the thousands of Civilian Conservation Corps members who lived at the ten camps located throughout the park. As Clarke had complained of the CCC on the Pacific Crest Trail, decisions regarding the nature of construction came rapidly, without any input from the PATC and other organizations with an interest in that section of trail. Woolman considered the Virginia construction "a precedent for having the Horse-Shoe Trail taken over." Although Virginia's aggressive use of eminent domain to secure park territory was interpreted by some trail builders as a positive precedent for future trailway acquisition, Woolman was concerned with the character of the relocated, CCC-constructed Appalachian Trail.[57]

Unlike traditional footpaths, which followed natural grades and—aside from brush clearing and antierosion techniques— appeared primitive, the CCC section was a carefully graded tread, created by building up the surface of the trail with a rock frame and filling it with gravel and dirt. Writing in the 1936 issue of *Appalachia*, the PATC vice-president and guidebook editor defended the CCC trail work against criticism. "This construction has been criticized as too 'artificial' in character, a criticism which raises the question of the requisites of a trail. Perhaps we are getting old, but we do not consider it essential to a true trail to have to step from rock to rock, over every fallen log, or to scramble down a talus slope, watching the ground all the while to avoid falls, or a sprained ankle or broken leg." After all, the men reminded readers, "graded trail, even in the East, is not a new undertaking." Appalachian Mountain Club members would

Graded CCC Trail, c. 1936. A portion of Shenandoah National Park's relocated Appalachian Trail, during and after construction, shows the smooth surface but unnatural appearance of graded path favored by the Civilian Conservation Corps. Courtesy of the National Park Service.

have been aware of the late nineteenth-century work of J. Rayner Edmands, a past club president who constructed a network of graded trails on Mount Washington and throughout the Presidential Range. They may have also sympathized with the hiker who complained that walkers on Edmands's trails "streamed up the mountain like a transplanted tea party," and applauded AMC councilor of improvements Parker Field's 1900 statement that "in no case has the Club undertaken to make the smooth graded paths or so-called 'boulevards.' Such work is left to others who have more time and means at their disposal than the Club can afford." In 1936, the PATC leaders supported the corps' relocation of the Appalachian Trail because they had little choice. Woolman, who had devoted time to developing primitive trails in the Smoky Mountains and had seen the changes firsthand, continued to worry about developments in Shenandoah.[58]

Woolman also monitored Appalachian Trail developments in south central Pennsylvania, where the PATC was working with the state to blaze a permanent through trail. This section of the Appalachian Trail crossed the Pennsylvania-Maryland border and passed through Michaux and Mont Alto State Forests and several state parks on its seventy-eight-mile path to the Susquehanna River, just north of Harrisburg. "Well-maintained trails traverse the valleys and ridges of both forests so extensively," PATC president Myron Avery then noted, "that the development of the through trail required little new construction." Still, the supervising state foresters consciously avoided graded trails. "The trail is to be cut open 9' wide," District Forester W. L. Byers reported to Avery, "all under brush to be removed and then a 3' strip of bare soil is to be constructed in which stones and stumps are to be removed." In contrast to Virginia's relocated trail, workers would clear a path or expand existing paths but do little more. "The marking party on this section was very enthusiastic about the location of the trail and the work done on the footway," wrote Avery after walking a stretch of completed trail. "There was just enough to make for a very easy walking without its being over-developed."[59]

More impressive to Woolman than the primitive character of the trail was that the men building it were employed through

New Deal relief work programs. From June 1933 to January 1937, an Emergency Conservation Work (ECW) camp operated out of the Caledonia section of Michaux State Forest, and Superintendent Oscar Book put his men to work on the Appalachian Trail. In return, Potomac Appalachian Trail Council members marked proposed routes, provided regular maintenance, and created maps and promotional materials for new trail sections. "We have a feeling that this relationship has not resulted merely to the benefit of the Trail Club," Avery wrote to Michaux's district forester, "but that our programs have made some contribution to the recreational activities of the forest." This working arrangement allayed Woolman's fears of losing autonomy, and in the fall of 1935, he wrote to Avery inquiring about the process of securing CCC, ECW, or Works Progress Administration labor for the Horse Shoe Trail. Aside from the few National Youth Administration participants who helped mark and clear the trail in 1934, however, Woolman failed to solicit New Deal aid.[60]

If contributions of federal labor would not be forthcoming, perhaps the government would incorporate the trail into its growing park system and thus ease the club's administrative burden. At an April 1938 meeting, Woolman expressed his hope that "some day the whole Trail, with a suitable amount of ground on either side, could be taken over as a State or National Park, in order to ensure permanency." As a first step, he suggested communicating the club's desire for takeover to the Eighteenth National Conference on State Parks. By 1942, the National Parks Association, the Pennsylvania Forestry Association, and various outdoors groups had passed resolutions recommending protected trailway status for the Horse Shoe Trail. One typical resolution praised the work of the HSTC in surveying and improving a trail "116 miles in length, with no fences or gates, no hot-dog stands or gasoline stations, and not more than two miles of hard surfaced roads." The resolution went on to argue that the Horse Shoe Trail should receive the same protections as the Appalachian Trail and requested that the secretary of forest and waters allocate one hundred thousand dollars for the project. The request went unfulfilled.[61]

Generating interest in the trail was a never-ceasing activity of the Horse Shoe Trail Club, more so than for hiking clubs maintaining portions of the Appalachian Trail, for which publicity came easily. It also cost HSTC a good deal of money. In March 1937, the club treasurer reported, "Our largest expenditures during the year have been in connection with publicity work, which," he quickly added, "has been more than justified by the increased amount of interest being shown in the trail by many individuals and groups of individuals." Most of the money was spent constructing exhibits for outdoor expos, such as the 1937 Philadelphia Sportsmen's Show, and publishing literature describing the club's efforts. But promotion did not stop there. At one point in 1938, Woolman, also the owner of a large farm, convinced the Dairy Council to promote the club in school lectures in and around Philadelphia. Further, in 1940, the HSTC directors formed a committee to "encourage the use of the Trail by the Boy Scouts, the Girl Scouts, YMCA and YWCA, and other organizations," just as Clarke was doing on the PCT at the very same time. Meanwhile, the club continued to divvy out maintenance work to regional hiking and equestrian clubs. These actions, taken together, represent a rather shrewd strategy of endearing the Horse Shoe Trail to the southeastern Pennsylvania outdoor recreation community and forging a diverse coalition with a stake in the protection of the trail. Throughout the 1930s and 1940s, support for the trail was certainly growing, but government protection would require millions of dollars in property buyouts, eminent domain lawsuits, and administrative fees. Such a program would require not only widespread public support but also influence with the state legislature in Harrisburg.[62]

Every few years, prospects for protection seemed promising, and HSTC mobilized with renewed enthusiasm. In 1945, the Directors encouraged members to contact State Attorney General James Duff, an influential cabinet member, "who has shown some interest in the matter." At the same time, HR-2142, a potential source of money for the trailway, was up for debate but eventually fizzled. By 1946, the new strategy was "to have articles appear about the Trail and what we are trying to do in

Philadelphia Magazine and other publications." In an effort to conduct a rudimentary economic impact study, some members were recruited to collect information about overnighters and out-of-state visitors to the trail. The HSTC went so far as to hire a "Publicity Director" and pay him a retainer of two hundred dollars to run the campaign to gain protection.[63]

When James Duff became governor in 1947, Woolman was pleased to report that the longtime ally was "becoming increasingly interested." This temporary optimism was stifled in 1949 when Milo Draemel, secretary of forests and waters, reported that "his Department has no time to work on the proposition at the moment as they are all tied up with land acquisition in connection with clean-up of the Schuylkill River." For a century, the Schuylkill River had served as a conduit for coal shipments coming down from the mountains and into Philadelphia, severely polluting the river with an estimated 38 million tons of culm. Beginning in 1945, the Commonwealth of Pennsylvania and the federal government initiated an environmental remediation effort, known as the Schuylkill River Desilting Project. Engineers, using dams and land acquired from the Schuylkill Navigation Company in the 1930s, hydraulically dredged river water and sediment into a series of large holding basins, where the water slowly seeped back into the river, leaving coal solids behind. The coal was then reclaimed for a variety of uses, and the basins were conserved as green space. Considered one of the first major environmental river cleanups undertaken by a government agency, the project was innovative and successful. Yet, for members of the Horse Shoe Trail Club, eager to implement their own version of green space conservation, it was another obstacle to the campaign for state funding.[64]

Hopes for government protection were certainly dampened, and, when Woolman passed away in December 1953, the campaign lost its most aggressive proponent. While longer and more prominent trail projects received increased government protection and technical assistance in the postwar period, the HSTC continued to operate with volunteer labor and handshake agreements with landowners. As a result, the trail suffered from sporadic closings and relocations, and quality of its maintenance

Hikers on the Horse Shoe Trail, 1938. Pennsylvania's Horse Shoe Trail is one of many successful trail projects overshadowed by the longer and better-known Appalachian Trail. Maintained by volunteers, without significant public funding, the trail represents a grassroots model of trail building practiced by clubs throughout the nation. Courtesy of the Horse Shoe Trail Conservancy.

could vary greatly. The HSTC, however, remained an enthusiastic and highly-skilled group of trail builders and organizers without whom the trail would have simply reverted back to nature.

The experience of the HSTC and the Horse Shoe Trail was common in the early twentieth century. Despite the fame of the Long, Appalachian, and Pacific Crest Trails, most trail projects were intended to serve the recreational needs of nearby residents and could be regional trails of twenty-five or fifty miles or local trails as short as one mile. These hundreds of trails escaped the national recognition received by their longer counterparts, even as local hiking clubs devoted countless hours to their construction and maintenance. As the clubs worked, they mimicked the trail construction standards and methods professed by the AMC, PATC, the Forest Service, and other authorities. But they also made their own innovations and developed regional styles of trail construction that best suited the landscape through which they passed.[65]

The capacity of hiking clubs to organize activities, including trail building, varied widely between regions of the country. There was no significant trail development in large portions of the South and Southwest because there were very few hiking clubs to lead the effort. Even in the Midwest, which had large clubs in Chicago, Madison, Milwaukee, and Cleveland, trail building was slow to begin. For example, the influential, Chicago-based Prairie Club had a limited, although interesting, engagement with trail building. In 1926, the club formed an "Indian Trails Committee" to investigate the existence of Indian Trails around the city. Committee members did research at the Chicago Historical Society, where they made tracings from old maps and tried to identify remaining traces of the trails in the field. "We came across a number of trees that had been bent in the early days by the Indians," one member remembered, "but it was not possible to follow any definite trail and only fragments of them could be found in the Forest Preserve, the main ones were long ago made into our radiating highways and of no interest to the Prairie club hikers."[66]

Subsequently, the committee was renamed the "Trails Committee," and the focus shifted from historic trails to "that of marking a continuous trail through the [City of Chicago's Forest] Preserves." The plan for a continuous trail was altered by the chief forester of the preserve, who requested that they instead focus on "marking half day and all day walks and small circular walks." "The first trail marked led from the club house at Palos to the Swallow cliff where hundreds of swallows make their home, and in a very short time became a beaten path," a committee member wrote. Following their first successful trail, the club organized "several scouting trips . . . the making of signs, carrying of paint, mixing colors, painting on bark, all of which meant time and work; but with the help of a splendid committee, it was not irksome." In all, the club blazed twenty-five miles of trails in the preserves, which—if not on the scale of eastern trail building—still provided the region's hikers with new ways to access the forests.[67]

In the absence of a grand vision for a long trail and a regional organizing entity to coordinate trail development, most Midwestern clubs simply pursued their own local interests, mostly revolving around the social aspects of hiking rather than trail construction. In states along the East Coast, the development and maintenance of the Appalachian Trail helped otherwise-independent hiking organizations feel like they were part of a regional or national movement. Meetings of the Appalachian Trail Conference, the New York—New Jersey Trail Conference, and chapters of the Green Mountain Club helped hikers and trail builders network with like-minded people and develop a culture of trail and hiking expertise. While Midwestern hiking clubs certainly benefited from developments in the East, the lack of a long-distance hiking trail or regional trail networks undoubtedly stifled growth of the trails community. It also prevented clubs from entering into the type of technical land stewardship projects that would come to define eastern clubs' trailway protection efforts and allow them to play an increasingly influential role in regional conservation initiatives during the postwar period. Although the Cleveland Hiking Club helped enhance existing trails in the city's Metroparks, the Milwaukee GO Club built some short footpaths in Wisconsin's Kettle Moraine State Park, and the Chicago Prairie Club mapped Indian trails and blazed a small trail network, the professionalization and institutionalization of trail building would not come to the Midwest until the 1970s and 1980s, when the Ice Age Scenic Trail and the North Country Scenic Trail became important projects to the regional and national trails community.

In the early twentieth century, many hiking clubs turned their attention to marking or clearing trails for the use of the public, and most members gained direct experience with the blood, sweat, and bug bites required to create new places to hike. In most regions, if hikers wished to travel away from city streets, country lanes, and lumber roads, they literally had to create the trails as they went. By the 1960s and 1970s, however, the growing popularity of hiking and the expanding network of trails throughout the nation meant that most hikers would rarely spend time building or maintaining the paths on which they traveled. Like the early through-hikers, they thrived on being alone and self-sufficient in the woods and covering as much distance as possible. They would take for granted that trails existed for their pleasure and that someone—presumably someone receiving a government paycheck or with more time, more energy, and less responsibility—would maintain it on their behalf. Of course, most Americans continued to view trail builders as "public benefactors," just as the group of Harriman State Park hikers did on that Sunday in 1921, but their growing detachment from the act of trail building would only contribute to the decline in American hiking club culture in the coming decades.

5 HIKING ALONE

"THE woods are overrun," Colin Fletcher, the famous walker, once quipped, "and sons of bitches like me are half the problem." Between the end of World War II and the late 1960s, the size of the American hiking community grew exponentially, as millions of people went to the nation's trails for the first time. In a crucial departure from previous trends, most of these new hikers eschewed membership in a club and instead hiked alone or in small, informal groups. The result was that by 1968 the authority of traditional hiking clubs was on the decline and more than a century of American hiking culture had begun to dissolve. The typical American hiker evolved from a net producer—of information, maps, well-maintained trails, advocacy, outings, and club culture—to a net consumer—of equipment, national magazines, and federally subsidized trails. Fletcher jokingly blamed himself—and the millions of new backpackers and hikers who, like him, hit the trails in the 1960s—but a number of factors contributed to the decline of traditional hiking club culture.[1]

Fletcher, to be sure, played a role. His 1968 *Complete Walker* was a massive tome that laid out in exhaustive detail the how-tos of hiking and backpacking without the aid of others. The book became an immediate hit: a bible for backpackers looking for self-sufficiency on the trail. By the time *The Complete Walker* was published, however, Fletcher was already a well-known name.

His 1964 *Thousand Mile Summer* had chronicled an epic walk along the eastern border of California that took him through the High Sierra and Death Valley and along the Colorado River. In 1965, Fletcher appeared on NBC's *Today Show* to discuss his walk and the book, and his publisher placed advertisements in the *New York Times* and other major news outlets.[2]

By 1963, Fletcher had become the first person to walk the entire length of the Grand Canyon below the rim—a journey he chronicled in *The Man Who Walked through Time* (1967). Inspiration for the walk came during a trip with a friend to the canyon's edge. "All afternoon I sat on the Rim and looked down into the burning and apparently waterless waste of rock," Fletcher remembered. "It was mysterious and terrible—and beckoning. And some time during the afternoon, as I sat on the brink of this strange new world, it came to me that if a route existed I would walk from one end of the Canyon to the other. Once the idea had crystallized, no hideously sensible doubts reared up to plague me. And I did not need such fragile props as 'reasons.'"[3]

It took a year for Fletcher to plan the journey, during which he resisted learning about the canyon for fear of replacing his wild dream with facts. "Then," he wrote, "late one mid-April day, the dream faded quietly away and the reality was born," as he took the first few steps of the walk. The journey itself was dangerous and difficult. In turns, Fletcher squeezed through side canyons, scrambled across narrow and crumbling rock ledges high above the canyon floor, and picked his way through boulders and along sandbars at the turbulent river's edge. While his through-hike was the first of its kind, most of the sections Fletcher walked had been scouted previously by Harvey Butchart, an Arizona State University mathematics professor who had section-hiked almost every mile of the canyon. Although Butchart did not produce a guide or map, Fletcher's confidence benefited immeasurably from the idea that a physical route existed. "I knew, or half-knew, that one man had already crossed that forbidding amphitheater," Fletcher noted, as he surveyed a scrub-covered talus slope perched above a fifteen-hundred-foot sheer drop. "Instead of hanging back on my mental heels and wondering if the thing were really possible I just checked the route through binoculars and then moved out onto the terrace."[4]

Butchart's presence was a matter of conscience; in reality, Fletcher was alone in the canyon wilderness and believed that the solitude led to daily enlightenment. A brief stop at Phantom Ranch—the sole hotel operating below the rim—only reminded Fletcher that telephones, mail, and other connections to the outside world disrupted the more natural rhythms he could develop on the trail. Despite his many sour words for modern life, however, *The Man Who Walked through Time* was not a call to live permanently in the wild. Immersed as he was in the hiking culture of the early and mid-twentieth century, Fletcher echoed the decades of previous hikers who believed that brief periods spent in wilderness restored one's soul to better conquer the rigors of daily life. "You cannot escape the age you live in," he reflected at the end of his journey. "You have to stand back from time to time and get your perspective right." He believed that the hike "had made me fitter for the outside world. Had made me a fitter contributor."[5]

Publication of *The Man Who Walked through Time* enhanced Fletcher's national prominence through reviews, advertisements, and television appearances. A detailed *New York Times* review called it a "passionate book" and *Publisher's Weekly*, a "rare adventure." Another critic was less charitable. He liked the narrative of the journey but not Fletcher's many philosophical tangents that revolved around the metaphor of penetrating time by entering the canyon and communing with nature. "This malarkey, which is not original and of which there is far too much, mars an otherwise estimable book."[6]

The Man Who Walked through Time stood on its own as an adventure narrative, but it was even more compelling in light of the broader environmental issues with which it engaged. In 1963, as Fletcher traveled down the Colorado, plans were already in the works for taming the river. He passed a potential construction site and noted testing gauges related to the proposed Pacific Southwest Water Plan, which would have added two dams and a diversion tunnel to the river. Fletcher believed that the dams, slack water pools, access roads, rubble, effluent, diesel trucks, humming generators, and other signs of development would undermine the captivating solitude of the canyon. "If the dams and the tunnel were built, in fact, the Canyon would not, from the rim, look so very different," he admitted. "But the heart of the place would be gone. The living river—the superb mechanism that has created the Canyon—would vanish." A Sierra Club book, *Time and the River Flowing*, published at the same time Fletcher was making his journey, used almost identical language. "The dams the bureau plans to build . . . would destroy not only the living river but also the unique life forms that through the ages have come to depend upon the river's life," the club's executive director, David Brower, wrote. "The major part of the canyon walls would still be there, but the pulsing heart of the place would be stopped." Ultimately, the project floundered on dubious engineering and economic plans as well as widespread opposition led by the Sierra Club and others, who argued that the project violated the sanctity of the national park that supposedly protected the canyon.[7]

Fletcher's personal hiking feats and role in promoting backpacking highlight the two central ironies that defined the evolution of the hiking community between World War II and 1968. The first irony is that beginning in the late 1940s, surplus military equipment, better technology, improved access, and new ideas about nature led to a proliferation in the number of Americans hitting the trail. Yet many of them eschewed club membership in favor of hiking alone, as Fletcher did, or with small, informal groups. Although many Americans view the late 1960s as the formative period for hiking, backpacking, and camping, it was actually the end of an extremely vibrant period for a national hiking culture rooted in clubs.

The second irony is that many of the new hikers were motivated by the environmental movement to protect and experience natural places but, in their enthusiasm, ended up degrading them in the process. Overuse of the nation's trails and other hiking terrain led to a new ethic of low-impact hiking and backpacking that ultimately reinforced the autonomy of the individual hiker and ensured federal and state activism in trail development and maintenance.[8]

The National Trails System Act of 1968 was a watershed moment for the hiking and trails movement but also a contributing factor in the decline of the traditional hiking community. As Americans came to expect government to provide accessible trails as a taxpayer-financed service, the volunteer ethic that had defined the hiking community for more than one hundred years was lost. New hikers believed that they were entitled to clean, well-maintained trails. Why, they wondered, should they be asked to do more?

World War II played a determinative role in expanding the American hiking community. Many returning veterans agreed with Appalachian Trail through-hiker Earl Shaffer, who found the nation's trails and wilderness areas to be welcoming, restorative places to "walk the army out" of his system. The war's impact reached much further, however, in that surplus equipment, new technologies, and expanded infrastructure also led to a rapid proliferation of hikers between 1945 and the late 1960s.[9]

During the war itself, rationing of rubber tires and gasoline restricted outings, and some clubs floundered for lack of leadership and members. The Allentown Hiking Club, for example, disbanded for the duration. Other clubs kept up a healthy schedule of walks and trail maintenance trips. Potomac Appalachian Trail Club members chartered buses and carpooled across the state to visit their section of the Appalachian Trail, and the club actually added members during the war. In some cases, hikers made direct contributions to the war effort. In 1942, the Sierra Club's Winter Sports Committee, headed by David Brower, assembled material for the *Manual of Ski Mountaineering*. The manual was one of the first how-to guides for backcountry skiing and, in the absence of official military training guides, was quickly adopted by the United States military to train soldiers for combat in Italy's rugged alpine terrain. Brower himself served in the Tenth Mountain Division, the military's first unit specializing in mountain and arctic warfare. He led groups of soldiers into the Rocky Mountains for training expeditions and to test the resilience of gear in the backcountry. American hikers found that by equating the health of individuals with national strength and aligning their activities with military needs, they could justify outings even during times of sacrifice.[10]

Time spent in the military exposed millions of Americans to life in the outdoors and encouraged them to hike and camp after returning to civilian life. Whether in domestic camps or on the war front, the argument goes, soldiers regularly walked long distances over varying terrain and in all weather conditions. Marches of up to fifteen miles each day while carrying a heavy pack were not uncommon. Soldiers learned the logistics of camp life, from pitching tents to cooking over fires or stoves to navigating by map and compass. They learned how to be comfortable in the outdoors, whether that meant protecting against blisters, warding off mosquitoes, or staying dry in a downpour. On returning to civilian life, veterans likely responded in different ways to these experiences. Compared to forced marches and combat conditions, the requirements of a pleasant Sunday walk or weekend camping outing seemed trivial. Armed with well-honed hiking and camping skills and conditioned to overcome discomfort, millions of veterans and their families could potentially join the outdoor recreation community.[11]

However appealing this argument may be, there is no way of knowing whether military experience really led to civilian hiking or camping. A veteran with horrific memories of the war could be forgiven for avoiding long-distance walking or camping in the future and question why such pastimes were appealing. Historians Laura and Guy Waterman support this reasoning, arguing that returning veterans eschewed dangerous or uncomfortable pastimes. "They came back from war to go to work, not to escape to the backcountry. These people had already 'gotten away from it all'—and were anxious to get back to it all."[12] In any case, millions of Americans did learn essential outdoor skills from their military experiences, whether they put them to recreational use or not.

More convincing is the argument that military technology and surplus helped to grow the hiking, camping, and backpacking community. Nylon and polyester were the most influential of these innovations. Both fabrics had their origins in scientific research at DuPont in the late 1930s and were being manufactured by the early 1940s. Nylon was a promising substitute for Asian silk, the supply of which had been cut off during the war. Silk was important for the domestic clothing industry, especially in the production of women's hosiery, but was also the primary material used for parachutes. Nylon would allow the U.S. military to continue to produce parachutes using a domestically produced fiber with theoretically infinite supply. Polyester had a wide range of applications from textile fiber to the bodies of planes and hulls of boats.[13]

Following the war, nylon and polyester became common elements in a variety of products, many of which proved useful in the outdoors. Nylon's lightweight and water-resistant characteristics made it the ideal material for tents. Traditionally, tents were made of heavy canvas that made them difficult to pack and carry for long distances. In combat, nylon provided "lightweight and compact tents suitable for use by airborne troops." After the war, the same characteristics were useful for hikers making overnight trips in the woods, and domestic outfitters recognized the promise of nylon tents, sleeping bags, and other products. Advertisements sold nylon products alongside traditional canvas and wool products, touting their "lightweight" and "waterproof" qualities in order to justify charging up to 30 percent more than in the past.[14]

Freeze-dried food was another influential technology that emerged from the war. The military needed to supply large quantities of serum to Europe to care for wounded soldiers, but inconsistent refrigeration led to the loss of many shipments. Freeze-drying—the method of quickly freezing a substance and placing it in a vacuum to sublimate the ice—preserved the serum without need for refrigeration. The process quickly extended to other perishable items, including food. Dehydration had been a traditional means of storing perishable food for long periods and reducing weight, but freeze-drying and vacuum packaging resulted in food with a shelf life of many years that maintained its nutritional value and could quickly and easily be reconstituted with water. In the postwar period, these characteristics made freeze-dried food useful to the U.S. space program, Americans preparing for civilian defense, and—of course—hikers.[15]

The food lists contained in early guides and the accounts of Appalachian Mountain Club and Sierra Club outings were daunting for their weight and required heavy cooking equipment for their preparation. One extreme example comes from the Sierra Club's 1922 High Trip. The three-week journey included 287 hikers who consumed more than thirty thousand pounds of food, including twenty-three thousand pounds of fresh and dried fruit, two thousand pounds of ham, four hundred pounds of chocolate, and at each breakfast fifty pounds of bacon. "The outdoorsman today is more fortunate," a guide from the early 1960s noted in reflection. "He may choose from a wide variety of deliciously seasoned, concentrated, moisture-proof, non-perishable foods that need no refrigeration and will keep for years. . . . A few ounces of carried weight yields pounds of prepared food whenever you want it." The U.S. Forest Service promoted freeze-dried foods in its guide to the use of the National Forests, writing, "Dehydrated food has progressed a long way in the last few years, both in taste and variety," and listing some of the more lavish offerings, including "shrimp supreme" and "turkey tetrazinni."[16]

Another reason for the growth in hiking following the war was the large shipments of military surplus that re-entered the domestic market on demobilization. The words "army used reconditioned" and "repaired reconditioned" appeared in many ads, indicating that the equipment came from the more than one hundred billion dollars in surplus war materials. These items, which included traditional materials as well as nylon, were marked at half the cost of brand-new equipment. Military equipment, especially clothing and packs, had always been important to American hikers. As early as the 1870s, John Meade Gould recounted the regular use of decommissioned Civil War equipment during White Mountain Club outings, including a leather haversack worn "as our solders did in war times." Gould's 1877 *How to Camp Out* recommended a number of army items, such as duck wall-tents, sheet-iron cooking stoves, cast-iron

Dutch ovens, and mattresses made of rubber cloth. Horace Kephart's 1906 classic *Camping and Woodcraft* expanded on Gould's list by recommending decommissioned or surplus leggings, shoes, neckerchiefs, shirts, trousers, bedrolls, blankets, dispatch cases, tents, stoves, gloves, cots, whistles, and entrenching tools. Kephart's contemporaries Elmer Kreps and Edward Breck also recommended military items in their popular guides. In 1913, thirty-four Appalachian Mountain Club members attended a "very interesting and valuable" presentation on the topic of "Army Shoes" and their applicability to hiking. A popular hiking guide from 1919 included several military items in its recommended hiking kit, including gabardine puttees, 1918 army campaign boots, and a military pack-bag. Hikers used World War I surplus for the next two decades. The end of World War II created another unprecedented scale of decommissioned surplus, and as in the past, hikers quickly adopted the clothing and equipment for civilian use.[17]

The influx of surplus equipment coincided with the growth of new outfitters. National chains, such as L. L. Bean and Abercrombie and Fitch, continued to dominate the market for serious outing equipment and grew rapidly during the immediate postwar period. L. L. Bean, for example, had steadily increased mail-order sales since its founding in 1912. However, business spiked in 1946 after the *Saturday Evening Post* ran an article and color photos describing "The Discovery of L. L. Bean." The article noted that Bean's appeal was in the reliability of its eclectic product line. "No doubt a chief reason for the success of the business," reflected Bean, "is the fact that I tried on the trail, practically every article I handle. If I tell you a knife is good for cleaning trout, it is because I found it so. If I tell you a wading boot is worth having, very likely you have seen me out testing it out in Merrymeeting Bay." The article resulted in fifteen thousand new inquiries about products and a 46 percent increase in sales. Despite the emphasis on field-tested, firsthand knowledge by Bean, by the early 1950s, his catalogs also included surplus military equipment alongside traditional items, many of which Bean never tested.[18]

There were many other sources for equipment. Abercrombie and Fitch had been formed as an upscale New York City sportsmen's outfitter in the early 1890s and by 1909 had a catalog circulation of more than fifty thousand. In 1929, the company had $6.3 million in sales and branch stores in Chicago and other major cities. Although the company's product line was broad—the 1909 catalog even included hot-air ballooning equipment—it was best known for its hunting and fishing equipment and clothing. In contrast, Recreational Equipment Co-Op (REI) began business in 1938 on a thirty-dollar loan and specialized in climbing and hiking equipment that national chains did not carry. Eventually, REI moved into space beside the Mountaineers' office in downtown Seattle and began a mail-order catalog in 1948. Business increased rapidly from that point on, and by 1970, the REI co-op had two hundred thousand members purchasing and renting equipment. One of the products REI sold was Kelty backpacks, the first nylon and external aluminum-frame backpacks to replace the wooden, U-shaped packs issued by the military. The design, which included a padded waist belt, shifted pack weight from the shoulders to the hips and made it more comfortable to carry larger loads on longer hikes. Dick Kelty began producing the backpacks at his living room table in 1951 and quickly expanded the business through mail order and wholesale. The successes of these companies—not to mention Eastern Mountain Sports (1967) and Patagonia (1973)—were repeated many times over, as entrepreneurs found ways to reach the new—but rapidly growing—niche market of hikers and backpackers.[19]

The proliferation of equipment and outfitters made consumption a central part of the hiking experience. In 1919, Appalachian Mountain Club president Allen Chamberlain had noted, "One of the beauties of tramping is that it does not call for an expensive or elaborate outfit." Following World War II, a hiker may have been able to find inexpensive military surplus, but the equipment that hiking "called for"—no matter the source—was certainly becoming more elaborate.[20]

Another critical outcome of the war was an increase in automobile access to natural areas. The armistice that ended

World War II led almost immediately to the Cold War. One of many responses to the perceived threat from the Soviet Union was further development of the Interstate Highway System, the origins of which dated to the prewar period. President Dwight D. Eisenhower's previous military experience had exposed him to the inadequacies of the American highway system as compared to Germany's *Reichsautobahn*. He believed that an interconnected network of interstate highways would aid in civil defense in the case of a foreign invasion and the need to evacuate cities threatened by nuclear attack. The Federal Aid Highway Act of 1956 authorized construction of the system, which would eventually require thirty-five years and $114 billion to complete. The interstate highways allowed Americans to visit national parks and forests more easily and independently than previously permitted by railroad service or circuitous trips on local roads. These highways provided access to the dense network of park roads constructed by the Civilian Conservation Corps and the Works Progress Administration during the 1930s and another flurry of road construction launched in the postwar period—with mixed results for those seeking wilderness experiences. The National Park Service, for example, initiated Mission 66 in 1956 with a ten-year plan to vastly increase access and amenities within the parks. More people than ever before could visit the nation's wilderness areas, but they often found that the natural landscape had been significantly altered to accommodate their visit. Regardless of Eisenhower's original intentions, the interstate highway system would become an important means of introducing Americans to the beauty of their country and delivering them to trailheads.[21]

All of those developments—more equipment, better technology, and easier access—led to rapid growth in the number of Americans hiking during the postwar period. Existing hiking clubs enrolled new members. The Appalachian Mountain Club, for example, experienced rapid growth from 6,000 members in 1955 to 22,700 members by 1975. Between 1960 and 1975, the Adirondack Mountain Club grew from roughly 2,000 to 9,000 members. The Green Mountain Club grew from 1,000 to 3,500.

Road construction in Great Smoky Mountains National Park, 1950s. An expanding network of park roads, funded as part of Mission 66, and a growing system of interstate highways encouraged millions of Americans to experience their national parks for the first time during the 1950s and 1960s. Courtesy of the Library of Congress.

Even local hiking clubs experienced fantastic growth, albeit at a much smaller scale. The Allentown Hiking Club, which had disbanded during World War II, re-formed with roughly 60 members in 1954 and doubled its membership to 129 by 1970.[22]

Meanwhile, new hiking organizations formed throughout the country, especially in places left behind by the interwar boom in hiking. The Tennessee Eastman Hiking Club, for example, began in 1946 as an outgrowth of the Eastman Kodak Company's recreation club. The club regularly held Sunday walks, with the usual mix of social events, including lobster bakes, open air concerts, and dancing. Based in Kingsport, a large town in the northeastern corner of the state, the club had easy access to Smoky Mountain National Park and the Appalachian Trail. By 1947, the club had assumed maintenance of the AT from the Carolina Mountain Club and Roan Hiking Club, and its leaders— first Frank Oglesby and then Stan Murray—became influential members of the Appalachian Trail Conference's board of directors. During the 1960s, the club responded to surging interest by scheduling its hikes on Saturdays, which was perceived as being more family friendly, with some of their larger outings attracting as many as fifty-five hikers.[23]

Other organizations formed specifically to build trails, as the Horse Shoe Trail Club had done in the 1930s. In October 1958, Merrill Gilfillan wrote an article in the *Columbus (Ohio) Dispatch* calling for a trail spanning the state from the Ohio River to Lake Erie that would be modeled on the Appalachian Trail. By May, a fifteen-member executive committee had formed the Buckeye Trail Association to bring the twelve-hundred-mile trail to fruition. Roy Fairfield, a political science professor at Ohio State University, had learned trail construction techniques by helping to build portions of the AT in Maine and serving as director of the Bates Outing Club. He would lead the club as its president during the first six years. By 1963, five hundred miles of trail were open. Perhaps the most famous club member was Emma "Grandma" Gatewood, mother of eleven and a licensed nurse who in 1955—at the age of sixty-seven—became the first woman to through-hike the AT. When the Buckeye Trail was completed in 1981, it ran 1,444 miles in a circular loop throughout the state.[24]

A decade later and to the south, real estate broker Jim Kern founded the Florida Trail Association in 1966 to fulfill his vision of building five hundred miles of continuous walking trail across the state, which would become known as the Florida Trail. Kern was frustrated with the lack of hiking opportunities in Florida, which until that time did not have a large hiking or trail organization. On hearing the unlikely proposal, the incredulous U.S. Forest Service gave Kern permission to do as he pleased on federal land, thinking that he would never be successful. Because the

region lacked historic logging and mining roads or other abandoned corridors, much of the Florida Trail had to be cleared and
blazed foot by foot. Florida's heavy rainfall and temperate cli-
mate meant that maintenance of adjacent foliage required thousands of volunteer hours. The completed trail was a thousand
miles long.[25]

Dozens—perhaps hundreds—of hiking and trail organizations were founded in the decades following World War II, many
resembling their prewar predecessors. For example, in Pennsylvania alone, at least seven hiking clubs were founded between 1941
and 1970, joining the ten organizations already active in the state.
Clubs were also founded in places with few existing organizations,
such as the Southwest, where a group of Albuquerque-based hikers interested in climbing the nearby Sierra Ladrones and hiking
throughout the region founded the New Mexico Mountain Club in
1952.[26]

As impressive as this growth in hiking clubs seemed, however, many new hikers sidestepped club membership, choosing
to walk alone or with small, informal groups. By 1970, there were
at least twenty million Americans participating in some form of
backpacking, while even a generous estimate of hiking club
membership barely approached 150,000. "There is evidence that
postwar hiking was more of an individual or family activity, less
dominated by hiking clubs," argue Laura and Guy Waterman. In
the postwar period, "it was easier to learn about the outdoors
and acquire experience without dependence on a hiking club, as
the outdoor press and equipment suppliers reached the hiking
public directly. Improved highways and broader automobile
ownership made trail-heads more accessible. Social clubs were
generally in decline in American culture." In other words, by the
1960s, there seemed to be few incentives to pay the dues and,
perhaps more important, make the significant commitment of
time and effort that traditional club membership required. Many
hikers simply did not join.[27]

The Watermans' observation is supported by Robert Putnam's study of the decline of American community in the postwar
period. Putnam finds that membership in national chapter–based

organizations flourished in the immediate postwar period but that "across all of these organizations, membership began to plateau in 1957, peaked in the early 1960s, and began the period of sustained decline by 1969." Hiking club membership peaked slightly later than many civic organizations simply because of the overwhelming interest generated by Earth Day, the environmental movement, and the founding of new clubs. While some of the larger clubs, such as the Appalachian Mountain Club, Green Mountain Club, and Adirondack Mountain Club, grew their membership rates rapidly through the mid-1970s, the majority of hiking organizations followed the national trend and grew only slowly, considering the overall increase in outdoor use. This decline in membership rate was very difficult to perceive, especially for hiking clubs growing at rates as high as 100 percent each year during the hiking "boom." During the late 1960s, club secretaries had every reason to believe that they would continue to add ever-increasing numbers to their membership lists. Only in later decades would they realize that the growth in their organizations paled in comparison with the numbers of new hikers.[28]

One prominent exception to this trend is the Sierra Club. The Sierra Club evolved to a greater extent than any other American hiking organization. In the 1910s, the club captured national attention through its opposition to O'Shaughnessy Dam in Yosemite's Hetch Hetchy Valley. "Dam Hetch Hetchy!" an impassioned John Muir wrote in the concluding lines of the *Yosemite*, "As well dam for water-tanks the peoples' cathedrals and churches, for no holier temple has ever been consecrated by the heart of man." During the 1950s, the club again led an antidam campaign, this time at Echo Park on the Green River, a tributary to the Colorado River. The proposed dam site—one of several slated for development as part of the Colorado River Storage Project—was located within Dinosaur National Monument. David Brower, hired in 1953 as the Sierra Club's first executive director, collaborated with other national conservation leaders to bring attention to the dam project, which they feared would set a precedent for future intrusions on federal lands protected as national parks and monuments. Ultimately, the U.S. Bureau of Reclamation compromised by removing the Echo Park dam from the proposal and, instead, built a dam downstream at Arizona's Glen Canyon, which the Sierra Club agreed not to oppose. At the time, the victory appeared to demonstrate the club's political savvy and grassroots organizing power, although the loss of Glen Canyon would haunt the club in the future.[29]

During the 1960s, the Sierra Club expanded its reach through innovative publications and marketing campaigns. Under Brower's direction, the club published a series of "exhibit format" books that matched wilderness photography with quotations from outdoor writers. The first book, *"In Wildness Is the Preservation of the World,"* featured photography by Eliot Porter and selections from Henry David Thoreau's writing. In contrast to the club's traditional focus on the rugged peaks and isolated wilderness of the West, *"In Wildness"* focused on the natural places of the Northeast, potentially engaging a new geographic audience ready "to discover how new and beautiful the familiar can be if we actually see it as though we had never seen it before." At the same time, the club hired publicists to help them wage compelling advertising campaigns. A full-page ad from the 1960s opposing a new dam in the Grand Canyon famously asked in language reminiscent of Muir, "Should We Also Flood the Sistine Chapel?"[30]

Most notable of all, the Sierra Club sought to attract the growing numbers of countercultural youth rejecting society, industry, environmental degradation, and the escalating war in Vietnam. For example, in 1967, the club published *On the Loose*, an account by brothers Jerry and Renny Russell of their outdoor adventures in the Pacific Northwest, Sierras, Utah, and Colorado. The book was similar to the exhibit format series in that it matched brief poetry and literary selections from Thoreau, Walt Whitman, George Bernard Shaw, and Aldo Leopold with the Russells' own writing and photography. The style, however, clearly drew from Jack Kerouac and other Beat poets, as the final lines of the book's introduction suggest. "Terry and Renny Russell, planet Earth, twentieth century after Christ. We live in a house that God built but that the former tenants remodeled—blew it up, it looks like—before we arrived," the Russells wrote.

"Poking through the rubble in the odd hours, we've found the corners that were spared and have hidden in them as much as we could. Not to escape from but to escape to: not to forget but to remember. We've been learning to take care of ourselves in places where it really matters. The next step is to take care of the places that really matter. Crazy kids on the loose; but on the loose in the wilderness. That makes all the difference."[31]

The book privileged the countercultural youth perspective to a remarkable extent, given that the Sierra Club was a seventy-five-year-old institution led by affluent adults. In a brief note tucked into the final pages of the book, David Brower—himself fifty-five— claimed that "to describe *On the Loose* is to deprive the reader of a freshness that ought to be self-discovered, and turned to often and remembered." The language on the back cover was more explicit, describing *On the Loose* as "a book you will be pleased to own and perhaps even more pleased to give—to the youth who will understand, and to their elders who will always be trying to."[32]

The club carried this praise for youth culture into its other publications. In 1970, at a time when concern for the environment had mobilized millions of Americans to participate in the first Earth Day, the club published *Ecotactics*, a handbook for activists that included essays on the environmental movement and methods, based on case studies, to advance it. Like the field organizers who made Earth Day a success, the contributors to *Ecotactics* were young—most under forty, many under thirty— and newcomers to the movement. "This is no anthology of tomes resurrected from the past," the editors noted, in an apparent critique of the club's previous photo and quotation books. "Since it is the earth environment that concerns us here, then the youth must be heard. This is *their* earth more than anyone else's: they will have to live with it longer, for better or for worse. And perhaps it is also appropriate that we listen to and learn from young people now because they are the ones who currently seem to be making the most sense out of a very bad environmental situation." The writing seemed to suggest that youth, like wilderness, was an untapped source of wisdom typically disparaged and degraded by modern society.[33]

The Sierra Club's new approach to publishing, advertising, and courting youth was highly effective and allowed the club to ride the rising tide of environmental concern during the late 1960s and early 1970s. There was a dramatic impact on membership. The club had approximately 4,000 members before World War II and saw that figure increase exponentially with each new campaign. By 1975, the club had more than 165,000 members, with nearly 100,000 of those members joining between 1965 and 1970 alone.[34]

As a result of its rapid growth and increasing prominence in national environmental politics, the original structure of the organization changed dramatically. Before World War II, the Sierra Club had truly functioned as a relatively close-knit club that relied on personal endorsements for approval of membership. In the years following the war, however, the club voted to allow chapters beyond California and accept members with no previous club affiliation. The growth also meant that volunteers alone could no longer conduct the club's official business. Brower became the first executive director in 1953, and the professional staff expanded quickly after that. As political scientist Christopher Bosso notes, "The tradition of leadership by volunteer was being eclipsed by the emergence of a new generation of professional managers." This was true of environmental organizations—and many other voluntary associations—throughout the nation, many of which enjoyed similar growth during the late 1960s.[35]

Despite its success in environmental politics, the Sierra Club's evolution had an ambiguous effect on the American hiking community. The club's innovative publications mostly ignored recreation. *"In Wildness,"* for example, features dozens of color photographs—none of which include people. *Ecotactics* focused on advocacy and a host of environmental problems but, aside from a few lines, did not promote or influence hiking. Perhaps most troubling, even *On the Loose*, the club's attempt to lure youth with the promise of adventure, focused on the Russells' spiritual rather than physical journey and said little of what hiking or backpacking was actually like. Of course, collectively the publications would lead people to hike, but the shift in emphasis was not that simple. "If, in the mid-1960s, three-quarters of the members joined for the outings program and only a quarter for the conservation program, by the early 1970s the ratio was reversed," historian Michael Cohen argues in his definitive history of the Sierra Club. "Members were paying their dues to see an effective conservation program." In short, the Sierra Club increased and maintained membership rates because it was no longer primarily a hiking and climbing organization.[36]

The evolution of the Sierra Club was less clear at the local level. Many state chapters founded in the early 1970s provided regular outings for their members and resembled traditional hiking clubs. However, in most cases, even these local chapters never emphasized hiking and climbing in the way that the Sierra Club did between its founding and World War II or as traditional hiking clubs continued to do in the postwar period. The national club itself continued to organize outings as well—twenty-six backpacking trips and several expeditions in 1973 alone—which engaged its membership in meaningful ways. However, as the club adopted low-impact camping principles, it tried to limit group sizes to fifteen people, significantly limiting the portion of members who could participate. Nonetheless, Sierra Club membership served as an entry point for thousands of hikers and backpackers in the 1960s and 1970s, even if the club was being pulled in other directions.

As the hiking community evolved—both within and outside of clubs—it became clear that, in part thanks to better equipment, increasing numbers of hikers were carrying large packs into the woods with food, cooking ware, tents, sleeping bags, and all of the gear needed for a long outing. In other words, they began backpacking, and this was an important development for the hiking community. Although day walks would remain at the heart of the hiking experience, backpacking provided a new way to experience the backcountry that appealed to many Americans, especially those who preferred to walk alone or in small groups. In 1962, one observer described backpackers as "a different breed of outdoor camper": "He usually is, or will soon become, a good woodsman and mountaineer," wrote W. K. Merrill, in his guidebook *All about Camping*. "He may belong to a hiking club or he may be a free lance. In any event, he is eager to get away from the crowd and the beaten paths, and to roam at will through the wilderness back country of our national parks and forests. The area he covers is only limited by the supplies he can carry comfortably on his back or secure along the route."[37]

By 1971, the *New York Times* recognized an outright "backpacking boom that has practically revolutionized American outdoor life." "What sort of breed are the backpackers?" the author asked. "To begin with, despite the fairly widespread notion, they are not exclusively or even mainly hippies, the long-haired people of Harvard Square, the East Village, and Berkeley's Telegraph Avenue. They represent every segment of American life. . . . In addition to the long-haired spiritual descendants of the Dharma Bums, today's backpacking battalions include their sisters and their cousins and their uncles and their aunts—persons of all ages and from all walks of life." Indeed, one of the appeals of backpacking was that "unlike tennis or golf, it is not a class sport in which costume and protocol play a large part. A hiker dressed in Levis, a work shirt, and boots, as are all men, women, and children on the trail, is hard to classify in terms of education, profession, or economic position. . . . The woods are open to all, regardless of age, sex, or race."[38]

The accessibility and appeal of hiking and backpacking, however, were precisely the problem. The most attractive places to hike tended to be natural, fragile places that could not accommodate a large number of visitors. Many of the newcomers flocked to state and national parks, which—thanks to the work of the Civilian Conservation Corps during the 1930s—provided new accommodations and easy automobile access to some of the most spectacular scenery in the world. Edward Abbey described this type of auto-based recreation as "industrial tourism." Over about ten years, Abbey watched visitation to Arches National Park increase rapidly. "Where once a few adventurous people came on weekends to camp for a night or two and enjoy a taste of the primitive and remote," he noted, "you will now find serpentine

streams of baroque automobiles pouring in and out, all through
the spring and summer . . . from 3,000 to 30,000 to 300,000 per
year, the 'visitation,' as they call it, mounts ever upward." Parks
across the nation felt the strain of overuse. In 1950, fewer than 50
million Americans visited national parks each year. By 1974, as a
result of road building and investment programs, such as Mission 66, visitation surpassed 217 million.[39]

Thoughtful hikers began to struggle with the idea that their
passion for wilderness was causing its destruction. "Where did
all these damn hikers come from?" Harvey Manning asked know-
ingly from the pages of *Backpacker*. Peter Noone, manager at the
Ski Hut in Berkeley, admitted, "We're a bunch of hypocrites.
We're trying to save the mountains and, at the same time, sell as
many backpacks as possible." The irony of hiking's popularity
frustrated many longtime advocates, but others channeled their
concerns into a new ethic of low-impact recreation that attempted to balance use with stewardship.[40]

William Kemsley became one leader in this movement. On a
drizzly morning in 1963, the corporate writer who would found
Backpacker magazine a decade later, woke up at a campsite along
the Appalachian Trail. As he made his morning coffee over a
small fire, he was vaguely aware of a small group of young men
camping nearby through a stand of trees. As the drizzle turned
into a brief downpour, the young men quickly gathered their
packs and headed down the trail, leaving their burning fire behind. In disbelief, Kemsley rushed over to their site and doused
the flames. If the hikers' carelessness with fire were not enough,
"I saw that they had scattered tin cans, paper plates, cups, forks,
spoons, scraps of food, assorted plastic containers, and wrappers
all around their campsite. It took me almost an hour to pick up
the rubbish."[41]

The seasoned hiker was furious. "I entertained all sorts of
sadistic ideas, like, say, shoot them, strangle them, or at least toss
them in a pokey until they learned better trail manners." But, as
his head cooled, Kemsley realized that was precisely the problem. No one had taught these "newbies" proper trail etiquette.
How were they to know the ethics of hiking and backpacking if

they did not have mentors to model good behavior? The problem, Kemsley knew, went well beyond this group of young men. He remembered that in the years immediately following World War II, he had the trails pretty much to himself, and during the 1950s, he would occasionally run into other experienced hikers in the backcountry. By the 1960s, however, the trails were becoming overrun, and the evidence of increased use was everywhere. "With increased numbers came increased trashing," Kemsley observed. "It was common to find a long string of gum and candy wrappers strewn along a popular trail, not to mention tissues and cigarette butts." As he witnessed that morning in 1963, campsites, especially those along the Appalachian Trail and other popular trails, were worn, muddy, and littered from overuse. By 1971, the *New York Times* reported that "a backpacking backlash has set in. Deep ruts have been worn into some trails, others have been hacked and littered." In Kemsley's mind, then, the question quickly turned from how to punish the group of careless young campers to how best to educate them—and the millions of other new hikers—in the proper principles of low-impact recreation.[42]

As a professional writer, Kemsley was drawn to the idea of a magazine. He was aware of the Sierra Club's success with *This Is the American Land* and other exhibit-style, coffee table books, as well as their innovative and provocative advertising campaigns. Further, he worked for the publishers of *Newsweek* and could regularly pick the brain of publishers, editors, and writers on how best to reach a national audience. Kemsley recognized that an abundance of glossy photos, engaging stories from what he called "heroes" of conservation and recreation, and relevant, nuts-and-bolts information would be the key to the magazine's success. Following discussions with Laura and Guy Waterman and other outdoor writers, he decided to target the content at the "elite of the hiking community."[43]

Advocates of low-impact recreation recognized that "new" backpackers were not necessarily the problem. As late as 1965, major hiking and backpacking guides included little to no information on how to limit one's impact on the land. Indeed, many

continued to perpetuate ideas about woodcraft and camp traditions that starkly contrasted with the new ethic. Bradford Angier's 1965 guide *Home in Your Pack*, for example, contained an
entire chapter on how to "Enjoy the Fires You Build." "What remains most fondly in our mind after a wilderness hike are the
campfires. The handful of twigs that boil the kettle at noon. . . .
The flames behind whose sanctuary you sit while darkening forests come to life. Then there is that fire at dawn. . . . Much of the
success of a hiking trip, as well as a considerable deal of the pleasure, is going to depend on you having the right kinds of cooking
fires." In this context, the new environmental ethic and its limits
on gathering wood for open fires would have appeared as an assault on what made hiking fun in the first place. By focusing on
people like Angier who were already backpacking at an advanced
level, Kemsley and the magazine's contributors could reach the
most influential group of backpackers without encouraging new
users to visit the backcountry.[44]

The inaugural spring 1973 issue of *Backpacker* indicated this
was a difficult balance to strike. Kemsley opened with a remarkably frank letter saying that the magazine would be limited in
circulation, would not be sold at stands or stores, and would not
contain content that taught newcomers how to get started. This,
he hoped, would allow *Backpacker* to foster a dialogue within the
hiking community without exacerbating the problems it set out
to solve. "I think this magazine is great," one reader wrote in support of Kemsley. "I'm glad to hear there are people around who
will limit their circulation even if it means losing money." Other
readers were less convinced. "A pox on your magazine which will
only encourage more abuse no matter how good your inten-
tions," wrote one. "I will not subscribe to or support a magazine
which will serve to further popularize the mass destruction of
our wilderness areas," wrote another. A more thoughtful letter
noted the key tension *Backpacker* represented. "Your mission, as
you call it, may hurt the general cause of conservation and wilderness preservation," wrote John Martin of Syracuse, New
York. "Granting that an effort must be made to keep what remaining areas of the wilderness and forest preserve we do have,

the one way not to do this is to further divide the conservation forces in our country." Also troubling were Kemsley's repeated claims—in the first issue of *Backpacker* and later—that the publication was not concerned with advertising revenue and therefore represented an objective voice for the backpacking community. From its first issue, however, *Backpacker* contained dozens of advertisements for high-end outdoor equipment and routinely included stories about new equipment and gear. The idea that equipment and expertise were equivalent appealed to those able to afford the advertised products but ostracized and discouraged those who thought of hiking and backpacking as relatively simple and inexpensive. By focusing on backpackers as a subset of hikers and the elite as a subset of the public, Kemsley perpetuated the mounting division between the traditional hiking community and the growing group of backpacking elite—many of whom had no club affiliations.[45]

During the 1970s, *Backpacker* and its contributors emerged as the most influential advocates of what later became known as "Leave No Trace" principles, but they were certainly not alone. In 1972, the Boy Scouts of America revised its handbook to reflect the new principles, eschewing more than sixty years of woodcraft education that had emphasized camping skills, building fires, constructing shelters, and felling trees. In that year, 6.2 million Scouts—the next generation of hikers, backpackers, and campers—learned that their enjoyment of the land could cause serious ecological problems if not wisely conducted. Beginning in 1965, college-age students could learn similar skills through the National Outdoor Leadership School, founded by mountaineer Paul Petzoldt to teach environmental ethics and outdoor skills. In 1974, Petzoldt published *The Wilderness Handbook*, which included chapters on "Camping for Conservation" and other ecologically friendly approaches to recreating in the backwoods. "Our wilderness needs protection from lovers of the outdoors," Petzoldt noted, in terms similar to Fletcher. "The wilderness can be traveled without harm. . . . Camping with techniques of practical conservation is the answer." Petzoldt's focus on extreme "semiexpedition"-style outings limited his appeal, but by the late 1970s, interested hikers could choose from a number of accessible and relevant books on the topic, including John Hart's *Walking Softly in the Wilderness*, published by the Sierra Club. Within a decade, low-impact principles had made their way into most hiking and backpacking guides.[46]

Low-impact hiking was an amalgamation of environmental ethics and high-tech equipment that sought to balance use of natural places with stewardship. These noble goals were often obscured, however, by overt consumerism. As historian James Morton Turner argues, "This shift toward a modern, consumer-oriented wilderness ideal calls into question the effectiveness with which some of America's most ardent environmentalists—its wilderness recreationists—have engaged the environmental challenges posed by the consumer economy." In seeking a solution to one recreational problem—environmental degradation—many advocates of low-impact hiking promoted a reliance on technology that discouraged some Americans, namely those not affluent enough to afford the technology, from hiking, and threw up artificial—literally synthetic—barriers between humans and the natural world they were supposed to be enjoying. The new principles suggested that to hike one must consume.[47]

By the mid-1960s, the growing popularity of hiking and concern for the overuse of the nation's trails prompted government action. As trail use increased, many trails began to experience closures as the handshake agreements that once allowed them to cross private property gave way to landowners' concerns about liability and the intrusion of outsiders. The need to protect routes indefinitely through public ownership became a motivating factor for government intervention.[48]

In 1965, President Lyndon Johnson delivered his Natural Beauty address to Congress in which he called for wide-reaching government action on a variety of environmental issues, including air and water quality, river cleanups, and solid waste reform. He also included—on equal footing—an entire section on trails. "The forgotten outdoorsmen of today are those who like to walk, hike, ride horseback, or bicycle," he noted. "For them we must have trails as well as highways." Johnson announced that he had

directed Secretary of the Interior Stewart Udall to work with federal and state leaders to recommend "a cooperative program to
encourage a national system of trails, building up more than
[one] hundred thousand miles of trails in our national forests and
parks." But Johnson went further, envisioning a trail network
that reached well beyond federal lands. "As with so much of our
quest for beauty and quality, each community has opportunities
for action," Johnson noted. "We can and should have an abundance of trails for walking, cycling, and horseback riding, in and
close to our cities. In the back country we need to copy the great
Appalachian Trail in all parts of America, and to make full use of
rights-of-way and other public paths." Johnson's vision was extremely ambitious. Federal agencies had assisted local groups
with trail building on an ad hoc basis for decades, but a concert-
ed effort to foster, organize, and fund trail building throughout
the country represented a monumental shift in policy.[49]

In fact, Johnson's proposal was not new. Hiking clubs and
their allies had encouraged Congress to pass national trails system legislation as early as the 1940s. Congressman Daniel Hoch
introduced a bill to create a "National System of Foot Trails" on
February 13, 1945. Hoch represented a district centered on Reading, Pennsylvania, that included a ridgeline section of the Appalachian Trail. As a member and past president of the Blue Mountain
Eagle Climbing Club and its land acquisitions arm, the Blue
Mountain Wilderness Preservation Association, he had developed
a relationship with Myron Avery and other Appalachian Trail Conference officials. He therefore recognized the need to fund the acquisition, development, and maintenance of long-distance trails.

Hoch and his allies decided that their best chance for funding was to amend the Federal-Aid Highway Act of 1944. The
amendment sought an appropriation of fifty thousand dollars
each year for "the construction and maintenance within the
continental United States of a national system of foot trails, not
to exceed ten thousand miles in total length, to be devoted solely
for foot travel and camping, which activities will develop the
physical fitness and self-reliance of, and an appreciation of nature in, the people of this Nation." The bill envisioned the trail

network serving "as part of the basic training of our youth in the armed services." The system would be developed as a partnership between the Departments of Agriculture and Interior and the political subdivisions through which the trails passed. The Appalachian Trail would be the first officially recognized trail in the system.[50]

In October 1945, Hoch's bill was given a hearing in front of the Roads Committee at which Hoch and Avery testified, along with representatives of the Potomac Appalachian Trail Club, the American Planning and Civic Association, and the U.S. Forest Service. Each spoke at length about the benefits of the nation's major trails and the minimal investment required for their care. However, the Federal Public Works Agency submitted written testimony strongly condemning the bill. "The development of a national system of foot trails as proposed does not seem to be an undertaking upon which the Federal Government should embark," the overburdened and war-weary agency argued. "It is not apparent that there can be any substantial need for such trails. The extension and improvement of public highways which have taken place throughout the States would seem definitely to make such system of trails unnecessary." Americans already had access to scenic areas via roads, and the government already funded the National Park Service and Forest Service to create trails within their jurisdictions. In a line of reasoning that must have driven the assembled trail advocates wild, the testimony noted that "it is becoming more and more the practice of the States and their subdivisions to provide for pedestrian traffic along highways as part of the highway construction projects." Hoch responded in his testimony by saying that the agency "completely failed to grasp the intention of this project." "I don't need to labor this point," he said with indignation. "There is no pleasure in walking along an open hot road in the area of gas fumes, with the constant danger of being hit by cars. We want to walk away from roads."[51]

Hoch's bill also met with some ridicule in the press. One journalist objected to the argument that trails helped preserve the "pioneer flavor" of the backcountry. "Why don't they grab an ax and go out in the woods and do what the frontiersmen

did, which was build their own trails?" he asked. "Do they
think that a construction gang, at 50 cents or so an hour, went
ahead of Boone when he plunged into the 'dark and bloody
ground' of the Kentucky Plains? Do you think that Kit Carson
refused to traipse through the Southwest until a bulldozer
had cleared the way?" Myron Avery, who had been serving as
Hoch's cheerleader behind the scenes, clipped the article for his
personal files.[52]

Despite the generally favorable hearing, the Public Works
Agency's testimony proved damning, and the bill never emerged
from committee. Hoch lost reelection in 1946, but he reached
out to fellow Congressman Francis Walter to keep the legislation
moving in the next session. Walter was an unlikely standard-
bearer for the trails movement. In the 1950s, he would become
best known as an anticommunist crusader and member of the
House Un-American Activities Committee. Although he, too, had
a section of the Appalachian Trail in his district, Walter seemed
most motivated by his friendship with Hoch. "I am surprised
that you would even entertain the thought that I wouldn't be willing to introduce a bill for you," he wrote in response to Hoch's
request. "I am dropping it [off for introduction] today." The local
paper—a regular critic of Walter—was not pleased, arguing that
"Mr. Walter was too busy promoting trails to give any attention
to tax reduction and other measures intended to benefit his
constituents." The bill again died in committee. Hoch was not
perturbed, writing to Avery, "In all such movements, one will run
up against those who do not have the vision."[53]

The thankless spadework done by Hoch, Avery, and other
trail leaders during the 1940s paid off in the early 1960s, when
the broader environmental movement and rapid growth of the
hiking community made investment in trails much more likely.
Following Johnson's "Natural Beauty" address, Secretary Udall
directed the Bureau of Outdoor Recreation to conduct a nationwide trails study that would describe existing trails and programs, assess their adequacy in meeting demand, consider the
role of federal agencies, and recommend national trails system
legislation.[54]

Even as the report committee conducted its research, there were signs that the findings would shift trail development policy toward urban areas. Most of the nation's major trails were located in rural areas, but in his address, Johnson had specifically mentioned the need for more trails near cities. Unwilling to wait for federal legislation, Udall took action that signaled a shift in the geographic focus of trail development. In July 1966, he announced that twelve urban areas would receive more than $367,000 in land and water conservation funds to develop trails. "I detect an awakening on the part of many urban areas, as they seek to counterbalance buildings with open space, to provide cleanliness instead of clutter, and to develop walkways, and trails, as well as highways," Udall said, in announcing the grants. "The trail plans announced today are indications of this growing desire for outdoor recreation and natural beauty within our cities." The projects, which ranged from thousands of feet to hundreds of miles in length, were located in major cities throughout the country, including New York, Detroit, Chicago, Phoenix, and San Francisco. Notably, all but a few were intended to accommodate bicyclists as well as hikers, reflecting the federal government's growing preference for multiple-use trails. These were distinctly government projects that even the most capable group of volunteer trail builders could not tackle. As a result, although hiking clubs could help inform decisions about the projects and use the final product, they had little role to play in the trails' construction and thus no "sweat equity" in the projects once completed. Similarly, the maintenance of these trails would require graders, paving equipment, heavy machinery, and significant funding, ensuring that hiking clubs would have a minimal role in their future operation. The choice to focus on multiuse trails effectively limited the traditional role of hiking clubs in constructing and maintaining the nation's trails. While the government remained committed to long-distance footpaths, Udall warned, "We should regard these urban trail projects as the first solid brushstrokes in painting a vastly greater concept of recreation and conservation."[55]

The committee's resulting report, *Trails for America*, was a testament to how far the trails community had come since its

Breaking ground for the Schuylkill River Trail, 1979. Beginning in
the 1960s, federal assistance for trails favored multiuse paths
typically located in urban areas. Abandoned rail corridors offered
readily available space and a well-engineered, graded route.
Courtesy of the Montgomery County Planning Commission.

origins in the mid-nineteenth century. The report found more
than 87,000 miles of trails on federal lands and another 14,865
miles managed by states. State governments alone were expected
to construct another 12,000 miles of trail during the next decade.
In keeping with Johnson's and Udall's rhetoric, the committee
found that trail development was accelerating most rapidly in
urban areas. "Trails located in or near metropolitan areas and
adapted to the use of walkers, hikers, horseback riders, and cy-
clists are among the best means of accommodating urban recreationists," the report noted. "Where population pressures are
greatest, efforts to provide the types of outdoor recreation that
trails afford should be intensified." The resulting system would
ideally balance rural and urban trail opportunities.[56]

Even before its publication, *Trails for America* provided the rationale and framework for the national trails system legislation introduced on March 31, 1966. The bill would establish the national trail system based on three designations. "National Scenic Trails" were the nation's most important and exceptionally scenic long-distance trails that connected the many shorter trails in between. Only Congress had the authority to designate these trails, and the first two included in the legislation were the Appalachian Trail and Pacific Crest Trail. The bill authorized the National Park Service and Forest Service to receive funding to acquire and maintain the trail corridors and manage the scenic trails. Although the federal agencies would be given the power to identify the official trail route, Congress placed significant limits on their ability to acquire land. The cap amounted to a maximum two-hundred-foot corridor protecting the land on both sides of the trail, and limited funding for acquisition made even this narrow buffer difficult to achieve. The federal agencies were also tasked with conducting feasibility studies of additional proposed national scenic trails.[57]

"National Recreation Trails" were those with the potential to provide recreational opportunities to large numbers of people, especially in urban areas. These were more common than scenic trails and could be created at the discretion of the secretaries of agriculture and the interior. They received less funding and protection but could leverage their official inclusion in the national system to compete for grants and attract new users. Most important, they fulfilled the vision to create a balanced system between rural and urban trails. "Connecting and Side Trails" were those with special potential to provide access to natural areas or link trails together and served as a catch-all for trails that did not appear to fit the "scenic" or "recreational" categories. In addition to supporting the three types of designated trails, the bill authorized the federal government's various agencies to include trail planning and promotion in their activities, including housing and urban development policy, forest management, reclamation projects, and other areas not typically associated with trail development.[58]

In congressional hearings, various iterations of the bill received much broader support than the 1940s legislation. Representatives of most national environmental organizations spoke in support of the bill, as did the federal agencies involved in its implementation. Since the legislation had originated with Johnson and Udall, there was little threat that a federal agency would come out strongly against it. But the bill also had its critics from outside government. For example, during hearings over Senate Bill 827—a companion version of the legislation—E. P. Harvey of the American National Cattlemen's Association raised "sincere and serious questions" about the cost of the bill and the effects on adjacent landowners. In addition to reasonable questions about the trails' management, Harvey suggested a number of spurious concerns, such as the need to erect fencing on both sides of each trail for their entire length. Representatives of citizen groups complained about the effect of trail corridor acquisition on property rights and real estate values. "Condemnation without the consent of the owner, at the discretion of an appointed, not even an elected official is rather unpalatable fare for independent and proud Americans," objected John Chesley of the South Potomac Citizens Council. "We trust that this will be put aside." Representatives of the lumber and tree farm industries and of railroads with large landholdings made similar requests. The outcry was a preview of the stronger antitrail sentiment that would emerge in the late twentieth century as a result of private property concerns. Overall, however, the idea of a national system of trails received widespread support and was considered less controversial than other conservation measures of the day, such as the creation of Redwoods National Park.[59]

On October 2, 1968, Johnson signed Public Law 90–543, the National Trails System Act, and the federal government became permanently invested in the development of trails throughout the nation. For individual trails, such as the Appalachian Trail, the result was not a government takeover but rather the creation of a unique public-private partnership that had been in the works for several decades. The Appalachian Trail Conference would continue to serve as the clearinghouse for AT information and advocacy and organize local hiking clubs to maintain sections of the trail, but they would do so with support from National Park Service staff and considerable federal funding, especially for acquisition of lands adjacent to the trail. The same would be true of the Pacific Crest Trail Conference, which worked closely with the Forest Service to maintain the trail and protect the surrounding corridor. To longtime hiking club members and trail builders, these working relationships were not new. The National Trails System Act simply formalized relations that had been in place by the early twentieth century, in which federal, state, and local governments regularly assisted volunteers with construction of trails. Given their past experiences, however, the pragmatic trail builders could anticipate the weaknesses of government support and recognized that thousands of volunteer hours would still be required to keep trails in good shape. Clubs building or maintaining trails outside of the national system—of which the majority were—would still be on their own. The new law represented progress, but club members knew they still had lots of work ahead.

For the millions of Americans new to hiking and trails in the 1960s, the National Trails System Act, the federal government's involvement in trail development, and policymakers' rhetoric all contributed to the idea that trail access was a right. Just as Americans had the right to clean air, clean water, and safe workplaces, they were entitled to well-maintained and easily accessible trails, and after 1968, they could justifiably argue that their taxes were paying to maintain that right. This expectation quickly extended to state governments, which developed comprehensive outdoor recreation plans and put considerable manpower and funding behind their trail and greenway systems during the 1970s and 1980s. It was remarkable that simple, cleared paths through the woods had become invested with such profound meaning and elevated to the same level as some of the most pressing environmental concerns of the period.

But this was also problematic for the trails community. If trail access was an entitlement—a government service supported through taxation—why should the millions of new hikers be

National Trails System Act signing ceremony, 1968. President
Lyndon Johnson, center, and Secretary of the Interior Stewart
Udall, left, survey a map of the proposed national trails system.
Courtesy of the Appalachian Trail Conservancy.

asked to devote additional time, energy, and wealth to maintaining or expanding trails? Most new hikers bypassed club membership and were therefore inexperienced with the realities of trail
work or the policies that made the trails possible. The misleading
simplicity of trails obscured the significant investment of volunteer time, energy, and wealth provided by traditional hiking clubs.
Millions of hikers passed over trails with little concern for how
they were created or by whom. They approached trails as consumers—willing to pay taxes for trails and perhaps mail a mem-

bership fee to an environmental organization—but not to make hiking club membership or trail work an important part of their lives.

As millions of Americans began hiking in the 1960s, the culture of hiking developed by clubs in the previous century began to change dramatically. The traditional hiking community had relied on clubs as net producers of hiking culture but evolved into a loose gathering of millions of Americans consuming equipment, information, and physical trails produced by private businesses, professional environmental groups, and government. The evolution of the producing, or "citizen," hiker—to use historian Lizabeth Cohen's terminology—to the consuming hiker meant that most hikers would spend almost no time investing in the clubs or trails they used. Of course, this transition was never really complete. "Rather than isolated ideal types," Cohen suggests, "citizen and consumer were ever-shifting categories that sometimes overlapped, often were in tension, but always reflected the permeability of the political and economic spheres." In fact, hikers of the 1960s were concerned for the public good, in terms of both access to recreation and the protection of nature. Influenced by the environmental movement, they hoped to increase the use of natural areas to build a larger constituency for stewardship while mitigating the impact of their activities through low-impact principles. They believed that more trails and preserved lands provided opportunities to engage new hikers, and they were willing to pay membership fees to organizations and write letters to legislators to aid in this effort. At the same time, their focus on high-tech equipment, payments for environmental advocacy, and sense of entitlement to government-funded trails and parks assured that consumption would define hiking.[60]

Previous generations of hikers assumed that they would need to work hard to produce expert information, engaging outings, and well-kept trails. Hiking clubs served as clearinghouses for trail information, natural and cultural history, and even scientific research on mountains, geology, and meteorology. They conveyed this information through self-published maps, guides, newsletters, and journals that were, in turn, reprinted in other clubs' publications. Members built, field-tested, and shared equipment recommissioned from their military service and pulled out of their closets. The clubs constructed trails—committing countless hours to blazing, clearing, grubbing, and maintaining narrow paths through the woods—and then they organized outings to walk on them. This culture of hiking, which emphasized communal, volunteer service and a commitment to the social aspects of club life, served the hiking community well through the 1950s and reinforced a national culture of hiking based on shared beliefs about its benefits.

For the hundreds of hiking clubs active and growing during the 1960s, this culture seemed stable, and it continued to guide and provide a context for their work. At the same time, the largest and most historic institutions—the Appalachian Mountain Club, Mountaineers, Mazamas, Adirondack Mountain Club, and the Green Mountain Club—evolved to meet changing conditions. They added professional staff and tweaked programming to include backpacking, low-impact principles, and generally court the new breed of recreationists. They grew rapidly—sometimes adding three to five times the members they had before the boom. Smaller, local hiking clubs also formed and grew during this period, adding members and programming. They held regular hikes, scheduled trips to build and maintain trails, and enjoyed social events. The clubs appeared to be thriving, and they promulgated the same communal, volunteer-based culture of hiking that they had since the early twentieth century.

As the popularity of hiking grew, however, these hiking clubs lost their hegemony over national hiking culture. In the postwar period, American civic life in general experienced a decline, and new hikers found little value in hiking as a club. Indeed, many thought communal walks undermined their attempts to get back to nature and experience wilderness. Furthermore, the traditional reasons for joining a club were no longer relevant. Better and more abundant equipment—using new technologies—replaced the need to rely on camp cooks, porters, and the other accoutrements of club outings. National magazines, mass-market books, and a glut of guides assumed the traditional role of sharing knowledge and replaced the customary methods for exchanging knowledge. In the same way that freeze-dried food and aluminum cook kits had replaced the camp cook, mass-market media replaced the institutional knowledge of clubs. Members had valued clubs for the hands-on advice and encouragement of more experienced members, for the evening lectures that highlighted conservation issues or demonstrated the latest equipment, and for the interaction with likeminded hikers. By the mid-1970s, however, most hikers could purchase printed material to get this information. In the absence of physical meetings, they found a sense of community in the knowledge that others were reading the same publications and, in the case of periodicals, exchanging ideas through the "letters" section. Many readers reaffirmed this sense of community on the trail, where they met other hikers, participated in ad hoc volunteer service, or perhaps shared a lean-to with strangers. In general, however, the communal aspects of American hiking culture were being lost. The rich, club culture that had promoted hiking for the previous one hundred years had evolved into a culture that emphasized individual, therapeutic experiences loosely united through mass media and consumption. Ironically, as millions of Americans hit the trail in the late 1960s, many found themselves hiking alone in a crowd.

EPILOGUE

Hiking before and after 1968

THE evolution of the American hiking community since 1968 has been marked by both continuity and change. On one hand, organized hiking clubs remained popular throughout the nation, and formal clubs continued to attract hikers to their social functions, communal outings, and trail work events. On the other hand, the factors leading to the rise of the consumer hiker in the late 1960s continue to influence the community today, so that of the thirty-four million Americans who hiked in 2012, less than 1 percent were active club members. As a result, two generations of hikers have reached adulthood with minimal—if any—relationship to the club structure that defined hiking for more than a century.[1]

The rise of the consumer hiker in the late 1960s and early 1970s represented a monumental shift within the community. Nineteenth-century hiking emerged in the context of a transportation revolution, new ideas about the natural world and how best to experience it, rapid urbanization and expansion of cities, and the emergence of a class of Americans with disposable time and money to pursue leisure activities, including walking in the woods. But, despite the power of these forces, hiking would not have become a national phenomenon without the men and women who formed dozens of clubs between 1876, when a group of Boston climbers founded the Appalachian Mountain Club, and the post–World War II period, when millions of Americans began to hike, camp, and backpack. The popularity of hiking in the second half of the twentieth century and relative decline of club membership obscured the volunteer labor that went into producing American hiking culture. Most hikers simply took it for granted—consuming trails, maps, and ideas but not playing a significant role in their creation.

Hiking culture has always been about investing the simple act of walking with a variety of meanings, from religion and patriotism to health and communal ties. Rather than a lament for a bygone "golden age" of American hiking, *On the Trail* shows how those meanings have changed—and in some cases remained the same—since the nineteenth century. Even as the health benefits, deistic value, and aesthetics of hiking continue to motivate participants, the shift from producer hiker to consumer hiker took its greatest toll on the idea that hiking was a social activity both in terms of group hikes and social events and in terms of clubs' collective effort to build trails, publish newsletters, and advocate for legislation. In most cases, increasingly professionalized staff at nonprofit environmental groups and federal and state governments with substantial funding sources for trail construction filled this void in volunteerism.

The decline in club membership is part of a broader shift in American culture during the postwar period that saw many voluntary associations—once powerful and influential community institutions—stagnate or disband. The decline coincided with rapid suburbanization and the ideology of conscious seclusion that increasingly permeated many new suburban developments. In autocentric landscapes lacking public space, public transportation, and the other amenities of urban life, suburban Americans redefined community in new ways that minimized volunteerism, regular meetings with others, and communal outings. The experience of moving to and living in the suburbs could lead to a general awakening to environmental issues that contributed to the rising numbers of hikers, backpackers, and campers; however, most suburbanites chose to hike alone or with friends and family rather than contribute time, effort, and dues to a club.

For hikers, the results of this decline in community have been ambiguous. On one hand, this shift has been an overwhelming success: thousands of miles of new trail have been constructed, tens of millions of dollars have been invested in trails, federal and state agencies are more involved in trail development than ever before, and more Americans—tens of millions—are hiking. On the other hand, most Americans are unaware of the rich culture of hiking that has been lost, and there are no clear answers about what the rise of the consumer hiker means for the future of the hiking community. Hiking clubs have been progressive forces within the environmental community. As early as the mid-nineteenth century, women were invited to join—and in some cases lead—clubs, disseminate their ideas through newsletters and journals, and transcend contemporary norms to participate in outings to even the most daunting places. During a period of rampant industrialism and rapid urbanization, the leaders of hiking clubs called for protection of natural places and envisioned a more benevolent relationship with wilderness. The low cost of club membership, communal culture of helping others, and focus on introducing new people to nature all meant that clubs had an egalitarian outlook on their work that allowed members from many walks of life relative parity on the trail. The rich set of ideological justifications for hiking—its relation to patriotism, religion, and health—meant that middle-class hikers could subvert social norms and structures with minimal risk of being seen as countercultural.

There were also limits, however, to the democratic and progressive ethos of hiking culture. Hiking club leaders were typically pragmatic. Many came from backgrounds in engineering, business, law, and other fields that gave them central roles in the development of the modern United States. Even during the 1950s and 1960s, as the number of hikers increased, many of the new participants were able to hike thanks to the postwar economic boom, high levels of consumption, and associated increase in affluence and leisure time. As a result, hiking culture—like the modern environmental movement itself—was never a rejection of modern society. Rather, like the picturesque landscapes that early hikers of the nineteenth century found so appealing, it sought a balance between the natural and man-made worlds. Hiking was—and is—a means of experiencing nature that replenished the body and soul so as to better carry on the business of modern life. This made hiking an incredibly appealing pastime for Americans seeking brief, restorative engagement with nature and a sense of community but in effect limited the ability of hiking clubs to achieve the ideals they promoted.

The inequalities of society inevitably found their way into hiking clubs. Women, despite their prominence in many clubs, were sometimes limited to secondary roles as secretaries or newsletter editors rather than leaders, and traditional gender roles undoubtedly influenced—and in some cases restricted—how women experienced their time on the trail. The same held true for working-class and minority hikers. Many examples exist of clubs that were accepting of hikers of all backgrounds, including blacks, Hispanics, Asians, and others. Poor or working-class men and women could also participate in hiking clubs and, in some cases, take leadership roles based on their walking abilities rather than their income. In general, however, hiking clubs were composed of middle- and upper-middle-class whites who, consciously or not, developed a culture that discouraged participation by people unlike themselves.

Hiking culture, as a product of urbanization, industrialization, and modern America, struggled to fulfill its promise to mediate the human and natural worlds. The conservation and environmental movements achieved great victories in terms of preserving and expanding parks and open space, building trails, and protecting wildlife, but many of these achievements came at the expense of broader environmental protection and a cultural shift toward meaningful environmental stewardship. Hiking allowed many Americans to feel a deep sense of connection to the natural world—a sense of authenticity and primal knowledge—without really changing the way they lived their daily lives. Even with the rise of the Leave No Trace and low-impact ethic, few hikers recognized that their time on the trail required the consumption of gasoline, aluminum cook kits, and nylon tents, the printing of glossy magazines and maps, and the use of countless other products of modern life that contributed to environmental degradation yet made hiking possible.

The decline of hiking club membership during the 1960s and the transition from producer hiker to consumer hiker, therefore, was a shift from one rich—but potentially problematic—culture to another. Even within the organized hiking community, the meaning of hiking was contested as different groups argued that developments during the late twentieth century either improved or degraded the quality of hiking and trails in the United States. Individuals who began hiking in the 1940s and 1950s often watched significant changes unfold over their lifetime.

Earl Shaffer, the famous Appalachian Trail through-hiker, provides one example. On an early spring day in Georgia in 1948, Shaffer made his way through a series of knolls, some still sheathed in ice. The Appalachian Trail, which he had been following for about a week, was overgrown and poorly marked in this area, despite passing through Chattahoochee National Forest. Relying on road maps rather than a trail guide and, therefore, not knowing exactly where he was within the forest, Shaffer was surprised to come to a highway crossing near Wood Gap. Stashing his pack in the woods, he headed toward the nearby town of Suches, in the hopes of buying supplies. The only grocery store was small and poorly stocked, and when Shaffer asked for sugar, the cashier had to dig into her private supply. According to his journal, he also bought a quarter-pound of cheese, a loaf of bread—always brown bread, never the white, flimsy stuff—a box of matches, and a can of Vienna sausages. The presence of the strange man, heard to be traveling on the "Government Trail," attracted some locals to the store, and Shaffer made small talk with several of them. As he later remembered, "One was a little old mountain lady wearing an ancient shawl. 'You ain't agonna sleep on Old Bloody Mountain tonight, be ye?,' she queried. 'It's too wild lonesome up thar.'"[2] Since embarking from Mount Oglethorpe a week before, Shaffer had not gone a day without some type of exchange with a "mountain boy," a Forest Service crew, a farmer, or a picnicking family.

As Shaffer continued north from Georgia on what would become the first continuous through-hike of the 2,050-mile

Appalachian Trail, experiences passing along country roads and through small towns would play as meaningful a part in his journey as his time spent in isolated wilderness. In 1948, the trail ran for many miles along rural, dirt roads and through villages, often providing a social experience as much as a retreat from civilization. The result was that, although on the most brutal days Shaffer would refer to hiking as "an exquisite kind of torture," he did not find his journey especially difficult. In some sections blazing was poor, the trail was overgrown, and the going was rough, but Shaffer never questioned the actual route of the trail or the motives of the trail builders. Instead, he relished the periodic hardships and celebrated his communion with nature, chance encounters with other people, and the unique history of trailside communities. When he finished his 124-day journey at the summit of Mount Katahdin in Maine, the ensuing press rejuvenated the trail movement, encouraged subsequent throughhikes, and ensured that the Appalachian Trail would not fade into obscurity as some had feared.[3]

In 1998, at the age of seventy-nine, Shaffer walked the trail for a third and final time. A series of Associated Press articles and network television interviews documented the journey, which should have been yet another celebration of the trail and how far it had progressed since the years just following the war. Instead, Shaffer sent shock waves through the trails community by harshly criticizing changes to the trail. "In 1965 [the second time he walked the trail], the trail was perfect, but they were not satisfied. They [made] all these changes," Shaffer was quoted as saying. "They seem to be obsessed with the idea you have to make it as rough as possible." Elsewhere Shaffer referred to the trail as "an almost impossible trip" and "made up mostly of rocks, roots, and puddles." Of course, Shaffer continued to praise the ideals underlying the trail experience, but his overall impression of the trail was that "it was a good trip then [meaning, in 1948], better than it is now."[4]

Shaffer's observations about how the Appalachian Trail changed between 1948 and 1998 are suggestive of several major tensions in the American hiking community following the enactment of the National Trails System Act of 1968. Shaffer represented an element of the community that continued to think of hiking as a partially communal activity best practiced in a pastoral setting of deep forests interspersed with small towns, welcoming farms, and interesting characters. The majority of hikers in the nineteenth and early twentieth centuries shared this preference for hiking as a social experience. However, this preference began to shift toward solo or small group experiences in places envisioned to be wilderness. In contrast to Shaffer, these hikers interpreted preservation of the AT's wilderness character and similar changes on other trails to be significant progress. "The guidelines of the trail tell you you're supposed to be in the high country, looking at the landscape," David Field, a long-time trail maintainer responded to Shaffer's critique. "If you want to hike the shoulder of Interstate 95, that would be easier. But that's not what the trail is for."[5]

Contrary to Shaffer's overall impression of an increasingly wilderness experience on the Appalachian Trail, the trails movement of the late twentieth century tilted significantly toward urban and suburban regions and multiuse trails rather than rugged footpaths. President Johnson had hinted at this shift in emphasis in his February 1965 Natural Beauty message, and over the next few decades Congress responded with major legislation to fund multiple-use trails, primarily with federal transportation funds. Although there were significant funding sources throughout the 1970s and 1980s, including the Land and Water Conservation Fund, the first revolutionary funding cycle came in 1991, when President George H. W. Bush signed into law the Intermodal Surface Transportation Efficiency Act, which included a funding provision for nonmotorized commuter trails as part of the nation's intermodal transportation system. ISTEA—pronounced by most as "iced tea"—was followed by TEA-21, SAFETEA-LU, and MAP-21, each of which committed tens of millions of dollars to trails. Notably, the funding was available primarily to multiple-use trails that could claim eligibility as an alternative form of transportation. This meant that footpaths generally were left out of these funding sources.

Sometimes federal aid came in the form of changes to the law rather than funding. For example, in 1983, at a time when railroad companies were shedding unused lines, Congress amended the National Trails System Act of 1968 to allow municipalities and other entities to use the abandoned corridors for recreational trails. These well-engineered, graded, and wide paths became known as "rails-to-trails" paths or simply rail trails. This movement, which began in earnest during the 1980s, resulted in more than eighteen hundred rail trails totaling 21,600 miles by 2013, many of which were eligible for public funds during their construction.[6]

By the early twenty-first century, the new federal regime for trail building promised to revolutionize recreation and alternative transportation in the metropolitan regions that were savvy enough to secure grants. In 2010, for example, the U.S. Department of Transportation awarded twenty-three million dollars for the closing of ten critical gaps in Greater Philadelphia's regional trail network, including trails along canal towpaths and riverbanks, urban greenways, bicycle and pedestrian access ramps on busy highways, a bridge over two active railroad lines, and even a two-thousand-foot boardwalk suspended over the Schuylkill River. Even though the construction would result in only 16 miles of new trails, closing the gaps could potentially provide access to an interconnected network of at least 125 miles of multiuse paths. The proposal, which was drafted by two nonprofit advocacy organizations in partnership with Philadelphia mayor Michael Nutter's office, argued that the funding would "leverage decades of investment in walking and cycling trails, while recycling existing infrastructure, such as available right-of-way on existing urban streets." The funding came through the American Recovery and Reinvestment Act of 2009, which included $1.5 billion dollars for a new program that would become known as TIGER (Transportation Investment Generating Economic Recovery). TIGER was intended to support innovative transportation projects while stimulating the economy to create new employment opportunities. Philadelphia's proposal promised to provide jobs ranging "from senior engineers and planners that [sic] will serve as Project Managers; to engineering and planning

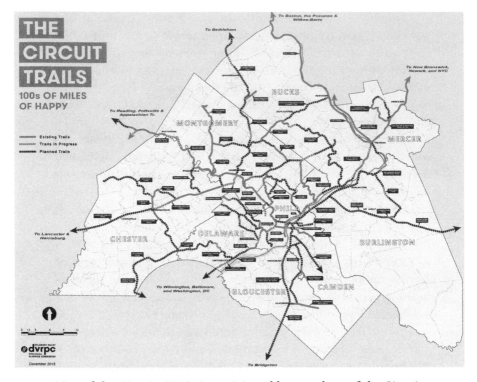

Map of the Circuit, 2015. As envisioned by members of the Circuit Coalition, the regional trail network will span southeastern Pennsylvania and portions of New Jersey. Major through trails, such as the East Coast Greenway, D&L Trail, and Schuylkill River Trail will connect the network to neighboring regions, states, and beyond. Courtesy of the Delaware Valley Regional Planning Commission.

graduates and interns retained at governments and non-profits, which will provide additional capacity for these organizations during project implementation." Furthermore, the enhanced trails would result in an estimated $970 million in mobility benefits, $19 million in recreation activity, and $542 million in public health savings. "The Circuit," as the trail network subsequently was branded, could potentially serve as a catalyst for the economic revitalization of the region.[7]

How could such lofty goals—economic renaissance, public health, alternative transportation—be associated with something as simple as a crushed limestone or paved path? As we have seen, the groundwork for the national trails movement had been set during the 1960s and institutionalized in the National Trails System Act of 1968. By the early twenty-first century, trails were widely regarded as a crucial element of recreation, transportation, and public health infrastructure that also—advocates noted—helped sustain a $646 billion outdoor recreation economy. As a result, individual communities and large regional coalitions across the country invested heavily to expand their trail networks. Minneapolis's park system, for example, included 50 miles of trails, while Des Moines, Iowa, and the surrounding region boasted a network of more than 450 miles. Fargo, North Dakota, built 90 miles of paths. Traverse City, Michigan, built 60. El Paso, Texas, built 20. The Carolina Thread Trail system consisted of 135 miles of trails spanning fifteen counties in North and South Carolina. Littleton, North Carolina, population 692, boasted of the world's shortest rail trail, at a quarter mile in length. Even the most unlikely of places, Brentwood, Tennessee—located in what has been called the most conservative county in America—had at least 20 miles of trails. Trails seemed to be everywhere.[8]

The proliferation of trails and large numbers of walkers masked an enduring problem. Although the hiking community became more diverse after 1968, hiking continued to be a pastime enjoyed by relatively affluent whites. In 2012, 70 percent of outdoor recreation participants were Caucasian, and 40 percent came from households earning more than seventy-five thousand dollars each year. Despite the work of the Sierra Club's Inner City Outings, the Appalachian Mountain Club's Youth Opportunity Program, YMCA services, Outward Bound trips, and numerous inner-city youth programs intended to encourage children of nonhikers to embrace the outdoors, the composition of the hiking community did not reflect the increasing diversity of the American population. In a January 2013 Internet discussion forum entitled "Why the Extreme Lack of Racial Diversity in the Hiking Community," a group of hikers guessed that the homogeneity resulted from a number of factors. Minorities "do not seek minimalistic entertainment to prove self worth," one commented. "It's hard for people who have been forced to do without to find pleasure in not having." Another hiker chalked it up to race: "We white Europeans grew up with a pioneering spirit. It's what our ancestors did." Others related it back to affluence and upbringing. "A large part of it is simply financial. Growing up in urban rather than suburban or rural settings with less exposure to the outdoors. Many white kids went to summer camps. Some parents had summer homes in the mountains, cars to be able to drive away from the cities. . . . Obviously it costs nothing to take a walk in the woods, but first you need to get to the woods." Last, one thoughtful commenter observed, "Even though [hiking] is somewhat of an anti-social activity, in the sense of getting away from society, it is still largely influenced by social factors." Although the hikers struggled to find answers, they were not alone. Reports by the National Park Service and commentary in national news outlets identified the same problem and similarly struggled to find a meaningful way forward in the face of complex structural factors that went far beyond recreation.[9]

The role of hiking organizations in national political discourse also became more complex during this time. Hiking clubs had traditionally played an important role in advocating for local and regional conservation issues and had at times, such as during the debate over the fate of Dinosaur National Monument, rallied for national preservation causes. They continued to do so during the era of environmentalism. For example, hikers joined canoers, fellow environmentalists, and displaced property owners during the 1960s to contest a proposed U.S. Army Corps of Engineers dam on the Delaware River at Tocks Island and the forty-mile-long reservoir it would have created. At nearby Sunfish Pond, a utility company purchased land from the state of New Jersey to build a pumped storage reservoir and hydroelectric project that would have inundated the pond, threatened its ecology, and disrupted the viewshed for the Appalachian Trail. In 1969, Supreme Court Justice William O. Douglas led more than a thousand supporters and journalists on a hike to the pond, where he declared, "Sunfish pond is a unique spot and deserves to be preserved." Both the dam at Tocks Island and the reservoir at Sunfish Pond were eventually defeated. Hikers led similar efforts throughout the nation in partnership with a growing coalition of environmental groups.[10]

For all of their successes, politics could also undermine the unity of the hiking community. Conflict within clubs could be especially troubling. The Sierra Club is the quintessential example. The club grew rapidly throughout the twentieth century thanks in part to its involvement with national preservation debates, but the club also established local chapters throughout the country that organized their own outings and focused on conservation causes specific to their area. The Pennsylvania chapter of the Sierra Club, for example, was established in the early 1970s and has since been an advocate for public land stewardship, air and water quality, and protective regulations. In the early twenty-first century, the chapter came to focus on the potentially harmful impact of hydraulic fracturing, or "fracking," which is a method used to release natural gas from the shale formations underneath portions of northern and western Pennsylvania. The chapter found an ally in the Keystone Trails Association (KTA), which shared its concern for recreation, trails, and opposition to fracking. A coalition of AT maintaining clubs had founded the KTA in 1956 to serve as an advocate for their shared interests, but in the 1970s, the organization expanded to cover all long-distance footpaths in the state. The coalition between the Sierra Club chapter and the KTA allowed the groups to focus public scrutiny on trails threatened by fracking, such as the Old Logger's Path, a twenty-seven-mile loop trail that follows former logging roads through what is now deep forest in Loyalsock State Forest. "As hikers and volunteer trail maintainers we believe in the responsible management of our public lands, that government will be transparent and fair, and that our volunteer work will be respected by Harrisburg," the coalition explained in a press release. "The Governor should not be working in secrecy to get the most money for drilling in this critical habitat; but rather should be working publicly to get the most protection for it."

Fracking in Loyalsock State Forest, Pennsylvania. In the twenty-first century, environmental politics have created divisions within the hiking community and elevated tensions between national environmental groups and their local chapters. Courtesy of Jane Partiger, EcoFlight.

This type of advocacy was similar to that practiced by hiking clubs for more than a century, as they sought to protect the landscapes through which they hiked.[11]

For the Sierra Club members, however, the local chapter's advocacy against fracking and criticism of the governor for accepting money from drillers highlighted a dissonance between local groups of hikers and the national organization. The national Sierra Club organization had long condoned natural gas as a transitional energy source between fossil fuels and renewables. Between 2007 and 2010, energy companies involved with fracking contributed more than twenty-five million dollars to the Sierra Club's Beyond Coal campaign, and the club's executive director, Carl Pope, toured the country with one company's CEO to tout the benefits of natural gas. The tour coincided with the rise of grassroots opposition in places like West Virginia, Pennsylvania, and New York. "Will the 20 percent of the membership that happens to live in places where drilling is happening be unhappy?" Pope asked. "I'm sure that's true." Pope's stance was a reversal of the argument put forward by John Muir and other early club members during the debate over Yosemite's Hetch Hetchy Valley, when they argued for the value of a specific and relatively small place over economic or regional imperatives. Now the national club seemed to be arguing that the old principles were no longer relevant. The national office's stance "makes us look like the extremists that the industry wants to call us anyway," said Beth Little, a board member of the Sierra Club's West Virginia chapter, which was also fighting fracking in its area. The outcry from members forced Pope to relinquish his role as executive director in 2010. He served on the board of directors for two years before resigning once and for all. The new executive director, Michael Brune, subsequently vacated all agreements with the energy companies. "The chapter groups and volunteers depend on the Club to have their back as they fight pollution from any industry," Brune noted, "and we need to be unrestrained in our advocacy." Whether the members of local chapters will remain loyal to the Sierra Club in the coming decades remains to be seen.[12]

Despite all of the developments noted above—from the rise of rail trails and federal transportation funding to struggles with diversity and national versus regional imperatives—most hiking clubs remained remarkably unchanged from the 1960s. Salt Lake City's Wasatch Mountain Club, for example, was founded in 1920 "to promote the physical and spiritual well being of its members and others by outdoor activities." More than eighty years later, the club continues to meet regularly, hosting an annual awards dinner, a Pink Flamingo Party, trail work trips, and—of course— regular hikes of varying difficulty throughout the Wasatch Mountains and the region around Salt Lake City. The same is true of clubs throughout the country—in Minneapolis, Anchorage, Boise, Hartford, Allentown, Atlanta, Austin, and hundreds of other cities and towns. When club members come together they are motivated by many of the same ideas that have always invested hiking with meaning. Many hike for health, for an outlet from modern life, for socialization with like-minded folks, for the natural beauty and curious places through which they pass, and—yes—some continue to think of hiking as a religious experience, as a means of experiencing God. As Flint, Michigan's ArrowHead Hiking Club motto puts it—in a succinct blending of old and new principles—"Leave no trace, and spread God's grace." Given the remarkable staying power of traditional clubs, we can expect them to remain essential to the hiking community in the future, even as a growing percentage of consumer hikers and backpackers forgo their ranks in preference of hiking alone.

It is not clear what the future holds for the American hiking community. We have seen that pleasure walking emerged when Americans were being freed from daily travel by foot. As an unstable economy and high gas prices compel more people to use self-propelled forms of transportation for the majority of their daily needs, many twenty-first-century Americans will return to the "walking city" model of the nineteenth century. Others will do so out of choice, as they return to revitalized cities or new planned communities where they can walk or bike instead of driving. In this new context, how easily will regular walkers romanticize the act of walking in the woods? Is it possible that, compelled to walk every day, they will no longer need to labor vicariously through recreation? Such a scenario is a long way off. For now, tens of millions of Americans are satisfied to hike, whether together or alone, on the trail.

NOTES

CHAPTER 1: THE ORIGINS OF AMERICAN NATURE WALKING

1. Henry David Thoreau, "Walking," *Atlantic Magazine* (June 1862): 658.

2. Leo Marx, *The Machine in the Garden: Technology and the Pastoral Ideal in America* (New York: Oxford University Press, 1964), 4.

3. Dorothy Wordsworth, *Journals of Dorothy Wordsworth*, 2nd ed., ed. Mary Moorman (New York: Oxford University Press, 1971), 133.

4. Ibid., 34, 127, 128, 129.

5. David Bjelajac, "Thomas Cole's *Oxbow* and the American Zion Divided," *American Art* 20 (Spring 2006): 60–83; Ellwood C. Parry, "Overlooking the Oxbow: Thomas Cole's 'View from Mount Holyoke' Revisited," *American Art Journal* 34 (2003): 6–61.

6. Paul Schneider, *The Adirondacks: A History of America's First Wilderness* (New York: Henry Holt, 1997), 157–159; Thomas Cole in Louis Legrand Noble, *The Life and Works of Thomas Cole*, 3rd ed. (New York: Sheldon, Blakeman, 1856), 206; Joel T. Headley, *The Adirondack; or, Life in the Woods* (New York: Baker and Scribner, 1851), 70.

7. Ralph Waldo Emerson, *The American Scholar: An Address Delivered by Ralph Waldo Emerson before the Phi Beta Kappa Society at Cambridge, August 1837* (New York: Laurentia Press, 1901), 58–59; Thoreau, "Walking," 658.

8. Henry David Thoreau, *The Maine Woods* (Boston: Ticknor and Fields, 1864), 60, 64.

9. Thoreau, "Walking," 658.

10. Aaron Sachs, "American Arcadia: Mount Auburn Cemetery and the Nineteenth-Century Landscape Tradition," *Environmental History* 15 (April 2010): 208–209.

11. Blanche M. G. Linden, *Silent City on a Hill: Picturesque Landscapes of Memory and Boston's Mount Auburn Cemetery* (Amherst: University of Massachusetts Press, 2007), 21; Henry Wadsworth Longfellow, *Outre-Mer: A Pilgrimage beyond the Sea*, 8th ed. (Boston: Ticknor and Fields, 1856), 85, 81.

12. Trustees of the Green-Wood Cemetery, *Exposition of the Plan and Objects of the Green-Wood Cemetery* (New York: Narine, 1839), 18.

13. David Schuyler, *The New Urban Landscape: The Redefinition of City Form in Nineteenth-Century America* (Baltimore: Johns Hopkins University Press, 1986), 42; *The Picturesque Pocket Companion and Visitor's Guide through Mount Auburn* (Boston: Otis, Broaders, 1839), 10, 23, 56, 59–60; Alexander Wadsworth, "Plan of Mount Auburn," map (Cambridge, Mass.: Pendleton's Lithography, November 1831).

14. *Guide through Mount Auburn*, 13.

15. Ibid., 14, 48.

16. "Greenwood Cemetery," *Knickerbocker* 14 (August 1839): 201; Wellington Williams, *Appleton's New and Complete United States Guide Book for Travelers* (Philadelphia: D. Appleton, 1850), 140.

17. Schuyler, *New Urban Landscape*, 37, 54–55; Andrew Jackson Downing, "A Talk about Public Parks and Gardens," *Horticulturalist* 3 (October 1848): 157; "Central Park," *Scribner's Monthly* 6 (September 1873): 529.

18. Patrick Malone and Charles Parrott, "Greenways in the Industrial City: Parks and Promenades along the Lowell Canals," *IA: Journal of the Society for Industrial Archaeology* 24 (1998): 19–40; "Shade Trees," *Lowell Offering* (April 1841): 233.

19. John Greenleaf Whittier in Malone and Parrott, "Greenways in the Industrial City," 30; Sidney and Neff, *Plan of the City of Lowell, Massachusetts*, map (Philadelphia: S. Moody, 1850).

20. National Canal Museum, *Delaware and Lehigh Canals: A Pictorial History of the Delaware and Lehigh Canals National Heritage Corridor in Pennsylvania* (Easton, Pa.: Canal History and Technology Press, 2005), 83.

21. Charles Rosenberg, *The Cholera Years: The United States in 1832, 1849, and 1866* (Chicago: Chicago University Press, 1962); Letter to the Editor, "A Central Park," *New-York Daily Times*, June 4, 1853.

22. Roy Rosenzweig and Elizabeth Blackmar, *The Park and the People: A History of Central Park* (Ithaca, N.Y.: Cornell University Press, 1992).

23. Frederick Law Olmsted and Calvert Vaux, "Greensward Plan" (1858), Central Park Conservancy, http://www.centralparkhistory.com/timeline/timeline_1850_greensward.html.

24. Rosenzweig and Blackmar, *Park and People*, 246.

25. Roy Rosenzweig, *Eight Hours for What We Will: Workers and Leisure in an Industrial City, 1870–1920* (New York: Cambridge University Press, 1983), 137.

26. Lucy Larcom, *A New England Girlhood: Outlined from Memory* (Boston: Houghton Mifflin, 1889), 163.

27. Samuel Pepys, *The Diary and Correspondence of Samuel Pepys*, 2nd ed., ed. Richard Braybrooke (Philadelphia: David McKay, 1889), 80; Peter Radford, *The Celebrated Captain Barclay: Sport, Money and Fame in Regency Britain* (London: Headline, 2001), 2; "Captain Barclay," *Maryland Gazette*, September 20, 1809.

28. Edward Weston, *"The Pedestrian": Being a Correct Journal of "Incidents" on a Walk from the State House, Boston, Mass., to the U.S. Capitol, at Washington, D.C., Performed in "Ten Consecutive Days," between February 22nd and March 4th, 1861* (New York: Edward Payson Weston, 1862), 5, 10, 30.

29. "The Great Walking Feat near St. Louis; Triumph of Curtis," *New York Daily Times*, October 12, 1855; "The 'Unknown' Won It," *Bethlehem Globe Times*, January 2, 1890.

30. Matthew Algeo, *Pedestrianism: When Watching People Walk Was America's Favorite Spectator Sport* (Chicago: Chicago Review Press, 2014).

31. "The Whortleberry Excursion," *Lowell Offering* (April 1841): 177–181.

32. Verplanck Colvin, "The Helderbergs," *Harper's New Monthly Magazine*, October 1869, 660.

33. "Obituary: Prof. John Torrey," *New York Times*, March 11, 1873.

34. Raymond Torrey, "Prefatory," *Bulletin of the Torrey Botanical Club* 1 (January 1870): 1; T. F. Allen, "The Oenothera of Montauk Point, Long Island," *Bulletin of the Torrey Botanical Club* 1 (January 1870): 2; I. H. Hall, "Trillium erectum, L., Var. album," *Bulletin of the Torrey Botanical Club* 1 (June 1870): 21.

35. T. F. Allen in Patrick Cooney, "Accumulated and Arranged Notes for a History of the Torrey Botanical Society" (Torrey Botanical Society, November 7, 2000), http://nynjctbotany.org/tbshist/histtofc.html.

36. "Obituary: Prof. John Torrey."

37. Laura Waterman and Guy Waterman, *Forest and Crag: A History of Hiking, Trailblazing and Adventure in the Northeast Mountains* (Boston: Appalachian Mountain Club, 1989), 185.

38. Sam Bass Warner Jr., *Streetcar Suburbs: The Process of Growth in Boston, 1870–1900*, 2nd ed. (Cambridge, Mass.: Harvard University Press, 1978), 15; Samuel Augustus Mitchell, "City of New York," lithograph engraving, *A New Universal Atlas Containing Maps of the Various Empires, Kingdoms, States and Republics of the World* (Philadelphia: S. Augustus Mitchell, 1850).

39. Warner, *Streetcar Suburbs*, 15; Clay McShane, *Down the Asphalt Path: The Automobile and the American City* (New York: Columbia University Press, 1994), 3–15; Charles Dickens, "Street Sketches No. 1," *Morning Chronicle* (London), September 26, 1834.

40. Henry C. Binford, *The First Suburbs: Residential Communities on the Boston Periphery, 1815–1860* (Chicago: University of Chicago Press, 1985), 126, 129, 137.

41. Waterman and Waterman, *Forest and Crag*, 190; "Introductory," *Appalachia* 2 (June 1876): 1; "Constitution," *Appalachia* 2 (June 1876): 3; "Officers and Members," *Appalachia* 2 (June 1876): 5–6.

CHAPTER 2: HIKING TOGETHER

1. Invitation, March 2, 1876, Papers of the Appalachian Mountain Club, Appalachian Mountain Club, Private Collection, Boston. Hereafter cited as AMC Papers; "Proceedings of the Club," *Appalachia* 1 (June 1876): 58; Charles Fay, "A Day on Tripyramid," *Appalachia* 1 (June 1876): 16; "Proceedings of the Club," 58.

2. Stuart Blumin, *The Emergence of the Middle Class: Social Experience in the American City, 1760–1900* (New York: Cambridge University Press, 1989), 192–229.

3. Edward Charles Pickering, "The Annual Address of the President," *Appalachia* 1 (March 1877): 63.

4. Alfred Goldsborough Mayor, "Samuel Hubbard Scudder, 1837–1911," *Memoirs National* 17 (Washington, D.C.: National Academy of Sciences, 1919), 82.

5. Samuel H. Scudder, "The Alpine Club of Williamstown, Mass.," *Appalachia* (December 1884): 46–48.

6. Ibid.

7. Ibid., 49.

8. Ibid., 47–48.

9. Ibid., 51.

10. Ibid., 54.

11. Ibid., 46–47.

12. Pickering, "Annual Address of the President," 64; Edward Elwell, "Ascent of Mt. Carrigain," *Portland Transcript*, September 13, 1873; Edward Elwell and G. Frederick Morse, "A Song of Mt. Carrigain" (1873), 7–9, 12.

13. Theodore Roosevelt, *The Strenuous Life: Essays and Addresses* (New York: Century, 1902), 3; Tom Lutz, *American Nervousness, 1903: An Anecdotal History* (Ithaca, N.Y.: Cornell University Press, 1991), 34, 78–80, 99; T. J. Jackson Lears, *Rebirth of a Nation: The Making of Modern America, 1877–1920* (New York: HarperCollins, 2010), 69.

14. John M. Gould, diary, June 8, 1875, available at https://www.mainememory.net/artifact/37321.

15. Ibid., June 9, 1875.

16. Ibid., June 9, 10, 11, 1875.

17. Ibid., June 9, 11, 1875.

18. William Henry Harrison, *Adventures in the Wilderness; or, Camp-Life in the Adirondacks* (Boston: Fields, Osgood, 1869); John M. Gould, *How to Camp Out: Hints for Camping and Walking* (New York: Scribner, Armstrong, 1877), 11, 14, 57.

19. Gould, *How to Camp Out*, 58–59; Julie Boardman, *When Women and Mountains Meet: Adventures in the White Mountains* (Lyme, N.H.: Durand Press, 2001).

20. Pickering, "Annual Address of the President," 64; "Proceedings of the Club," 58–59.

21. "Introductory," *Appalachia* 1 (June 1876): 1; "Reports of the Councillors," *Appalachia* 1 (June 1876): 45.

22. Charles Fay, "The Annual Address of the President," *Appalachia* 2 (June 1879): 3.

23. Edward Pickering, "Heights of the White Mountains," *Appalachia* 4 (December 1886): 305–322.

24. Ibid., 316; Charles Hitchcock, "Reports of the Councillors for the Spring of 1876," *Appalachia* 1 (June 1876): 41–43.

25. Fay, "Annual Address of the President," 11–12; "Secretary's Report for 1879," *Appalachia* 2 (June 1879): 152.

26. Edwin M. Bacon, *Walks and Rides in the Country round about Boston: Covering Thirty-Six Cities and Towns, Parks and Public Reservations, within a Radius of Twelve Miles from the State House* (Boston: Houghton Mifflin, 1897), 6.

27. Wilbur B. Parker, "Reports of the Councillors; Improvements," *Appalachia* 2 (June 1879): 76.

28. Laura Waterman and Guy Waterman, *Forest and Crag: A History of Hiking, Trailblazing and Adventure in the Northeast Mountains* (Boston: Appalachian Mountain Club, 1989), 202.

29. William G. Nowell, "Reports of the Councillors for the Spring of 1876; Improvements," *Appalachia* 1 (June 1876): 51–55.

30. Waterman and Waterman, *Forest and Crag*, 203; Nowell, "Reports of the Councillors for the Autumn of 1876; Improvements," 110–111.

31. A. E. Scott, "Report of the Councillors for the Spring of 1880; Improvements," *Appalachia* 2 (July 1880): 184.

32. John Muir, *John of the Mountains: The Unpublished Journals of John Muir*, ed. Linnie Marsh Wolfe (Madison: University of Wisconsin Press, 1979), 2; John Muir, "A Thousand Mile Walk to the Gulf," *John Muir: The Eight Wilderness-Discovery Books* (Seattle: Mountaineers Books, 1992), 119.

33. Muir, "A Thousand Mile Walk to the Gulf," 62.

34. Ibid., 129.

35. Michael Cohen, *The History of the Sierra Club, 1892–1970* (San Francisco: Sierra Club Books, 1988), 9; William Armes to John Muir, May 15, 1891, John Muir Correspondence Collection, University of California.

36. William Gladstone Steel, "Preliminary History of the Mazamas," *Mazama* 1 (1896): 12.

37. William Gladstone Steel, *The Mountains of Oregon* (Portland, Oreg.: David Steel, 1890), 69, 83–84; Harvey Scott, *History of Portland, Oregon with Illustrations and Biographical Sketches of Prominent Citizens and Pioneers* (Syracuse, N.Y.: D. Mason, 1890), 630; "The Olympic Range; A Member of an Exploring Party Tells of Its Wonders," *Spokane Falls Chronicle*, December 23, 1890.

38. John Muir to William Armes, May 26, 1891, John Muir Correspondence Collection, University of California; Susan Schrepfer, citing 1891 correspondence between Berkeley professor William Armes and John Muir, credits Armes with proposing the Sierra Club. Susan Schrepfer, *Nature's Altars: Mountains, Gender, and American Environmentalism* (Lawrence: University Press of Kansas, 2005), 23; Cohen, *History of the Sierra Club*, 8.

39. Cohen, *History of the Sierra Club*, 9.

40. "Proceedings of the Sierra Club," *Sierra Club Bulletin* 1 (January 1893): 23–24.

41. Cohen, *History of the Sierra Club*, 12; Hal Rothman, *The Greening of a Nation? Environmentalism in the United States since 1945* (New York: Harcourt Brace, 1998), 19; Stephen Fox, *The American Conservation Movement: John Muir and His Legacy* (Madison: University of Wisconsin Press, 1986); Donald Worster, *A Passion for Nature: The Life of John Muir* (New York: Oxford University Press, 2008), 330–331.

42. Allen Chaffee, *Adventures on the High Trail* (Springfield, Mass.: Milton Bradley, 1923), 54.

43. Charles D. Robinson quoted in Holway R. Jones, *John Muir and the Sierra Club: The Battle for Yosemite* (San Francisco: Sierra Club, 1965), 57; Cohen, *History of the Sierra Club*, 13–17.

44. Steel, "Preliminary History of the Mazamas," 13, 14; "Smoking Mountain; The Mazamas Will Soon Climb Mount Hood," *Morning Oregonian* July 8, 1894.

45. E. Fay Fuller, "Historian's Report for 1894," *Mazama* 1 (1896): 16.

46. William G. Steel, "President's Address for 1894," *Mazama* 1 (1896): 22; J. D. Newman, "The Invasion of Hood," *Morning Oregonian*, July 9, 1894.

47. "Plan of the 'Mazamas' for This Year," *Morning Oregonian*, April 4, 1895; "The Mazamas Happy," *Morning Oregonian*, May 2, 1895; "Letters to Mazamas," *Morning Oregonian*, April 25, 1895; "Words from the Sun," *Morning Oregonian*, April 14, 1895; T. Brook White, "Historian's Report for 1896," *Mazama* 1 (1897): 273.

48. E. Fay Fuller, "Historian's Report for 1894," *Mazama* 1 (1896): 17.

49. "Smoking Mountain"; Roosevelt, *Strenuous Life*, 3; C. H. Sholes, "President's Address for 1896," *Mazama* 1 (1897): 276.

50. John H. Cameron, "Shall American Climbers Adopt European Methods?" *Mazama* 2 (December 1905): 218; C. H. Sholes, editorial note in John H. Cameron, "Shall American Climbers Adopt European Methods?" *Mazama* 2 (December 1905): 219.

51. "Gathering of the Goats; First Annual Bleating Conclave of the Mount Hood Mazamas," *Morning Oregonian*, September 24, 1894.

52. C. H. Sholes, "President's Annual Address, 1904," *Mazama* 2 (December 1905): 260; Gertrude Metcalfe, "The Rainier Climb," *Mazama* 2 (December 1905): 230–231; M. W. Gorman, "The Complexities of the Diamond Hitch," *Mazama* 2 (December 1905): 42–47.

53. Sholes, "President's Annual Address, 1904," 260–261.

54. William Brooks, "With Sierrans and Mazamas," *Appalachia* 11 (May 1906): 114–117, 124; Charles Fay, "Through Appalachian Eyes," *Mazama* 2 (December 1905): 208–211.

55. "List of Members" *Mazama* 2 (December 1905): 281–284; "Report of the Secretary," *Sierra Club Bulletin* 6 (June 1907): 197; "Report of the Secretary," *Sierra Club Bulletin* 6 (June 1908): 316.

56. Brooks, "With Sierrans and Mazamas," 124.

CHAPTER 3: THE RISE OF AMERICAN HIKING CULTURE

1. *Republican* (Meyersdale, Pa.), June 19, 1921; "A Little History of Mt. Davis," *Meyersdale Republican*, September 16, 1950.

2. "Large Boulder Unveiled in Honor of Reading Man," *Reading Eagle*, June 26, 1933.

3. Frederick Jackson Turner, "The Significance of the Frontier in American History," in *The Frontier in American History* (New York: Henry Holt, 1921), 37.

4. Theodore Roosevelt, *The Strenuous Life: Essays and Addresses* (New York: Century, 1902), 3.

5. John Higham, "The Reorientation of American Culture in the 1890s," *Writing American History: Essays on Modern Scholarship* (Bloomington: Indiana University Press, 1970), 79–83.

6. William James, "The Moral Equivalent of War," *McClure's Magazine*, August 1910, 463, 465–468.

7. Char Miller, *Gifford Pinchot and the Making of Modern Environmentalism* (Washington, D.C.: Island Press, 2001), 338.

8. John Muir, *Our National Parks* (Boston: Houghton Mifflin, 1901), 1.

9. Donald Worster, *A Passion for Nature: The Life of John Muir* (New York: Oxford University Press, 2008), 433.

10. "September 26, 1978," CHC Camp Log, Book 1, 1933–1967, papers of the Cleveland Hiking Club, Western Reserve Historical Society, Cleveland, Ohio, hereafter cited as CHC Papers; "October 7, 1945," CHC Camp Log, Book 1, 1933–1967, CHC Papers.

11. For a detailed history of the Pennsylvania hiking community, see Silas Chamberlin, "'A True Recreation of Our Spirits, Our Courage, and Our Love': Hiking Ideology in Twentieth-Century Pennsylvania" (M.A. thesis, Lehigh University, 2008); and Chamberlin, "To Ensure Permanency: Expanding and Protecting Hiking Opportunities in Twentieth-Century Pennsylvania," *Pennsylvania History* 77 (Spring 2010): 193–216.

12. Simon Bronner, *Popularizing Pennsylvania: Henry W. Shoemaker and the Progressive Uses of Folklore and History* (State College: Pennsylvania State University Press, 1996), 57; Henry W. Shoemaker, *Black Forest Souvenirs* (N.p.: N.p., 1914), xv–xvii.

13. Bronner, *Popularizing Pennsylvania*, 26; Henry W. Shoemaker and Joseph S. Illick, eds., *In Penn's Woods: A Handy and Helpful Pocket Manual of the Natural Wonders and Recreational Facilities of the State Forests of Pennsylvania* (Harrisburg, Pa.: Pennsylvania Department of Forests and Waters, 1925), 77.

14. J. Herbert Walker, ed., *The Pennsylvania Mountaineer: Third Annual Publication of the Pennsylvania Alpine Club* (Altoona, Pa.: Times Tribune Press, 1921), 14; Barbara Wiemann, ed., *Pennsylvania Hiking Trails*, 12th ed. (Cogan Station, Pa.: Keystone Trails Association, 1988), 62.

15. Sheila Carmody, *York Daily Record*, February 16, 1998; Book I, 18, 95, [1934], papers of the York Hiking Club, York Heritage Trust, York, Pennsylvania, hereafter cited as YHC Papers; *Batona* vol. 30, no. 1 (Spring–Summer 1958), 6. One nearly complete run of *Batona* is located in the papers of Orestes Unti, Urban Archives, Temple University, Philadelphia; newsletter, 1941, papers of the Susquehanna Trailers Hiking Club, private collection; hereafter cited as STHC Papers.

16. Throughout Gifford's childhood and early training as a forester, his father, James Pinchot, emphasized the need "to see God in Nature," and Gifford even referred to his career as "God's work." Miller, *Gifford Pinchot*, 61, 100, 189.

17. "Meeting Minutes," September 29, 1940, papers of the Blue Mountain Eagle Climbing Club, Historical Society of Berks County, Reading, Pennsylvania, hereafter cited as BMECC Papers; "Large Boulder Unveiled in Honor of Reading Man," *Reading Eagle*, June 26, 1933; *Batona*, 1932; hike schedule, February 1959, STHC Papers.

18. Aron, *Working at Play*; Marguerite Shaffer, *See America First: Tourism and National Identity, 1880–1940* (Washington, D.C.: Smithsonian Books, 2001).

19. Newsletter, 1941, STHC Papers; *Batona* vol. 6, no. 1 (April 1934), 9.

20. Walker, *Pennsylvania Mountaineer*, 16.

21. "York Is on the March," 1942, YHC Papers; *Batona*, vol. 14, no. 1 (Spring–Summer 1942), 9; *Batona*, vol. 14, no. 2 (Fall–Winter 1942), 2; D. K. Hoch, President, to Members, October 8, 1942, BMECC Papers.

22. Emma Doeserich, Mary Sherburne, and Anna B. Wey, eds., *Outdoors with the Prairie Club* (Chicago: Paquin, 1941), vii; Cathy Jean Maloney, *Images of America: The Prairie Club of Chicago* (Chicago: Arcadia, 2001), 6–7.

23. Robert Grese, *Jens Jensen: Maker of Natural Parks and Gardens* (Baltimore: Johns Hopkins University Press, 1992); Jens Jensen, "The Dunes; Dawn," in Doeserich, Sherburne, and Wey, *Outdoors with the Prairie Club*, 77; Samuel A. Harper, *My Woods* (Chicago: Book Fellows, 1923), 22; Maloney, *Prairie Club of Chicago*, 104–105.

24. Edna K. Wooley, "D'You Want to Be a Hiker?" *Cleveland News,* March 17, 1919; "Hiking Enthusiasts Will Retrace Steps of First Journey," *Berea News,* March 10, 1950; "Constitution of the Cleveland Hiking Club," CHC Papers.

25. "Pleasure at a Walking Pace," *Milwaukee Journal,* May 12, 1968; "Minutes of the Organizational Meeting of the GO Club Held March 2, 1924," papers of the Wisconsin GO Club, private collection, hereafter cited as GO Club Papers; "Wisconsin GO Club," n.d., and speaking notes [1930s], GO Club Papers; Speaking notes [1930s], GO Club Papers; *Go Club News,* July–August 1935, GO Club Papers; Hike schedule [1920s], GO Club Papers.

26. Carl Hub, "To the Members of the Wisconsin GO Hiking Club," *GO Club News,* April 1935, GO club Papers; "Trail Blazer's Report, April 1934 to April 1935," *GO Club News,* April 1935, GO Club Papers.

27. Meeting minutes, May 29, 1925, GO Club Papers; "Seeing Nature on Foot," *GO Club News,* June 1935, GO club papers; "What Other Hiking Clubs are Doing," *GO Club News* [1936], GO Club Papers.

28. Doeserich, Sherburne, and Wey, *Outdoors with the Prairie Club*, vii.

29. "December 28, 1941," CHC Camp Log, Book 1, 1933–1967, CHC Papers; Florence Burrell and Chester Boron, "The Cleveland Hiking Club 55th Anniversary," [1974?] and N.p., 27, CHC Papers; "Automobiles and the GO Club," *Go Club News,* 1942, GO Club Papers; "From the Editor's Pen," *Go Club News,* December 1933, GO Club Papers.

30. Louise Cattoi, "Autumn Shows Treasures to Hiking Club Members," *Milwaukee Journal,* October 4, 1943; "Boys at Camp," *GO Club News,* April 1941?, GO Club Papers; Keepsake photo book, CHC papers.

31. Margaret Bruhlman, "Know Your Chicago Tours," in Doeserich, Sherburne, and Wey, *Outdoors with the Prairie Club*, 315–322.

32. Jensen, "Dunes; Dawn," 77; Carl T. Robertson, "Wildflower Conservation: Written for the Cleveland Hiking Club," 1919, CHC papers; Christmas party and installation banquet bulletin, 1940, Scrapbook of CHC Programs, 1924–1983, CHC Papers.

33. "Free Healing," *GO Club News,* 1934?, GO Club Papers.

34. "Seeing Nature on Foot," *GO Club News*, June 1935, GO Club Papers; Emma Ellefson, "Our Club," *GO Club News*, November 1934, GO Club Papers.

35. *Outing Magazine* 57 (1911).

36. Anna Marie Stefanick, "Smoky Mountains Hiking Club Diamond Anniversary, 1924–1999," www.smhclub.org/Diamond/diamond1.htm; Carol Niedzaliek, ed., *A Footpath in the Wilderness: The Early Days of PATC* (Vienna, Va.: Potomac Appalachian Trail Club), 8–29; Carolina Mountain Club, "History," www.carolinamountainclub.org/index.cfm/do/pages.view/id/39/page/History; Charles Foster, *The Appalachian National Scenic Trail: A Time to Be Bold* (Harpers Ferry, W.Va.: Appalachian Trail Conference, 1987), 99.

37. Jim Kjeldsen, *The Mountaineers: A History* (Seattle: Mountaineers Books, 1998), 13; "Recapitulation of Membership," *Trail and Timberline* 1 (April 1918): 11.

38. On climbing history, see Joseph Taylor, *Pilgrims of the Vertical: Yosemite Rock Climbers and Nature at Risk* (Cambridge, Mass.: Harvard University Press, 2010).

39. Fred Harris to the Editor, *Dartmouth*, December 7, 1909, papers of the Dartmouth Outing Club, Special Collections, Dartmouth University, Hanover, New Hampshire, hereafter cited as DOC Papers; Burt Boyum and Jamie LaFreniere, *The Ishpeming Ski Club: Over a Century of Skiing* (Ishpeming, Mich: United States National Ski and Snowboard Hall of Fame Museum, 2003); Fred Harris to the Editor, *Dartmouth*, DOC Papers.

40. Editorial, *Dartmouth*, January 11, 1910, DOC Papers.

41. "About Winter Carnival," n.d., 2, DOC Papers; Fred Harris, "Winter meet given by Outing Club, Ski and Snowshoe Championship, Golf Links," February 26, 1910, DOC Papers.

42. "Dartmouth Outing Club," *Aegis* 56 (1914): 372; Fred Harris, "Skiing over the New Hampshire Hills," *National Geographic*, February 1920, 160–161; "About Winter Carnival," DOC Papers; J. Kenneth Sullivan, "A History of the Finances of the Dartmouth Outing Club from 1910 to 1930," March 31, 1931, 4, 23.

43. Fred Harris, "Dartmouth Men Plan Line of Camps in White Mountains," *Boston Herald*, April 20, 1913.

44. Obituary, "Rev. John Edgar Johnson," n.p., November 2, 1934.

45. Christopher Johnson, *This Grand and Magnificent Place: The Wilderness Heritage of the White Mountains* (Lebanon: University of New Hampshire Press, 2006), 172.

46. John E. Johnson, *Help for the Hills; The Boa Constrictor of the White Mountains; or, The Worst "Trust" in the World: An Account of the New Hampshire Land Company, a Corporation Chartered to Depopulate and Deforest a Section of the White Mountains* (North Woodstock, N.H.:

John E. Johnson, 1900), 5; Leslie F. Murch to John E. Johnson, December 16, 1922, DOC Papers.

47. Carl E. Shumway to Dan P. Hatch, November 2, 1934, DOC Papers; Obituary, "Rev. John Edgar Johnson"; Shumway to Hatch, November 2, 1934.

48. Sullivan, "A History of the Finances of the Dartmouth Outing Club from 1910 to 1930," 13; John E. Johnson letter, February 13, 1915, DOC Papers; Johnson to Secretary, Dartmouth Outing Club, May 14, 1921, DOC Papers; Obituary, "Rev. John Edgar Johnson."

49. W. See Whule to John E. Johnson, September 15, 1915, DOC Papers.

50. Chairman, Dartmouth Outing Club Council, to John E. Johnson, November 22, 1920, DOC Papers.

51. Dartmouth Outing Club, *Dartmouth Out-o'-Doors* (Hanover, N.H.: Dartmouth College, 1931), 6; Sullivan, "History of the Finances of the Dartmouth Outing Club," 2; Cabin and Trail Meeting Minutes, February 23, 1928, DOC Papers.

52. Sullivan, "A History of the Finances of the Dartmouth Outing Club," 11; Johnson to Secretary, Dartmouth Outing Club, May 14, 1921, DOC Papers; Dartmouth Outing Club, *Dartmouth Out-o'-Doors;* Harris, "Skiing over the New Hampshire Hills," 151–152.

53. *Aegis* 56 (1914): 371; Johnson to President, DOC, April 7, 1915, DOC Papers; Johnson to Secretary, Dartmouth Outing Club, May 14, 1921, DOC Papers.

54. Chairman, DOC Council, to Johnson, November 22, 1920, DOC Papers; Sullivan, "History of the Finances of the Dartmouth Outing Club," 2.

55. Fred Harris to C. C. Throop, May 12, 1921, DOC Papers; Fred Harris to Dartmouth Outing Club, December 6, 1930, DOC Papers.

56. B. W. Gills to Johnson, February 24, 1915, DOC Papers.

57. Dartmouth Outing Club, *Dartmouth Out-O'-Doors*, 5–6.

58. Laura Waterman and Guy Waterman, *Forest and Crag: A History of Hiking, Trailblazing, and Adventure in the Northeast Mountains* (Boston: Appalachian Mountain Club, 1989), 452; "University Outing Club to Be Organized," *Main Campus*, November 3, 1920, 1.

59. Bob Peterson and Bill Thomas, "The Hoofer History," December 5, 1953, in papers of the University of Wisconsin Hoofers, Special Collections, University of Wisconsin, Madison, Wisconsin, hereafter cited as Hoofers Papers.

60. Porter Butts, "The Wisconsin Union: The First 75 Years, 1904–1979" (Madison, Wis.: Hoofers, 1979), 53–63; "Report of the Executive Committee on Promoting Outing Activities at the University of Wisconsin," in Scrapbook, "Hoofers, [1932–1940]," Hoofers Papers.

61. "Howdy Bulletin," *Hoofers' Bulletin* 1 (October–November 1935), Hoofers Papers; Scrapbook, "University of Wisconsin Hoofer Activities, 1937–1942," http://digital.library.wisc.edu/1711.dl/UW.UWHoof1937.

62. "Howdy Bulletin"; Scrapbook, "University of Wisconsin Hoofer Activities, 1937–1942"; Oscar Strichelz, "Interview for Becoming a Hoofer," n.d., Hoofer Papers.

63. *Hoofers Bulletin* 8 (November 1939), Hoofers Papers.

64. Doeserich, Sherburne, and Wey, *Outdoors with the Prairie Club*, 340.

65. "Cupid Hitches Hikers' Head to Boss of Bikers' Brigade," *Milwaukee Journal*, September 6, 1941; Louise Cattoi, "Autumn Shows Treasures to Hiking Club Members," *Milwaukee Journal*, October 4, 1943.

CHAPTER 4: BUILDING TRAILS

1. Raymond H. Torrey et al., *New York Walk Book* (New York: American Geographical Society, 1923), 170, 186.

2. Raymond Torrey, "Long Brown Path," *New York Evening Post*, October 28, 1921.

3. Jane and Will Curtis and Frank Lieberman, *Green Mountain Adventure: Vermont's Long Trail* (Montpelier, Vt.: Green Mountain Club, 1985).

4. "The Vermont Academy for Boys," advertisement, *Independent*, July 20, 1914; Curtis and Lieberman, *Green Mountain Adventure*, 11; Walter Collins O'Kane, *Trails and Summits of the Green Mountains* (Boston: Houghton Mifflin, 1926), 24–25.

5. O'Kane, *Trails and Summits of the Green Mountains*, 20, 22.

6. Ibid., 23–24.

7. "The Mountaineer," *Boston Evening Transcript*, February 11, 1911; Camel's Hump Club Huts, Herbert W. Congdon, Carton Three, Longtrail photos and slides, box 2, sub-box 5, http://cdi.uvm.edu/collections/item/hwccr03b02030; Louis J. Parker, *Along the Skyline over the Long Trail* (Green Mountain Club, 1915), 8; O'Kane, *Trails and Summits of the Green Mountains*, 23.

8. O'Kane, *Trails and Summits of the Green Mountains*, 26–28; Curtis and Lieberman, *Green Mountain Adventure*, 17–18; Allen Chamberlain, *Vacation Tramps in New England Highlands* (Boston: Houghton Mifflin, 1919), 86; O'Kane, *Trails and Summits of the Green Mountains*, 28.

9. O'Kane, *Trails and Summits of the Green Mountains*, 28–29; Parker, *Along the Skyline over the Long Trail*, 9.

10. Parker, *Along the Skyline over the Long Trail*, 19, 28; Chamberlain, *Vacation Tramps*, 83–84.

11. Parker, *Along the Skyline over the Long Trail*, 19; Chamberlain, *Vacation Tramps*, 56.

12. O'Kane, *Trails and Summits of the Green Mountains*, 28; Chamberlain, *Vacation Tramps*, 56.

13. O'Kane, *Trails and Summits of the Green Mountains*, 30.

14. Chamberlain, *Vacation Tramps*, 81–82.

15. Ibid., 80–81.

16. Parker, *Along the Skyline over the Long Trail*, 22–25.

17. O'Kane, *Trails and Summits of the Green Mountains*, 31–32, 34; Parker, *Along the Skyline over the Long Trail*, 6, 34.

18. O'Kane, *Trails and Summits of the Green Mountains*, 26, 36–37.

19. Ibid., 37.

20. O'Kane, *Trails and Summits of the Green Mountains*, 37–38, 40; Chamberlain, *Vacation Tramps*, 84.

21. O'Kane, *Trails and Summits of the Green Mountains*, 33–34; "Report of the Brattleboro, Vermont, Outing Club, Inc. and the U.S. Amateur Ski Championships," *Canadian Ski Annual: 1923–1924* (1924), 51, 54; "Winter Sports Bulletin," *Brooklyn Eagle*, January 10, 1923, 14; Chamberlain, *Vacation Tramps*, 55.

22. Chamberlain, *Vacation Tramps*, 9–10, 31–32.

23. Ibid., 6–7.

24. For histories of the Appalachian Trail, see Sutter, "Wilderness as Regional Plan: Benton MacKaye," in Paul Sutter, *Driven Wild: How the Fight against Automobiles Launched the Modern Wilderness Movement* (Seattle: University of Washington Press, 2002), 142–193; Sarah Mittlefehldt, *Tangled Roots: The Appalachian Trail and American Environmental Politics* (Seattle: University of Washington Press, 2014); Larry Anderson, *Benton MacKaye: Conservationist, Planner, and Creator of the Appalachian Trail* (Baltimore: Johns Hopkins University Press, 2008); Charles Foster, *The Appalachian National Scenic Trail: A Time to Be Bold* (Harpers Ferry, W.Va.: Appalachian Trail Conference, 1987); Benton MacKaye, "An Appalachian Trail: A Project in Regional Planning," *Journal of the American Institute of Architects* 9 (October 1921): 328.

25. "Major Welch Dies; Builder of Parks," *New York Times*, May 5, 1941; Glenn D. Scherer, *Vistas and Vision: A History of the New York–New Jersey Trail Conference* (New York: New York–New Jersey Trail Conference, 1995), 3.

26. Raymond Torrey in ibid., 4.

27. Robert Binnewies, *Palisades: 100,000 Acres in 100 Years* (New York: Fordham University and Palisades Interstate Park Commission, 2001), 143.

28. J. F. Schairer, "We Had Some Marvelous Times in the Old Days," in *A Footpath in the Wilderness: The Early Days of PATC*, ed. Carol Niedzaliek (Vienna, Va.: Potomac Appalachian Trail Club), 13–14.

29. Carol Niedzaliek, ed., *A Footpath in the Wilderness: The Early Days of PATC* (Vienna, Va.: Potomac Appalachian Trail Club), 8–29.

30. Foster, *Appalachian National Scenic Trail*, 12.

31. Ibid., 13. Sarah Mittlefehldt, *Tangled Roots: The Appalachian Trail and American Environmental Politics* (Seattle: University of Washington Press, 2014).

32. Donald Anderson, "Legacy of the American Frontier: A History of the John Muir Trail" (M.A. thesis, California State University, 1997); "Chapter 8: Tramping John Muir and the John Muir Trail," in Glynn Wolar, "The Conceptualization and Development of Pedestrian Recreational Wilderness Trails in the American West, 1890–1940: A Landscape History" (Ph.D. diss., University of Idaho, 1998), 286–311.

33. Allen Chaffee, *Unexplored!* (Springfield, Mass.: Milton-Bradley, 1922), 21–22.

34. Barney Mann, "Discovering Dad: A Dusty Trail Leads to Clinton Clarke's Handmade Journal," *PCT Communicator*, December 2010, 12–16; Clinton C. Clarke, *The Pacific Crest Trailway* (Pasadena, Calif.: Pacific Crest Trail System Conference, 1945), 1, 12.

35. Robert Foote, "Pacific Trail Challenges Hikers," *New York Times*, April 25, 1937; S. R. Winters, "Trails in Primitive Areas: Uncle Sam's Vast Network for Hikers Now Covers nearly 140,000 Miles," *New York Times*, September 20, 1936.

36. United States Forest Service, *The Use of the National Forests* (Washington, D.C.: United States Department of Agriculture, 1907), 32; Clarke, *Pacific Crest Trail*, 2.

37. Barney Mann, "Found: 1938 Relay Boy Marcus Moschetto," *PCT Communicator*, Spring 2013, 14–15.

38. "Long Trail thru Vermont Tempts Hikers," *Telegraph* (Nashua, Mass.), July 31, 1926; "Will Again Walk over Long Trail," *North Adams Transcript* (Roxbury, Mass.), June 28, 1927; Parker, *Along the Skyline over the Long Trail*, 53.

39. Parker, *Along the Skyline over the Long Trail*, 55.

40. Dick Barton in Scherer, *Vistas and Vision*, 4.

41. Earl Shaffer, "To Make a Real Marine," n.d., Earl V. Shaffer Papers, 1803–2007, Archives Center, National Museum of American History, Washington, D.C., hereafter cited as Shaffer Papers.

42. Earl Shaffer, *Walking with Spring: The First Solo Thru-Hike of the Legendary Appalachian Trail* (Harpers Ferry, W.Va.: Appalachian Trail Conference, 1983), 84; Shaffer, "To Make a Real Marine"; John Shaffer, correspondence with author, January 15, 2008.

43. For a brief history of the York Hiking Club, see Chamberlin, "'True Recreation of Our Spirits, Our Courage, and Our Love,'" 26–30.

44. Shaffer, "To Make a Real Marine."

45. *A History of West Manchester Township, York County, Pennsylvania, 1799–1999* (West Manchester Township, Pa.: Board of Supervisors, 1999).

46. Earl Shaffer, diary entry, 1948, Shaffer Papers; Shaffer, *Walking with Spring*, 8.

47. Appalachian Trail Conference, *Suggestions for Appalachian Trail Users* (Washington, D.C.: Appalachian Trail Conference, 1941), 3; Shaffer, *Walking with Spring*, 152.

48. Applachian Trail Conference, *Suggestions for Appalachian Trail Users*, 1.

49. Andrew Brown, "Skyline Trail from Maine to Georgia," *National Geographic*, August 1949, 219; Shaffer, *Walking with Spring*, 8; Martin Papendick, "Pacific Crest Trails," *Appalachia* 28 (1953): 374–376; Eric Ryback, *The High Adventure of Eric Ryback* (New York: Bantam, 1973).

50. A version of this Horse Shoe Trail Club history originally appeared as Silas Chamberlin, "To Ensure Permanency: Expanding and Protecting Hiking Opportunities in Twentieth-Century Pennsylvania," *Pennsylvania History* 77 (Spring 2010): 193–216.

51. Henry N. Woolman, "The Horseshoe Trail," *General Magazine and Historical Chronicle* 39 (January 1937): 174–75.

52. Ibid., 176.

53. "Minutes of the Meeting of Those Interested in a Hiking Trail," March 6, 1934, papers of the Horse Shoe Trail Club, private collection, hereafter cited as HSTC Papers; *The Horse-Shoe Trail*, 1st ed., American Guide Series (Philadelphia: William Penn Association, 1938), 8.

54. Woolman, "Horseshoe Trail," 176; *Horse-Shoe Trail*, 7–8; Horse-Shoe Trail Task Force and Trails Conservation Assistance Program, *The Horse-Shoe Trail Protection Plan: Report to the Horse-Shoe Trail Club* (Philadelphia: Trails Conservation Assistance Program, 1990), 2, 177.

55. "Minutes of the First Annual Meeting of the Members," May 12, 1936, HSTC Papers; "In the Court of Common Pleas in and for the County of Montgomery; April Term, 1935; No. 13; Articles of Incorporation, Horse Shoe Trail Club, Inc.," n.d., HSTC Papers; "Minutes of Directors' Meeting," July 24, 1935, HSTC Papers.

56. Woolman, "Horseshoe Trail," 178; "Minutes of Annual Meeting of the Members," April 30, 1937, HSTC Papers; "Minutes of the First Annual Meeting of the Members," May 12, 1936.

57. "Minutes of the Annual Meeting of the Members," April 28, 1938, HSTC Papers. That government interference was not Woolman's main objection is clear from his repeated calls for state oversight: "Mr. Woolman again reminded the meeting of his ultimate aim to have the Horse Shoe Trail Club taken over as a State Trailway and urged everyone to keep that end in mind." "Minutes of Informal Meeting," May 3, 1941, HSTC Papers.

58. L. F. Schmeckebier and Harold Allen, "Shenandoah National Park: The Skyline Drive and the Appalachian Trail," *Appalachia* (1936): 78; Laura Waterman and Guy Waterman, *Forest and Crag: A History of*

Hiking, Trailblazing and Adventure in the Northeast Mountains (Boston: Appalachian Mountain Club, 1989), 288–291.

59. Myron Avery, "The Appalachian Trail in Pennsylvania's South Mountain," *American Motorist,* April 1931; W. L. Byers to Myron Avery, February 15, 1935, papers of the Potomac Appalachian Trail Club, private collection, hereafter cited as PATC Papers; Myron Avery to Oscar Book, n.d., PATC Papers.

60. Myron Avery to R. E. Chamberlain, April 28, 1936, PATC Papers; Myron Avery to Henry Woolman, October 16, 1935, PATC Papers.

61. "Minutes of the Annual Meeting of the Members," April 28, 1938, HSTC Papers; "Minutes of the Annual Meeting," 1942, HSTC Papers; "Resolution adopted at a Joint Meeting, November 5, 1945, by the Garden Club Federation of Pennsylvania, the Pennsylvania Forestry Association, and the Friends of the Land, Pennsylvania Chapter," HSTC Papers.

62. "Treasurer's Report," March 31, 1937, HSTC Papers; "Minutes of the Directors' Meeting," March 31, 1937, HSTC Papers; "Minutes of the Annual Meeting of the Members," April 28, 1938, HSTC Papers; "Minutes of the Directors' Meeting," May 15, 1940, HSTC Papers.

63. "Minutes of the Directors' Meeting," April 30, 1945, April 2, 1946, January 31, 1947, January 20, 1948, HSTC Papers.

64. "Minutes of the Annual Meeting," 1948, HSTC Papers; "Minutes of the Directors' Meeting," April 4, 1949, HSTC Papers; *The Schuylkill River Desilting Project: Final Report of the Schuylkill River Project Engineers* (N.p.: N.p., 1951).

65. Michael Egan, "Visions of Arcadia: Wilderness and the Ecology of Trail Construction in the Coastal Pacific Northwest" (M.A. thesis, Simon Fraser University, 2000).

66. Margaret Cleveland, "Trails," in *Outdoors with the Prairie Club,* ed. Emma Doeserich, Mary Sherburne, and Anna Wey (Chicago: Paquin, 1941), 74.

67. Ibid., 74–76.

CHAPTER 5: HIKING ALONE

1. Colin Fletcher in Roderick Nash, *Wilderness and the American Mind,* 3rd ed. (New Haven: Yale University Press, 1967), 316.

2. Colin Fletcher, *The Complete Walker: The Joys and Techniques of Hiking and Backpacking* (New York: Alfred A. Knopf, 1968); Colin Fletcher, *The Thousand-Mile Summer: In Desert and High Sierra* (Berkeley, Calif.: Howell-North Books, 1964); "Television," *New York Times,* February 8, 1965; advertisement, *New York Times,* February 21, 1965.

3. Colin Fletcher, *The Man Who Walked through Time* (New York: Vintage, 1967), 6.

4. Ibid., 13, 57, 79.

5. Ibid., 228.

6. Brooks Atkinson, "The Mysteries of Grand Canyon," *New York Times*, January 28, 1968; advertisement, *New York Times*, February 11, 1968; "Books of the Times," *New York Times*, January 8, 1968.

7. Fletcher, *Man Who Walked through Time*, 234; David Brower, "Foreword," in *Time and the River Flowing*, ed. David Brower (San Francisco: Sierra Club and Ballantine Books, 1964), 5.

8. Nash, *Wilderness and the American Mind*, 316.

9. Earl Shaffer, *Walking with Spring: The First Solo Hike of the Legendary Appalachian Trail* (Harpers Ferry, W.Va.: Appalachian Trail Conference, 1983), 8.

10. "AHC Mailing Roster," January 1, 1966, papers of the Allentown Hiking Club, Lehigh County Historical Society, Allentown, Pennsylvania, hereafter cited as AHC Papers; Barbara Wiemann, "AHC History," Allentown Hiking Club, www.allentownhikingclub.org; David Bates, *Clearing Trail in Wartime: The PATC in World War Two* (Vienna, Va.: Potomac Appalachian Trail Club, n.d.); David Brower, ed., *Manual of Ski Mountaineering* (Berkeley, Calif.: National Ski Association of America and University of California Press, 1942); Peter Shelton, *Climb to Conquer: The Untold Story of World War II's 10th Mountain Division Ski Troops* (New York: Simon and Schuster, 2003), 23–24; Paul Petzoldt, *The Wilderness Handbook* (New York: W. W. Norton, 1974), 12.

11. See, e.g., Charles Foster, *A Time to Be Bold: The Appalachian National Scenic Trail* (Harpers Ferry, W.Va.: Appalachian Trail Conference, 1987), 14.

12. Laura Waterman and Guy Waterman, *Forest and Crag: A History of Hiking, Trail Blazing, and Adventure in the Northeast Mountains* (Boston: Appalachian Mountain Club, 1989), 558.

13. "New Silk Made on Chemical Base Rivals Quality of Natural Product," *New York Times*, September 22, 1938.

14. "Business World," *New York Times*, July 31, 1943; "Tents," advertisement, *New York Times*, May 21, 1950.

15. J. C. Harper and A. L. Tappel, "Freeze-Drying of Food Products," *Advances in Food Research* 7 (1957): 206.

16. Allen Chaffee, *Adventures on the High Trail* (Springfield, Mass.: Milton-Bradley, 1923), 211–213; W. K. Merrill, *All about Camping* (Harrisburg, Pa.: Stackpole Books, 1962), 265–266; United States Forest Service, *Backpacking in the National Forest Wilderness: A Family Adventure* (Washington, D.C.: Government Printing Office, 1971), 21.

17. John M. Gould, diary, June 9, 1875, available at https://www.mainememory.net/artifact/37321; John M. Gould, *How to Camp: Hints for Camping and Walking* (New York: Scribner, Armstrong, 1877), 79, 40, 63, 42; Horace Kephart, *Camping and Woodcraft*, 2nd ed. (New York: Macmillan, 1918), 15, 143, 153, 127, 172, 78, 62, 160, 170, 260, 115; Elmer

Krep, *Camp and Trail Methods* (Columbus, Ohio: A. R. Harding, 1910), 52; Edward Breck, *The Way of the Woods* (New York: G. P. Putnam's Sons, 1908), 25, 42, 49, 80, 120; "Proceedings of the Club," *Appalachia* 13 (October 1914): 220; Allen Chamberlain, *Vacation Tramps in New England Highlands* (Boston: Houghton Mifflin, 1919), 16, 18, 19.

18. Arthur Bartlett, "The Discovery of L. L. Bean," *Saturday Evening Post,* December 14, 1946; Leon Gorman, *L. L. Bean: The Making of an American Icon* (Boston: Harvard Business School Press, 2006), 16, 18.

19. Abercrombie and Fitch, catalog (1909), 218–219; Recreational Equipment Incorporated, "REI: Celebrating 75 Years of Adventure," www.reihistory.com; "Dick Kelty," obituary, *Telegraph* (London), January 23, 2004.

20. Chamberlain, *Vacation Tramps,* 12.

21. Tom Lewis, *Divided Highways: Building the Interstate Highways, Transforming American Life,* 3rd ed. (Ithaca, N.Y.: Cornell University Press, 2013); David Louter, *Windshield Wilderness: Cars, Roads, and Nature in Washington's National Parks* (Seattle: University of Washington Press, 2010); Paul Sutter, *Driven Wild: How the Fight against Automobiles Launched the Modern Wilderness Movement* (Seattle: University of Washington Press, 2002); Ethan Carr, *Mission 66: Modernism and the National Park Dilemma* (Amherst: University of Massachusetts Press, 2007).

22. Membership estimates based on figures 51.1 and 54.1 in Waterman and Waterman, *Forest and Crag,* 564–565, 595; "AHC Mailing Roster," January 1, 1970, AHC Papers; Wiemann, "AHC History."

23. Collins Chew, "History of the Tennessee Eastman Hiking & Canoeing Club," Tennessee Eastman Hiking and Canoeing Club. http:// tehcc.org/about/club-history.

24. "Announce Program for Appalachian Club Bates Meeting," *Lewiston Evening Journal,* May 4, 1951; Robert Pond, *Follow the Blue Blazes: A Guide to Hiking Ohio's Buckeye Trail* (Athens: Ohio University Press, 2003), 274–275; "Mrs. Emma Gatewood," *Sports Illustrated,* August 15, 1955.

25. The Florida Trail Association estimates that maintenance of the trail requires approximately sixty thousand volunteer hours each year. This history of the Florida Trail Association is drawn from the narrative and video documentary at http://www.floridatrail.org/about-us/history/.

26. Matt Samet, *Death Grip: A Climber's Escape from Benzo Madness* (New York: St. Martin's Press, 2013), 58–59; Robert Julyan, *The Mountains of New Mexico* (Albuquerque: University of New Mexico Press, 2006), 218.

27. Susan Sands, "Backpacking: I Go to the Wilderness to Kick the Man-World Out of Me," *New York Times,* May 9, 1971; Waterman and Waterman, *Forest and Crag,* 595.

28. Robert Putnam, *Bowling Alone: The Collapse and Revival of American Community* (New York: Simon and Schuster, 2000), 55.

29. John Muir, *The Yosemite* (New York: Century, 1912), 262; Robert Righter, *The Battle over Hetch Hetchy: America's Most Controversial Dam and the Birth of Modern Environmentalism* (New York: Oxford University Press, 2005); Russell Martin, *A Story That Stands Like a Dam: Glen Canyon and the Struggle for the Soul of the West* (New York: Henry Holt, 1989), 328; Mark Harvey, *A Symbol of Wilderness: Echo Park and the American Conservation Movement* (Seattle: University of Washington Press, 2000).

30. Joseph Wood Krutch, "Introduction," in *"In Wildness Is the Preservation of the World,"* ed. David Brower (San Francisco: Sierra Club Books, 1962), 13; Sierra Club, advertisement, "Should We Also Flood the Sistine Chapel?" *New York Times*, April 16, 1967.

31. Jerry Russell and Renny Russell, *On the Loose* (San Francisco: Sierra Club Books, 1967), 8.

32. Ibid., 124, back cover.

33. Adam Rome, *The Genius of Earth Day: How a 1970 Teach-In Unexpectedly Made the First Green Generation* (New York: Hill and Wang, 2013), 77; John Mitchell and Constance L. Stallings, eds., *Ecotactics: The Sierra Club Handbook for Environmental Activists* (New York: Trident Press, 1970), 5, 6.

34. Membership estimates based on "Table 3.1. Membership Trends of Selected Environmental Organizations, 1950–2003," in Christopher Bosso, *Environment, Inc.: From Grassroots to Beltway* (Lawrence: University Press of Kansas, 2005), 54.

35. Ibid., 34.

36. Michael Cohen, *The History of the Sierra Club, 1892–1970* (San Francisco: Sierra Club Books, 1988), 436; William Kemsley, "How the 1970s Backpacking Boom Burst upon Us," *Appalachia* (Winter–Spring 2007): 29–32.

37. Merrill, *All about Camping*, 202.

38. Sands, "Backpacking."

39. Edward Abbey, *Desert Solitaire: A Season in the Wilderness* (New York: Ballantine Books, 1968), 51; *Advancing the National Parks Idea: Connecting People and Parks Committee Report* (Washington, D.C.: National Parks Conservation Association, 2009), fig. 1 (p. 2).

40. Harvey Manning, "Where Did All These Damn Hikers Come From?" *Backpacker* 1 (Summer 1975): 36; Sands, "Backpacking."

41. Kemsley, "How the 1970s Backpacking Boom Burst upon Us," 22.

42. Ibid., 20; Sands, "Backpacking."

43. Kemsley, "How the 1970s Backpacking Boom Burst upon Us," 26–27.

44. Bradford Angier, *Home in Your Pack: The Modern Handbook of Backpacking* (New York: Collier Books, 1965), 149–150.

45. William Kemsley, "Why Backpacker: A Note from the Publisher," *Backpacker* 1 (Spring 1973): 4–5; "Letters," *Backpacker* 1 (Spring 1973): 6; Kemsley, "How the 1970s Backpacking Boom Burst upon Us," 29; "Letters," 6; James Morton Turner, "From Woodcraft to 'Leave No Trace': Wilderness, Consumerism, and Environmentalism in Twentieth-Century America," *Environmental History* 7 (2002): 462–484.

46. Boy Scouts of America, *Scout Handbook*, 8th ed. (N.p.: Boy Scouts of America, 1972); Petzoldt, *Wilderness Handbook*, 107–108; John Hart, *Walking Softly in the Wilderness: The Sierra Club Guide to Backpacking* (San Francisco: Sierra Club Books, 1977).

47. Turner, "From Woodcraft to 'Leave No Trace,'" 463, 477.

48. Foster, *Time to Be Bold*, 15; Mittlefehldt, *Tangled Roots*.

49. Lyndon B. Johnson, "Special Message to the Congress on Conservation and Restoration of Natural Beauty," February 8, 1965, available online at Gerhard Peters and John T. Woolley, *The American Presidency Project*, http://www.presidency.ucsb.edu/ws/?pid=27285; "Excerpts from Johnson's Special Message on Natural Beauty," *New York Times*, February 9, 1965.

50. H.R. 2142, A bill to amend the Federal-Aid Highway Act of 1944 to authorize the construction of a national system of foot trails; Myron Avery to Daniel Hoch, March 31, 1947, Appalachian Trail Conference Archives, Kearneysville, W.Va., hereafter cited as ATC Papers; Myron Avery to Henry Woolman, January 16, 1947, ATC Papers.

51. U.S. House of Representatives, Committee on Roads, "Hearings on H.R. 2142" (Washington, D.C.: Government Printing Office, 1945), 2, 7.

52. Henry McLemore, "A Hiker Who Wants a 'Lift,'" *New York Journal-American*, November 1, 1945.

53. Foster, *Time to Be Bold*, 14; Daniel Hoch to Francis Walter, February 14, 1948, Papers of Congressman Francis E. Walter, Special Collections, Linderman Library, Lehigh University, Bethlehem, Pa., hereafter cited as Walter Papers; Myron Avery to Daniel Hoch, January 16, 1947, ATC Papers; Francis Walter to Daniel Hoch, February 19, 1948, Walter Papers; Daniel Hoch to Appalachian Trail Conference, June 16, 1948, ATC Papers; Office of Francis Walter to Dorothy Crawford, Federation of Western Outdoor Clubs, July 21, 1948, Walter Papers; Daniel Hoch to Myron Avery, April 29, 1949, ATC Papers.

54. Jeanne Beaty, "There Are Some Long, Long Trails A-Making," *New York Times*, December 12, 1965; "Udall to Press 4 Outdoor Bills," *New York Times*, November 18, 1966.

55. Department of Interior News Release, July 24, 1966, reprinted in U.S. Senate, Committee on Interior and Insular Affairs, "Hearings on S. 827" (Washington, D.C.: Government Printing Office, 1967), 25.

56. Bureau of Outdoor Recreation, Department of the Interior, *Trails for America: Report on the Nationwide Trail Study* (Washington, D.C.: Government Printing Office, 1966), 93, 111, 120; William Blair, "4 Trails Sought as Scenic Trails," *New York Times*, January 15, 1967.

57. "Senate Unit Votes Trail Bill," *New York Times*, May 25, 1968.

58. U.S. Senate, "Hearings on S. 827," 9.

59. "National Trails Bill Gains," *New York Times*, June 19, 1968; "Conferees Back Plan for Recreational Trails," *New York Times*, September 11, 1968; "Udall to Press 4 Outdoor Bills"; "Hearings on S. 827," 108–111, 162; "Congress Returns," *New York Times*, September 5, 1968.

60. Lizabeth Cohen, *A Consumer's Republic: The Politics of Mass Consumption in Postwar America* (New York: Vintage, 2003), 8.

EPILOGUE

1. The figure for total hikers comes from the Outdoor Foundation's annual participation report. The percentage of club members is a generous estimate of national club membership totals divided by total participation. Outdoor Foundation, *Outdoor Recreation Participation Report, 2013* (Boulder, Colo.: Outdoor Foundation, 2013), 17.

2. Earl Shaffer, *Walking with Spring: The First Solo Thru-Hike of the Legendary Appalachian Trail* (Harpers Ferry, W.Va.: Appalachian Trail Conference, 1983), 14.

3. Ibid., 12.

4. "Challenges Taking Root on Appalachian Trail," *Boston Globe*, November 2, 1998; Jeff Strout, "79-Year-Old Finishes Hike along the Appalachian Trail," *Bangor (Me.) Daily News*, October 22, 1998; Mike Argento, "The Entire Appalachian Trail 50 Years after the First Time," *York Daily Record*, July 17, 1998.

5. "Challenges Taking Root on Appalachian Trail."

6. "National Rail-Trail and Trail Mileage Counts," Rails to Trails Conservancy, http://www.railstotrails.org/our-work/research-and-information/national-and-state-trail-stats/#national.

7. Sarah Clark Stuart et al., "Great PA/NJ: Generating Recovery by Enhancing Active Transportation in Pennsylvania & New Jersey," grant proposal narrative for 2010 Transportation Investment Generating Economic Recovery grant cycle (May 2010): 5, 9–10.

8. Outdoor Industry Association, *The Outdoor Recreation Economy* (Boulder, Colo.: Outdoor Industry Association, 2012), 1, 7; Aleksandra Kulczuga, "America's Most Conservative-Friendly County Is Williamson County: Horse Farms, Guitar-Shaped Pools and Low Taxes," *Daily Caller*, March 19, 2010.

9. "Why the Extreme Lack of Racial Diversity in the Hiking Community," Internet discussion forum, WhiteBlaze.Net: A Community

of Appalachian Trail Enthusiasts, January 1, 2013, http://www.whiteblaze. net/forum/showthread.php?90877-Why-the-extreme-lack-of-racial-diversity-in-the-hiking-community; Kirk Johnson, "National Parks Try to Appeal to Minorities," *New York Times,* September 5, 2013; Ryan Kearney, "White People Love Hiking, Minorities Don't, Here's Why," *New Republic,* online edition, September 6, 2013.

10. Richard Albert, *Damming the Delaware: The Rise and Fall of Tocks Island Dam* (State College: Pennsylvania State University Press, 1987); Frank Dale, *Delaware Diary: Episodes in the Life of a River* (New Brunswick, N.J.: Rutgers University Press, 1996), 151; "The Ecologist Plea: 'Save Sunfish Pond,'" *New York Times,* May 14, 1972.

11. "The KTA News," November 1958, April 1, 1957, Keystone Trails Association newsletters, private collection, Cogan Station, Pa.; "12,000 Pennsylvanians Demand: 'Protect Loyalsock from Fracking,'" press release, Pennsylvania Sierra Club Chapter, Keystone Trails Association, PennEnvironment, August 22, 2013.

12. Bryan Walsh, "How the Sierra Club Took Millions from the Natural Gas Industry and Why They Stopped," *Time,* online edition, February 2, 2012; Ben Casselman, "Sierra Club's Pro-Gas Dilemma," *Wall Street Journal,* December 22, 2009; Louis Sahagun, "Sierra Club Leader Departs amid Discontent over Group's Direction," *Los Angeles Times,* November 19, 2011.

INDEX

Note: Page numbers in *italic* refer to illustrations.